SPIRITUAL WARFARE

John Franklin and Chuck Lawless

LifeWay Press®
Nashville, Tennessee

© 2001 • LifeWay Press®
Seventh Printing August 2007

ISBN 0-6330-2903-3
Item 001114630

This book is the text for course CG-0621 in the
subject area Personal Life in the Christian Growth Study Plan.

Dewey Decimal Classification: 235.4
Subject Heading: SPIRITUAL WARFARE

Unless otherwise noted, Scripture quotations are taken from the Holy Bible,
New International Version, copyright © 1973, 1978, 1984 by International Bible Society.
Scripture quotations identified NKJV are from the New King James Version.
Copyright © 1979, 1980, 1982, Thomas Nelson, Inc. Publishers. Used by permission.
Scripture quotations identified KJV are from the King James Version.
Scripture quotations identified HCSB® are taken from the Holman Christian Standard Bible™,
© Copyright 2000 by Holman Bible Publishers. Used by permission.
Scripture quotations identified NASB are from the New American Standard Bible.
Scripture quotations identified RSV are from the Revised Standard Bible.
Scripture quotations identified NLT are taken from the Holy Bible, New Living Translation,
© Copyright 1996. Used by permission of Tyndale House Publishing, Wheaton, IL 60189. All rights reserved.

To order additional copies of this resource WRITE LifeWay Church Resources Customer Service;
One LifeWay Plaza; Nashville, TN 37234-0113; FAX order to (615) 251-5933;
PHONE 1-800-458-2772; ORDER ONLINE at *www.lifeway.com;*
or VISIT the LifeWay Christian Store serving you.

Printed in the United States of America.

Leadership and Adult Publishing
LifeWay Church Resources
One LifeWay Plaza
Nashville, TN 37234-0175

TABLE OF CONTENTS

MEET THE AUTHORS

Chuck Lawless

Chuck Lawless is associate dean and associate professor of evangelism and church growth at the Billy Graham School of Evangelism at Southern Baptist Theological Seminary. A frequent conference leader on church growth and spiritual warfare, Dr. Lawless is also the author of *Discipled Warriors: Healthy Churches Winning Spiritual Warfare* (Kregel, 2002). A graduate of Cumberland College, Chuck earned a Master of Divinity and Doctor of Philosophy in evangelism/church growth from Southern Baptist Theological Seminary. He and his wife Pam live in Louisville, Kentucky.

John Franklin

John Franklin is a pastoral ministries specialist in prayer in the Pastoral Ministries Department of LifeWay Church Resources. John came to LifeWay as prayer ministries specialist in the Discipleship Division and compiled the leadership book for church prayer ministries, *A House of Prayer: Prayer Ministries in Your Church*. He has also contributed articles on prayer for *Transformed Lives: Taking Women's Ministry to the Next Level* and *Forward Together: A New Vision for Senior Adult Ministry*. John has authored articles for *Light Magazine, Sunday School Leader, Stewardship Journal,* and *Single Pursuit*.

John is a graduate of Samford University, Southern Baptist Theological Seminary, and Beeson Divinity School. His passion is spiritual awakening and teaching leaders how to lead corporate prayer. John and his wife Kathy have three children, Daniel, Nathan, and Susanna. They live in Nashville, Tennessee.

ABOUT THE STUDY

Welcome to this study on spiritual warfare. Over the next eight weeks you will be exploring a topic of vital interest for all Christians. You will examine the relationship between God and Satan. How does God's sovereignty impact Satan's schemes? You will learn Satan's schemes for you and for your church. Each day will give you practical handles for knowing how to recognize spiritual warfare and how to respond victoriously.

Since much controversy surrounds the subject of spiritual warfare, your authors have limited this study to teachings that can be clearly seen in the Bible. The Bible will be the basis for our conclusions. The subtitle of this course, *Biblical Truth for Victory,* highlights the two main truths we wish to communicate over the next few weeks: the Bible contains truth that is essential for the believer to know and practice in order to successfully wage spiritual warfare, and victory does not always mean immediate deliverance from the evil around us. Sometimes victory requires endurance. Why does God allow warfare in a believer's life? That's the question we will begin with in week 1.

Week 8 introduces several contemporary issues in spiritual warfare and helps you understand the biblical position on such topics as warfare praying, territorial spirits, demon possession, and generational curses. Week 9 is an optional unit that helps you discern between the voice of God and the voice of Satan. Week 9 does not have video support.

During the introductory group session, you will meet your authors in a video interview that explains their interest in the topic of spiritual warfare. During each of the eight group sessions to follow, you will review the major concepts of the week's study with your authors by video. Then at the end of the session you will watch a dramatic vignette that you will discuss with your group. The dramatizations will help you understand spiritual warfare as it occurs in the lives of a typical American family.

The daily lessons in your member book should be completed on your own during the week. The learning activities will help you apply to your life what you learn. In the margins of each page you will find additional information, quotes from well-known persons, summaries of the content, and Bible passages.

The basis for victory in spiritual warfare is a personal love relationship with Jesus Christ. If you have not yet accepted Jesus' free gift of eternal life and acknowledged Him as Lord of your life, turn to page 182 and read "How to Become a Christian."

The Leader Guide beginning on page 183 will assist the group leader in planning and implementing each group session.

Why Warfare Exists

CASE STUDY

Pete's life seemed like one mountain to climb after another. He unexpectedly lost his job. Two of his children were struggling in school. His wife wrestled between getting a job to help pay bills or staying at home to care for their preschool child. Arguments became common. Stress led to temptations to sin, and Pete often gave in to the temptations. When he prayed about all of these issues, he felt his prayers went nowhere.

Then he read a popular book about spiritual warfare. Maybe the devil was behind all of these struggles. Maybe Satan was trying to weaken Pete's home and his faith. If so, all Pete needed to do was rebuke the devil—right? After all, the Bible says to resist the devil and he will flee.

But, Pete wondered, *how do I know if the devil is causing all of this trouble? When is the devil involved, and when is life just difficult? And, if the devil is responsible, where is God? Doesn't God care? If God were really in control, wouldn't He stop all of these problems?*

What possible reason could God have for allowing Pete to go through these battles?

How would you answer Pete's questions?

DAY ONE

LAYING THE FOUNDATION

What Do We Mean by Spiritual Warfare?

When you think of spiritual warfare, what do you mean by the term? Some people limit warfare to conflict with the devil and his forces. Others include enemies mentioned in the Bible such as the world and the flesh (Eph. 2:2-3). Since these influences cause a struggle in our spirits—even if we choose the good—many believers include the world and the flesh in their definitions of spiritual warfare.

In order to focus our thoughts in this study, your authors will primarily define *spiritual warfare* as it relates to Satan. Simply put, the definition of *spiritual warfare* we're using in this book is *the conflict of two opposing wills*—namely that of God and His followers versus Satan and his followers. God is good and seeks to do good; He cannot do evil. Satan is evil and seeks to do evil; he cannot do good. God's will always desires that which builds. Satan's will always desires that which destroys. God desires that which is right, pure, and lovely. Satan desires that which is wrong, corrupt, and perverse. In fact, regarding every aspect of God's nature, Satan proves to be the exact opposite. Therefore, they cannot ever be in agreement. Their wills, desires, and actions remain in a perpetual state of conflict.

In the chart below, list differences that separate the two opposing wills of God and Satan.

God's Nature	Satan's Nature
_____	_____
_____	_____
_____	_____

The wills of God and Satan are so diametrically opposed that *warfare* best describes their irreconcilable differences. Each has followers, and their followers reflect the nature of the one they serve. In our world, whenever the desires of God and His followers come in conflict with the desires of Satan and his followers, spiritual warfare occurs.

How Did God and Satan Come To Be at Odds?

In the Bible God often used an earthly life as a type, or reflection, of something or someone of greater spiritual significance. For example, Moses was a type of savior since he delivered the children of Israel from bondage. His life foreshadowed Christ who was the Savior who delivered us from the bondage of sin. Bible writers often interpreted the Bible in this way (for example: Matt. 2:15).

Ezekiel 28:11-19 is such a passage. Although it refers to the king of Tyre, many scholars believe it reflects the beginning and fall of Satan.

Spiritual warfare is the conflict of two opposing wills.

NAMES OF SATAN:

- *accuser*
- *adversary*
- *angel*
- *Beelzebub*
- *Belial*
- *demon*
- *devil*
- *dragon*
- *enemy*
- *evil one; evil spirit*
- *god of this age*
- *god of this world*
- *he who deceives the whole world*
- *Leviathan*
- *liar, father of lies*
- *Lucifer*
- *Morning star*
- *prince of demons*
- *prince of the power of the air*
- *prince of this world*
- *Ruler of the demons*
- *ruler of the kingdom of the air*
- *Ruler of this world*
- *Satan*
- *serpent*
- *son of the dawn*
- *tempter*
- *unclean spirit*

Therefore, this passage from Ezekiel records Satan's beginnings and gives us the clearest insight into how the warfare between God and Satan began.

Read Ezekiel 28:11-19. Fill in the blanks to explain Satan's beginnings. Compare your answers to those in the paragraph that follows.

Satan was originally created as an anointed _____ .

He was absolutely _____, full of _____

and exceedingly _____ .

Satan was originally created as an anointed cherub. A cherub was not only an angel, but an angel that guarded the throne of God. No other angel in heaven would have been closer to God, and probably no other angel excelled him in power. He was absolutely perfect, full of wisdom, and exceedingly beautiful (Ezek. 28:12). God adorned him with every possible jewel so that he was the perfection of beauty. Satan's splendor was exceptionally great—probably greater than any other created being, as would seem fitting for a guardian cherub.

How did someone so close to God become so corrupted? How could someone God blessed so superabundantly turn against Him? What could have possibly enticed him to rebel against God?

Read Ezekiel 28:17 and Isaiah 14:12-15. List at least two factors that caused Satan to turn from God.

1. _____

2. _____

Evidently, Satan became so enamored with himself and so focused on his beauty that he actually believed he deserved to be God. This beauty clouded his better judgment (Ezek. 28:17) until self became all-important. Notice that he used the word *I* five times in two verses (Isa. 14:13-14). Once he was consumed with self, even this perfect creation became corrupted. These two factors caused Satan to turn from God: 1) His heart was lifted up because of his beauty (Ezek. 28:17), and 2) He essentially said, *I will be like God* (Isa. 14:14).

Can God-given abilities and attributes become a temptation to focus on self? ❑ Yes ❑ No
List anything you've been given that could become a temptation to pride.

_____   _____

_____   _____

"Your heart became proud on account of your beauty, and you corrupted your wisdom because of your splendor. So I threw you to the earth; I made a spectacle of you before kings."
—*Ezekiel 28:17*

"How you have fallen from heaven, O morning star, son of the dawn! You have been cast down to the earth, you who once laid low the nations! You said in your heart, 'I will ascend to heaven; I will raise my throne above the stars of God; I will sit enthroned on the mount of assembly, on the utmost heights of the sacred mountain. I will ascend above the tops of the clouds; I will make myself like the Most High.' But you are brought down to the grave, to the depths of the pit."
—*Isaiah 14:12-15*

Satan had position, beauty, wisdom, and perfection. In spite of these gifts, or maybe because of them, he focused on himself and forgot the One who gave them to him. When God gives His children gifts or talents that distinguish them in particular areas, they must take care lest the temptation to pride becomes too great.

Does the War Still Occur Today?

The fact that you are reading this workbook indicates that you probably believe the answer to this question is yes. Revelation 12:7-12 provides a snapshot of what happens in our world today.

Although the battle started in heaven, God defeated Satan (v. 7), and he was cast down to earth (v. 9). A loud voice announced salvation and victory for those who follow Christ but gave this warning in verse 12: "Woe to the earth and the sea, because the devil has gone down to you! He is filled with fury, because he knows that his time is short."

Does spiritual warfare occur today? Absolutely! Paul confirmed this truth in Ephesians 6:12. Peter further admonished, "Be self-controlled and alert. Your enemy the devil prowls around like a roaring lion looking for someone to devour" (1 Pet. 5:8). Many other Scriptures bear witness to the fact that the battle continues. However, Revelation 12:7-12 records two significant truths that make this war unlike any other.

Satan Is Already Defeated

A war rages, but the final outcome has already been decided. "He was not strong enough, and they lost their place in heaven" (Rev. 12:7-8). Other Scriptures confirm this defeat. Paul noted in Colossians 2:15 that "having disarmed the powers and authorities, he made a public spectacle of them, triumphing over them by the cross." Revelation 20:10 describes Satan's final end: "The devil, who deceived them, was thrown into the lake of burning sulfur, where the beast and the false prophet had been thrown. They will be tormented day and night for ever and ever."

Since the war has already been won, Christians do not fight with uncertainty. We cannot follow God and ultimately lose. The final outcome is not determined by what we do.

How do you feel about Satan having already been defeated? (Check one.)
❑ confident   ❑ confused

The War Will Continue on Earth Until the End

Ironically, the fact that the war has been won does not mean that the war is over. Notice in Revelation 12:13,17 that when the devil saw he had been cast to the earth, he persecuted the woman. Some debate exists over the identity of the woman. Scholars suggest this woman refers to Mary, to believing Israel, or to the church. In any event, verse 17 reiterates that the devil "was enraged at the woman." As a consequence, "he went off to make war against the rest of her offspring—those who obey God's commandments and hold to the testimony of Jesus." Who is the rest of the woman's offspring? Believers in

"There was war in heaven. Michael and his angels fought against the dragon, and the dragon and his angels fought back. But he was not strong enough, and they lost their place in heaven. The great dragon was hurled down—that ancient serpent called the devil, or Satan, who leads the whole world astray. He was hurled to the earth, and his angels with him. Then I heard a loud voice in heaven say: 'Now have come the salvation and the power and the kingdom of our God, and the authority of his Christ. For the accuser of our brothers, who accuses them before our God day and night, has been hurled down. They overcame him by the blood of the Lamb and by the word of their testimony; they did not love their lives so much as to shrink from death. Therefore rejoice, you heavens and you who dwell in them! But woe to the earth and the sea, because the devil has gone down to you! He is filled with fury, because he knows that his time is short.' "
—*Revelation 12:7-12*

"Our struggle is not against flesh and blood, but against the rulers, against the authorities, against the powers of this dark world and against the spiritual forces of evil in the heavenly realms."
—*Ephesians 6:12*

Christ. The witness of Scripture is that this conflict ultimately continues until Satan launches a final battle and meets his demise in the lake of fire where he will be tormented day and night forever (Rev. 20:7-10).

Are You Ready?

Perhaps you are asking, *if God has already defeated Satan, why does He allow him to continue promoting evil? Why doesn't He destroy him now?*

A proper understanding of spiritual warfare views all circumstances through the lens of God's sovereignty. Satan may use tactics that are pleasant or troublesome, but ultimately the will of God determines His criterion. Warfare continues or ends depending on whether or not God's purposes are being accomplished.

God in His sovereignty does not exempt His children from the war. The question, therefore, is not whether I want to be involved—but rather, when I become involved, will I be ready? Will I understand God's pattern and prescription for victory? That's the question that you will answer during this study. Day 2 will examine the fundamental question that determines ahead of time how you will respond when encountering spiritual warfare.

Write a prayer in the margin for God's guidance during this study. Pray for yourself as you seek to answer the fundamental question raised in day 1, *Am I ready?*

Warfare continues or ends depending on whether or not God's purposes are being accomplished.

DAY TWO

IS GOD IN CONTROL?

Today's lesson throws the searchlight of Scripture onto a foundational question of spiritual warfare. Everything that you believe about spiritual warfare, the way you act, the way you pray, and the counsel you give others will be determined by your answer to the following question: *What is the relationship between God's sovereignty and Satan's freedom?* What you believe about each player's role will determine your positions on various topics and issues related to warfare.

God's Sovereignty vs. Satan's Freedom

If you believe Satan is completely free to attack at will, then you will expect constant attacks with no greater purpose than Satan's attempts to hinder the will of God and personally destroy you. This belief will impact how you likely would pray for the attack to cease.

On the other hand, if you believe God is sovereign, then you will assume that Satan had to first obtain permission, and God has a greater purpose in mind for the warfare. Your response would be to pray that God would show you His purpose for the attack. Therefore, getting the answer right to this question is absolutely critical to developing a proper understanding and response to spiritual warfare.

What's your answer? Since the Bible is our standard, think of biblical characters who encountered warfare. One of the clearest passages occurs in Job 1–2.

Read the conversation between God and Satan in Job 1:6-12; 2:1-6. What do you conclude about the relationship between God's sovereignty and Satan's freedom? (Check one.)
- ❏ Satan is free to do whatever he wants to God's children when he wants to do it.
- ❏ God's sovereignty means Satan must obtain permission before he can act in the life of a believer.

In the margin list evidences from the passage that support your belief.

Notice that Satan's freedom does not mean he is free to do anything he wants. If you chose the second response, you believe that God's sovereignty means Satan must obtain permission before he can act in the life of a believer. The evidences from the passage include:
- God made a hedge around Job that Satan couldn't violate (v. 10).
- Satan asked God to touch Job. He did not volunteer to do it himself. In effect, he acknowledged God's sovereignty over Job and his own limitations. He could not cross the boundaries God had set (v. 11).
- God Himself had to grant permission before Satan could touch Job's things (v. 12).
- Even in granting permission, God set a limit on Satan. He could not touch Job himself, and Satan had to obey (v. 12).

Clearly, the throne belongs to God. He and He alone exercises authority. In the conversation in Job 2:1-6 we again see the sovereignty of God and the subservience of Satan. Satan had to appeal to God to touch Job. Once again, when God granted permission, He exercised sovereignty in setting a limit on what Satan could do in Job's life.

Does this passage line up with the rest of the Bible? Is this only an Old Testament reality? Numerous passages in the New Testament confirm the same pattern. In Luke 8:32 the demons could not go into the pigs without permission. In 1 Corinthians 5:5 Paul counseled the church to deliver an unrepentant believer over to Satan, which implies the granting of permission before Satan could work. In 1 Timothy 1:20 Paul delivered two men over to Satan to teach them not to blaspheme, again implying the granting of permission. In Revelation 13:7 the beast was given permission to war against the saints.

Perhaps the clearest New Testament picture of Satan's obtaining permission comes from the life of the Lord Jesus and His disciples. In Luke 22:31-32 Jesus made a startling announcement immediately after the Lord's Supper. " 'Simon, Simon, Satan has asked to sift you as wheat. But I have prayed for you, Simon, that your faith may not fail. And when you have turned back, strengthen your brothers.' " This Scripture is another example of Satan asking before he can act.

> "The devil, full of subtlety, and malice, and determination to spoil the work of God in the human soul, could nevertheless not touch a single hair upon the back of a single camel belonging to Job until he had asked God's leave."[1]
>
> —G. CAMPBELL MORGAN

The Scripture is clear. Satan cannot arbitrarily do anything he wants to you at any time. If you are experiencing warfare, the biblical evidence confirms Satan cannot do it without first obtaining permission.

How do you feel about spiritual warfare in light of God's sovereignty? (Check one or more.)
❑ I feel confident. I am unafraid. Bring on the battle.
❑ I feel relieved. I never understood that He is in such control. It gives me great comfort having such an anchor.
❑ I'm still trying to take it all in. I have a lot of questions.
❑ I'm uneasy. I thought God was supposed to deliver me from evil. Why would He grant Satan access in my life?

How you feel will be determined by your focus. If you drew comfort, courage, or a sense of freedom from these Scriptures, you probably recognized that God's sovereignty means you are never at the mercy of Satan. He has limits that he cannot cross. He cannot randomly access you or your family. God's loving protection will always determine the boundaries of what he can and cannot do. The battle is always the Lord's. God is the one who ultimately fights our battles. (See 1 Sam. 17:47 and 2 Chron. 20:15 in the margin.)

You don't have to panic and suddenly call God into the situation as if He were caught off guard. Instead, you recognize that He remains absolutely sovereign, in charge, and in complete command of the situation, Satan, and you. Things do not just happen to you, but God works them out for His greater purposes. If God is sovereign and the battle is His, then you cannot ultimately be defeated.

If God's sovereignty does not give you this confidence and comfort, then maybe it's because the last answer reflects your feelings. Certainly, the idea of God's granting Satan access to your life on occasion raises a number of questions. For example, if Satan is evil and he seeks our demise, then why would God let him test us? Why did Jesus knowingly let Satan test Peter, especially when he knew that Peter would fail? Why did God let Job be tested and lose everything important to him? Even more disturbing, if God let a true servant such as Job be tested, then how much testing will He allow in your life?

Understanding that the sovereignty of God is always accompanied by the love of God should allay any fears a believer may have about warfare. Love by nature seeks the welfare of others. Spiritual warfare is not some chess game in which God dispassionately, mechanically moves you and Satan in some grand scheme called His "will." Instead, the love of God means that He is looking out for your best interests. This truth sets you free to take refuge in God's sovereignty as a strong tower.

But, What If ...
Perhaps you are still feeling a little unsure about God's purposes for you. What if your authors' scholarship is flawed? What if Satan could attack at will? We really might feel like pawns on a giant chessboard. Look at the following chart and consider the implications.

"All those gathered here will know that it is not by sword or spear that the Lord saves; for the battle is the Lord's, and he will give all of you into our hands."
—1 Samuel 17:47

"He said: 'Listen, King Jehoshaphat and all who live in Judah and Jerusalem! This is what the Lord says to you: "Do not be afraid or discouraged because of this vast army. For the battle is not yours, but God's." ' "
—2 Chronicles 20:15

The Implications of a Sovereign God
1. God has a greater purpose in spiritual warfare.
2. The focus would be on God, not Satan, in the midst of the attack.
3. The confidence for victory depends on God, not me and my performance.
4. The standard of evaluating success depends on whether or not God accomplished His purposes through my life.

The Implications of an Unsovereign God
1. There would be no purpose in spiritual warfare, only random attacks.
2. The focus would have to be on Satan's evil plots instead of God's purposes.
3. The confidence for victory would depend on me and my performance.
4. The standard of evaluating success would depend on whether we were able to remove Satan.

God's sovereignty does not mean that you have no responsibility in spiritual warfare. Although the ultimate outcome is not in question, what happens in your life will be affected by how you respond. Adam and Eve's failure had negative consequences. Paul's obedience had positive consequences. God's sovereignty means your focus, expectations, and responses are radically altered so that you cooperate with God.

Do you see why trusting God's sovereignty is freeing? If God has a purpose for warfare, everything changes about the way you deal with the warfare. Instead of suddenly reacting to Satan's machinations, you immediately focus on God to seek His perspective. You don't get rattled and respond hysterically. Instead, you ask God what He is up to and respond accordingly. You recognize that He is not in heaven sitting on His hands waiting for Satan to come up with something. Instead, He is the pacesetter, the leader, the one who is more actively at work in your life than any created being in existence. God in His sovereignty knew every encounter you would have with evil before it ever happened.

Satan is not dictating the tempo of your life. God has predestined those whom He foreknew to experience the purposes He has for them (Rom. 8:29). God knows His own purposes for allowing the enemy access to your life, and His purposes can only be good. Although on occasion God chooses not to reveal His purpose in warfare, most of the time He does. His main desire is that we increasingly know and cooperate with Him. Days 3-5 will explore three of the overarching purposes for why God allows warfare in a believer's life.

Summarize how confidence in God's sovereignty helps us as we approach times of testing.

_____

_____

DAY THREE

REVEALING HIS WILL AND GLORY

If you were God, what would spiritual warfare look like from your perspective? Think of it—your sovereignty means you would have complete foreknowledge from all eternity of every single encounter with evil that any of your children would ever have, know every possibility of every outcome, already be completely present, and be all-powerful to do whatever you wanted. Concerning your feelings, you would love your children completely and would never let anything contrary to their best interests come into their lives. What, then, could possibly motivate you to allow Satan access to your children's lives?

The next three lessons will examine God's intentions when He allows warfare in a believer's life. Learning these three truths will help you respond correctly to God, keep a confident spirit, and experience God's victory. Today's lesson will focus on this first truth: God uses warfare to accomplish His will and reveal His glory. Admittedly, someone could list this statement as two separate truths because some distinctions are unique to both. However, we have chosen to list it as one because they are like two sides of the same coin. Let's look at the first side of the coin.

God Uses Warfare to Accomplish His Will

"The chief priests and the teachers of the law were looking for some way to get rid of Jesus, for they were afraid of the people.
Then Satan entered Judas, called Iscariot, one of the Twelve. And Judas went to the chief priests and the officers of the temple guard and discussed with them how he might betray Jesus."
—Luke 22:2-4

In the Bible, the cross is the clearest example of this truth. Consider the cross from the standpoint of warfare. We know that Satan orchestrated the arrest of Jesus. Read Luke 22:2-4.

Not only did Satan lay the groundwork for arresting Jesus, but also he was diligent to insure his plan succeeded. We know he was even present at the Last Supper because John 13:27 records, "As soon as Judas took the bread, Satan entered into him. 'What you are about to do, do quickly,' Jesus told him."

He continued to be active after the supper because Jesus told Peter in Luke 22:31 that Satan was going to sift the disciples. We see that sifting when Peter denied the Lord three times while Jesus was on trial at the high priest's house. Finally, Jesus foretold Satan's presence at the crucifixion by His statement in John 14:30, " 'the prince of this world is coming.' " Therefore, the cross and the events around it were unmistakably warfare.

Now ask the original question again with a twist. What would motivate a holy, sovereign, loving God to grant Satan access to His Son's life, even to the point that Satan succeeded in his plan of inflicting extreme torture and cruel death? Why would God do that? Precisely because God was in the process of working out His plan for world redemption. God used Satan to accomplish His will.

What does this reality mean for your life? What can you expect when you encounter warfare? (Check one.)

❑ God will never allow Satan to severely test me. Since I have Christ's authority, the moment Satan attacks, all I have to do is claim the blood of Jesus, and he can't touch me.

❑ If God turned Satan loose on Jesus, then I guess I'm in for it too. I probably should never expect Him to protect me; I will just have to endure random attacks while God accomplishes His will.

❑ That was just for Jesus—after all, He was the Son of God. He's in a different league. His experience doesn't apply to me.

❑ The moment Satan attacks, my confidence in God causes me to focus on Him as I seek to know Him and His purposes. My faith remains strong that a loving, sovereign God is up to something great, and I have the honor of being chosen for what He wants to accomplish.

Did you check the last choice? Many people encountering warfare get cocky or prideful because they misunderstand the nature of authority. Others adopt a fatalistic approach of just suffering through it. The attitude of Jesus was one of confidence in His God as He focused on the joy set before Him (Heb. 12:2). This faith in God means Christians never need be subjected to defeatism, panic, disorientation, or a sense of abandonment when encountering warfare.

Rate your level of confidence in God on a scale of 1 (shrinking) to 10 (growing). Indicate with an arrow whether it is growing or shrinking.

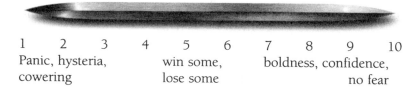

1	2	3	4	5	6	7	8	9	10

Panic, hysteria,   win some,   boldness, confidence,
cowering   lose some   no fear

Three biblical pictures give us reasons to have confidence in God. **First,** whenever Satan commits or perpetuates evil against the children of God, God uses that evil to accomplish His will. God used the persecution and scattering of the early church as a way of spreading the gospel. God used the death of Jesus to accomplish salvation. God used Satan's sifting of Peter and the disciples to break their pride about who would be the greatest.

Second, God turns into good what Satan means for evil. Saul's persecution of David (1 Sam. 18:10; 19:9) only strengthened his relationship with God and prepared him to be the kind of ruler who could lead the nation to depend on God. Satan's scheme of crucifying Jesus led to the salvation of the world. In each instance the very evil Satan committed became the very thing that God used for good. Satan must be the most frustrated being in existence. Not only does he lose, but whatever evil he commits becomes the very thing that God changes into good to defeat him. Dueling with the mind of God means that he must always fear in the midst of his apparent successes because at any moment God may reveal how He has redeemed Satan's wiles for His own purposes.

> "Spiritual warfare is a way of characterizing our common struggle as Christians. Whether we want to think about it or not, the truth is that we all face supernatural opposition as we set out to live the Christian life. … There is virtually no part of our existence over which the Evil One does not want to maintain or reassert his unhealthy and perverse influence. Conversely, Jesus longs to reign as Lord over every area of our lives. This is the locus of intense struggle for all believers. And it is a power struggle. To which kingdom—and source of power—do we yield?"[2]
>
> CLINTON ARNOLD

OUR CONFIDENCE IN GOD:
- *God uses evil to accomplish His will.*
- *God turns into good what Satan means for evil.*
- *Satan's machinations cannot thwart the purposes of God.*

Third, Satan's machinations cannot thwart the purposes of God. Numerous people in the Bible suffered setbacks. David went from being anointed king and killing Goliath to being hunted regularly by Saul. Jesus went from being proclaimed Messiah at the triumphal entry to being crucified in less than a week. However, Satan's initial success in no way implied that God's purposes were being hindered. The rest of the story reveals that David was anointed king, and Jesus rose from the dead. In fact, from God's perspective, setbacks are re-defined as experiences to develop character and accomplish His will.

Have you experienced setbacks? injustices? wrong? In light of these three truths, how should you respond the next time something evil happens? (Check one.)
- ❑ When I encounter trouble, I should assume that I didn't hear God correctly.
- ❑ When I encounter trouble, I should quit what I'm doing and try another approach.
- ❑ When I encounter trouble, I should attack Satan in return.
- ❑ When I encounter trouble, I should stay angry at the person who caused it.
- ❑ When I encounter trouble, I should focus on God and seek His perspective on how to respond. In the meantime, I will rejoice because I know that God will bring about victory in the end.

Living your life by the last answer is more difficult but brings tremendous freedom in the end. Ask God to enable you to walk in these new truths. Now let's look at some truths about God's glory.

God Uses Warfare to Reveal His Glory

Have you ever tried to define *the glory of God?* Describing it is a very difficult task. Even the dictionary has multiple definitions for the word *glory*, and none really seems comprehensive when applied to God.

Glory is the outshining, the reflection, the effulgence, the radiance of what it means to be God.

Glory is the outshining, the reflection, the effulgence, the radiance of what it means to be God. Glory is bound up with the essence of who God is because it comes from who He is. Understanding that God's glory cannot be separated from His person means one must walk a very careful tightrope when making the statement, "God uses warfare to reveal His glory." On one hand, neither Satan, demon, angel, nor man can add to or subtract from this glory. If God were dependent on another to reveal His glory, then He would be less than God because He would not be self-sufficient.

On the other hand, God has chosen to use the actions of Satan and man to reveal His nature and character. For example, when Satan succeeded in His scheme of the cross, what did it demonstrate about God? The moment God accomplished atonement for sin, we came to know Him in ways we would not have otherwise. Who would have guessed that God's love was that great? Who could have understood the depth of His compassion and forgiveness? Conversely, who really fathomed the fear of God until that event? Could we have guessed the extent to which His holiness demanded satisfaction had He not poured His wrath out on His own Son? The glory of His character was revealed by the context of the evil in which it occurred. Because God allowed warfare, all creation can understand Him in ways it could not have before.

God allows warfare in the lives of His children in order that believers can know Him in new and deeper ways. Perhaps we miss this central truth because of the way we view the will of God. Typically, when we pray "thy will be done on earth just as it is in heaven," we define His will as the action, the plan, the goal, or the thing that He wants to accomplish. God's will does include what He wants to accomplish, but we often forget that the heart of His will focuses on developing a relationship with His children. Think about it—if it were simply a matter of getting things done, He would just use the angels. They would immediately respond without quibble or reservation, unlike what we believers succumb to from time to time. Instead, the heart of God's will relates to what happens in our relationship with Him through the process.

Therefore, God does not want us to contract tunnel vision, to myopically focus on a set of activities to obey, but rather to know Him in the process of obeying. Our skill, ability, and efficiency motivate Him not one little bit, but the intimacy from a love relationship does. He allows the trials of Satan so that He can reveal His glory in ways that a sanitized, sterile environment could not afford. Our fresh encounters and newfound discoveries of Him help fuel a love relationship. God's motive explains His actions, making sense of what does not make sense. What joy would it be to God if He always shielded us from temptation, yet our relationship with Him was not strengthened? This desire for a love relationship explains why God uses warfare to reveal His glory.

Reflect on a time when you encountered warfare. Tell how you came to know God better as a result.

_____

_____

Take a moment and praise God for the overwhelmingly wonderful reality of your love relationship with Him. Ask Him to reveal His glory to you and through you.

A MISPERCEPTION ABOUT SPIRITUAL WARFARE

Many people mistakenly call every single bad event in their life spiritual warfare. This belief reveals a deadly error in thinking.

1. *A person with this viewpoint believes the whole nature of warfare revolves around how self is impacted. They view good and evil solely through the lens of whether or not it troubles them.*

2. *This viewpoint does not seek to interpret accidents, mistakes, and troubles of life through the lens of the purposes of God. Never assume it is warfare unless the accidents, mistakes, and troubles hinder a person from doing the will of God.*

3. *This viewpoint does not take into account the consequences of the fall. Man inherited a sinful nature, and much evil committed in the world results from the wickedness of his own heart. Death also was a consequence of the fall. We know of a man who actually referred to the death of an aged family member as spiritual warfare!*

4. *This viewpoint does not allow for the discipline of God. Many things we might consider to be bad happened in the lives of Bible characters because God was disciplining His children.*

5. *My irresponsibility does not equal warfare.*

DAY FOUR

ADVANCING THE KINGDOM

Yesterday's study revealed that all warfare results in God accomplishing His will and revealing His glory. Today's lesson focuses on a second reality that always happens whenever Christians successfully handle warfare: the kingdom of God advances in some way.

The kingdom is the rule and reign of God over all that is under His dominion.

What Is the Kingdom?

We first need to define what we mean by *kingdom*. Simply put, the kingdom is the rule and reign of God over all that is under His dominion. On one level that includes everything in creation because God is over all. Surprisingly, however, God has limited His rule in the human heart to the consent of each person. God does not force anyone to involuntarily submit to His Lordship. Therefore, when the Bible speaks of the kingdom, it is more concerned with the heart than geo-political boundaries.

How Is God's Kingdom Advanced?
Conversion
On the most basic level the kingdom advances whenever someone is saved. Salvation is accepting the rule of God. Prior to being born again, a sinner rejects God's rule. The moment he recognizes his sin (rebellion against God's rule), repents (turns from self-rule), and believes (trusts God and His Word), he is converted. As more people turn to God, the the kingdom advances more.

The Influence of Salt and Light
The kingdom advances when God's people persuade society to accept God's moral standard. Culture is affected as the salt and light perform the function Jesus intended (Matt. 5:13-16). Three examples of American Christians influencing their country are the shaping of the values upon which the government was founded, abolishing slavery, and reducing the evils of alcohol abuse. This influence should not be mistaken as a substitute for conversion, but it does increase the welfare of society and the likelihood that people will be converted (1 Tim. 2:2-4).

The Increase of Love and Unity Among Christians
The kingdom not only extends roots outward but downward as well. As believers walk with the Lord, He transforms the propensity to gratify self first with a desire to put others first. The more believers conform to the ways of love and unity, the sweeter life becomes in the kingdom. Love and unity among Christians influence the world toward conversion as well. Jesus said all men would recognize that they are His disciples by their love (John 13:34-35). The increase of love results in the lost being converted, because they want what believers have.

How does your church primarily seek to advance the kingdom? (Circle one.)

conversion   influence   love and unity

If your church does not have a burden for advancing the kingdom, what do you feel is the reason for this attitude?

_____

_____

How Does Kingdom Advance Relate to Spiritual Warfare?

If Christians remain focused on God when Satan attacks, the kingdom will advance in at least one of these three ways. God capitalizes on the opportunity to impact hearts by redeeming the devil's scheme for good. Therefore, when Satan begins to attack believers, a child of God ought to expect that God will accomplish a victory either immediately or in due time.

The victory, however, requires cooperation. Although God could act unilaterally, He has chosen to use His children in the process of advancing the kingdom. The responsibility He delegates is so great that the kingdom will be positively or negatively impacted by our obedience. For example, if Christians fight with each other and live immorally, the watching world will not be drawn to Christ. If believers sacrifice for each other, forgive, and love one another, many will be drawn to Christ because they see a difference. Therefore, we must know the ways of God to cooperate with Him.

Be on Mission with God to Advance the Kingdom

Our hope of victory in warfare is determined ahead of time by whether or not we are on mission with God. Everyone in the Bible whose life was characterized by victory sought the kingdom ahead of his or her own interests. Typically, a four-step process occurs for the kingdom to advance through warfare. Acts 16 presents an example of this process from the life of the apostle Paul. Read it in your Bible.

Paul's second missionary journey had been delayed by the Spirit Himself, but Paul refused to become discouraged. Finally, in verse 9 he had a vision of a man asking for help in Macedonia, a Roman province. He eagerly went, concluding that the Lord had finally opened a door for him to preach the gospel. After arriving, he found a place where women regularly gathered to pray. He spoke to them, and a woman named Lydia and her household were converted. This inroad into Satan's kingdom soon resulted in conflict, but the foundation for victory in Paul's life was established ahead of time because of his obedience to God. If he had not been on mission with God, he would have been disobedient to the Great Commission, and he could not have had much expectation of God's answering his prayer.

What does this experience from the life of Paul mean to you? When can you have absolute confidence that God will accomplish a great victory through your life?

Not every person has to be an evangelist or missionary, but every person does need to seek the advance of the kingdom by using the gifts God has given him. Fortunately, God often chooses to be gracious and helps believers even when they have not put Him first. However, the point is that believers cannot have full confidence unless they are walking in obedience.

A four-step process occurs for the kingdom to advance through warfare.
1. Be on mission with God to advance the kingdom.

A four-step process occurs for the kingdom to advance through warfare.
1. *Be on mission with God to advance the kingdom.*
2. *Conflict and testing always occur*
3. *Obey God and do His work His way*

Conflict and Testing Always Occur

When Christians seek to advance the kingdom, conflict must ensue because two opposing kingdoms clash. Satan and those under his influence will resist the message. Notice in Acts 16:16-18 that a slave girl with a spirit began to follow Paul. Presumably, she was disrupting his message because her antics would have drawn attention to herself, even if she were saying the right thing. Whatever the reason, Paul cast out the spirit.

The exorcism upset her masters, and they dragged Paul and Silas to the authorities where they began falsely accusing them (vv. 19-24). Satan may have lost the slave girl's mind, but he obviously retained the minds of her masters. They so stirred up the crowd that Paul and Silas were beaten, thrown into prison, and shackled.

Their experience was representative of people in the Bible who set out to be on mission with God. Moses, the prophets, all the apostles, and the early church all encountered opposition of varying kinds. Their message threatened Satan's kingdom, and he fought back. Based on this reality, Christians should not be surprised by trouble.

Satan's resistance takes various forms depending on the avenues available to him. For example, on a national scale he can use government structures to persecute, squelch the message, or dissuade people from faith. On an individual scale he may use peer pressure, antagonism, or the seduction of ease. Whatever the case, the demands of the gospel will be in direct opposition to the self-rule that Satan encourages in peoples' hearts. Many will resist it.

On a national scale how is Satan fighting Christians?

_____

_____

How does Satan oppose believers individually?

_____

_____

Where is God when the conflict begins? He is the One who leads us into the battle in the first place. He doesn't need to be suddenly called into the situation. He's not shocked and scrambling for a plan. No, He led us there because He knows how He will advance the kingdom through us. Our job is to focus on Him and seek His perspective.

Obey God and Do His Work His Way

Victory does not come by intelligence, power, or formulas. Victory comes by doing God's work God's way. Read James 4:6. Did you notice that submission precedes resistance? If we are not obeying the Lord, can we have any hope for victory? God never promises His power to

"God opposes the proud but gives grace to the humble. Submit yourselves, then, to God. Resist the devil, and he will flee from you."
—*James 4:6*

Christians who resist on their own terms. The only defense a Christian has against Satan is obedience to God.

How did Paul and Silas resist? Acts 16:25 says they were praying and singing hymns to God. They were not cursing or threatening their jailers. Instead, they were focused on God, confident in Him. They did not whine and throw a pity party; the joy of the Lord was their strength. When the earthquake jarred the prison doors open, Paul immediately asked the jailer not to kill himself. Obviously he had forgiven the injustices they suffered and sought the man's well-being. Paul gladly proclaimed the way of salvation and willingly received the hospitality the new convert offered them.

The only defense a Christian has against Satan is obedience to God.

God Advances the Kingdom

God advanced His kingdom in three ways as a result of Paul's and Silas's prison experience. **First,** advancement came through conversions. The Philippian jailer and his household entered the kingdom as a direct result of Paul and Silas cooperating with God in the midst of their warfare. **Second,** a door opened for Christians to proclaim the gospel that would not have happened without this incident. In verses 37-39 Paul made the magistrates escort them out publicly. The effect was to publicly legitimize Christianity and discourage the persecution of new converts because everyone would know they had beaten Roman citizens. The potential for the influence of the gospel increased in Philippi.

Third, as Christians experienced trials together, their love for one another was strengthened. Philippians 4:15-18 reveals just how special the relationship was between Paul and these believers. When he was in Thessalonica, they sent him aid on at least two occasions, perhaps more (v. 16). In the Philippian letter Paul acknowledged another gift through Epaphroditus whom they sent to minister to Paul. Obviously, their trials and experiences had only served to strengthen the bond between them.

A four-step process occurs for the kingdom to advance through warfare.
1. Be on mission with God to advance the kingdom.
2. Conflict and testing always occur
3. Obey God and do His work His way
4. God advances the kingdom

List a time in your life when you saw this pattern at work.
What individual or group was on mission?

_____

What opposition resulted?

_____

How did the person or group stand the test by doing God's work God's way?

_____

How did God advance the kingdom?

_____

Reflect on Your Readiness

What's your spiritual warfare readiness? Are you on mission with God? Are you seeking ways to advance the kingdom? Do you reach out to the lost through the gifts God has given you? If so, are you prepared for opposition? Are you willing to do God's work God's way?

DAY FIVE
_____

CONFORMING TO CHRIST'S IMAGE

Thus far this study has explained how God generally uses spiritual warfare to accomplish His will, to reveal His glory, and to advance His kingdom. This lesson will examine how God uses warfare to achieve His overall goal in the lives of His children: to make them like Christ.

Becoming like Christ

People use the term *Christian* in many ways. For some, a Christian is simply a good person who goes to church. Others equate *American* with *Christian*. In some parts of the world, anyone who isn't Muslim or Jewish is called *Christian*.

The word *Christian* literally means "of Christ" or "like Christ." A Christian has been "born again" by God's grace and now is a child of God (John 1:12; 3:3; Eph. 2:8-9). God expects His children to become increasingly more like Jesus as they grow in their faith—and sometimes He uses spiritual warfare to make them like Jesus.

Read Romans 8:18-37. In this text, the apostle Paul told how to respond to the struggles we face in this world. Answer each of the following questions, paying attention to Paul's understanding of what God is doing in our lives as He leads us through battles.

If we struggle in this world, how do these sufferings compare with what God will provide in heaven? (v. 18)

_____

When we don't know how to pray in the midst of struggles, who

prays for us? (v. 26) _____

When the Spirit prays for us, does He ever pray in opposition to God's will in our lives? (v. 27) ❏ Yes ❏ No

When God works all things together for good in our lives (v. 28), what is His goal? (v. 29)

_____

Can anything—including the powers—separate us from the love of God? (vv. 31-39) ❑ Yes ❑ No

Paul knew that when the battles were intense, believers would not always be sure how to pray. The Holy Spirit prays for believers, and He always prays according to God's will. Because God's will is that His children be conformed to the image of Christ, the Spirit must be praying that God will allow whatever it takes to make them like Jesus. However, believers know that nothing can separate them from the love of God.

God always has a goal—to make us like His Son. If He allows spiritual battles to occur in our lives, He does so for our good. He wants us to turn to Him, trust Him, follow Him, and become more like Him through the battle. This process gives us hope.

If He allows spiritual battles to occur in our lives, He does so for our good.

How do you respond to this truth? (Check all that apply.)
❑ I need this truth right now—I'm in a battle.
❑ I didn't know how God uses spiritual battles in my life.
❑ I'm glad God has a purpose, but I still don't like battles.
❑ Usually I try to run from the battles. Maybe I need to see what God might be teaching me in my battles.

Paul Lived this Process

The apostle Paul struggled with a "thorn in the flesh" that he attributed to Satan (2 Cor. 12:7). Paul didn't identify the thorn, but it clearly caused anguish. In fact, the word translated *torment* in verse 12 suggests persistent, repetitive slapping.[3] Satan was continually attacking the apostle through this weakness.

Yet when Paul asked God three times to remove the thorn, God did not do so. Instead, He taught Paul that His grace would always be sufficient (2 Cor. 12:8-9). The apostle would be strengthened only when he realized that God would be his strength. The battle was difficult for Paul, and the pain of battling the enemy was real, but in the end, Paul learned to lean upon God even in his weakness. He learned to say as Jesus had, "Not my will, [God], but yours be done [in my life]" (Luke 22:42).

Do those words sound familiar? Jesus voiced similar words when He struggled with the reality of His impending death (Mark 14:36). He was in a spiritual battle, but He chose to remain in the battle if God willed it. When Paul learned to accept his thorn because God chose to leave it there, he was being conformed to the image of Christ. He was learning to trust and depend on God.

When we fight spiritual battles, we are wise to follow Paul's example. God may choose to leave us in the battle because He is always in the process of molding us to the image of His Son. Indeed, while we likely won't enjoy the battle, we can experience joy in the battle as we become more like Christ.

In the margin describe a time when God left you in a spiritual battle so you could learn to depend on Him. Tell how you became more like Christ in the process.

> When I (Chuck) was a young believer, I asked God to remove all my temptations so that I could best serve Him. God didn't do so; in fact, temptations sometimes were stronger. What God taught me was that temptation should cause me to depend on Him for strength—and that I needed to learn dependence to be like Jesus.

Believers Can Depend Upon God to Defeat the Enemy Because We Are "In Christ"

In the process of learning dependence through spiritual battles, Christians also learn the significance of Christ's living in them. We aren't strong enough in our own strength to defeat Satan, but Christ who lives within us gives us strength to do all things (Phil. 4:13).

In the first three chapters of Ephesians—the same book that calls believers to "put on the whole armor of God" (6:11)—Paul clearly laid this theological foundation for victory in spiritual warfare. Christians experience spiritual victory because we are in Christ.

The phrase *in Christ* occurs often in Ephesians.

- He chose us in Him (1:4).
- In Him, we have redemption (1:7).
- We have our hope in Him (1:12).
- We have been included in Him (1:13).
- We have been marked in Him with a seal (1:13).
- We are created in Him to do good works (2:10).

The first three chapters contain other great truths. God has adopted us as His sons (1:5). He has forgiven our sins (1:7). He has guaranteed our inheritance, securing our salvation forever (1:13-14). He has expressed His kindness to us (2:7). Because we are in Christ, we may "approach God with freedom and confidence" (3:12).

Read each Scripture and match the text with its corresponding truth of who we are in Christ.

___ 1. Romans 8:17   a. We are His children.
___ 2. 2 Corinthians 1:21-22   b. He has made us a new creation.
___ 3. John 1:12   c. He has rescued us from darkness.
___ 4. 2 Corinthians 5:17   d. We are heirs with Christ.
___ 5. Colossians 1:13   e. He has sealed us with His Spirit.

Take some time to meditate on all of these New Testament truths. Do you realize how important you are to God? Do you understand all that God has done for us? Can you see why Paul felt confident in struggles to say, "No, in all these things we are more than conquerors through him who loved us" (Rom. 8:37)? The answers are 1. d; 2. e; 3. a; 4. b; 5. c.

Because Christ lives in us, we are promised victory in spiritual battles. At the same time, God uses the battles to make us more like Christ. Christ within us becomes evident in our outward actions and attitudes as we remain faithful in spiritual warfare. Thank God that you are in Christ and that He uses your battles to make you more like Christ.

---

[1]Warren W. Wiersbe, *Classic Sermons on Spiritual Warfare* (Grand Rapids: Kregel, 1992), 91.
[2]Clinton Arnold, *Three Crucial Questions About Spiritual Warfare* (Grand Rapids: Baker, 1997), 27.
[3]David Garland, *New American Commentary,* vol. 29 (Nashville: Broadman, 1999), 522.

VIEWER GUIDE

1. God is absolutely _____ over all things, yet we are

   _____ for our actions.

2. God's plan is to make us like _____.

   Sometimes He uses the devil, demons, and evil to accomplish that in our lives.

   For example, Paul's thorn in the flesh was a messenger of _____.

   Paul learned that God left the thorn to teach Paul _____

   _____.

3. God allows the devil to interrupt our lives, but He's working even in using the

   devil for His _____.

4. When we wrestle with struggles in life, we go to the book of _____

   to find out that God's in control in even these struggles.

5. The main two issues that get in the way of our living victorious Christian lives are

   1) the _____   2) the _____

6. The Bible doesn't give the devil the priority. The Bible is about _____.

7. Being in Christ makes all the difference in battling the devil. When I learn to live

   on the basis of that truth, I can stand firm against the _____.

Authority and Character

CASE STUDY

Sally was in trouble. A wayward teen, she had created heartache after heartache for her single mother. Now she'd been expelled from school, and the counselors recommended that she be placed in a school for difficult teens. Sally's mother agreed to sign the papers.

Sally's response was quick: "You have no right to do this to me. I can take care of myself, and you can't make me go to that school."

Her mom tried to explain her decision, but Sally's next response was cutting: "When you were young, you did the same things I'm doing. No one put you in a special school. Why should you, of all people, tell me how to live?" As a parent, Sally's mother had the authority to send her daughter to the school. But, because of her own questionable character, she lacked authority in Sally's eyes.

For all of us, our authority to influence and lead others can't be separated from our character. Few people will follow us—and the devil doesn't get too worried about our authority in Christ—if our character lacks credibility. This week's lessons will address the relationship between our authority in Christ and our character as they relate to spiritual warfare.

DAY ONE

THE NATURE OF OUR AUTHORITY

Have you ever wondered why God hasn't already taken you to heaven? What an infinitely better place to be! No more pain or suffering—just perfect bliss. Instead, misery, injustice, disease, wars, and wickedness surround you. If God loves you, why does He leave you here?

We Cooperate with God

The reason is amazing. Read Colossians 1:28-29. Obviously Paul believed that God wants believers to work with Him to impact the world. He has chosen to accomplish His will by involving His children in the process. What a staggering thought!

"We proclaim him, admonishing and teaching everyone with all wisdom, so that we may present everyone perfect in Christ. To this end I labor, struggling with all his energy, which so powerfully works in me."
—*Colossians 1:28-29*

When God wants to save someone, He looks for one of His children. When He wants to put a marriage back together, He calls upon a Christian. When He wants to feed the hungry, He motivates one of His own. When He wants to impact a nation, He stirs His people. When God moves against the kingdom of Satan, He involves His church. Although God could do it without anyone else, He has chosen to work through us.

List one way God has involved you in His work.

_____

We Have Been Given Authority to Cooperate with God

Romans 8:32 teaches that since God did not withhold the most precious possession He had (His Son), then He will give His children anything else He has. Ephesians 2:6 lists one of those "anything else" things He has given us. God has "raised us up with Christ and seated us with him in the heavenly realms in Christ Jesus." Sitting together with Jesus implies reigning on the throne with Him. God has actually given us His authority, the right to rule with Him!

What does this authority imply when it comes to spiritual warfare? Do we have authority over the devil just as Jesus has authority over the devil? Yes! In Luke 9:1 Jesus gave His disciples power and authority over demons. Upon returning from their second tour (Luke 10:17), they proclaimed an amazing discovery, "Lord, even the demons submit to us in your name!" He then reiterated to them, " 'I have given you authority to trample on snakes and scorpions and to overcome all the power of the enemy; nothing will harm you' " (v. 19).

In that hour Jesus rejoiced in His Spirit and thanked God that He had revealed these things to His disciples (v. 21). Why did He rejoice so? He meditated on the upside-down ways of His Father. God had made babes wiser than the wise. He had made the simple profound. He had made the weak stronger than the strong. When it came to spiritual warfare, those once under Satan's authority now had authority over him. In God's upside-down world, the mighty Satan was no match for the lowliest disciple.

Does God play favorites? Were biblical characters privy to certain things withheld from believers today? Of course not! What Jesus did for

EXAMPLES OF AUTHORITY IN THE BIBLE

1. *The absolute power and freedom of God to act as He wishes (Luke 4:36; John 17:2).*
2. *The power and ability of Jesus to do the Father's work (Matt. 9:6-8; 28:18-20; Mark 6:7; John 10:18).*
3. *The right given to church leaders to build up the church (2 Cor. 10:8; 13:10).*

them, He has done for us. The authority we have in Christ today is no less than the authority the disciples had 2,000 years ago.

What do you think authority over the devil implies?
❏ I can limit the activity of Satan by using my authority in Christ.
❏ I can protect others under spiritual attack through the use of my authority.
❏ I can remove Satan's presence by claiming my authority in Christ.
❏ Satan must submit to me whenever I tell him to do anything.

Scripture presents us with a paradox.

Whether you checked one or all four, remember that nothing creates disillusionment like understanding only half the truth. Admittedly, authority in Christ creates the possibility of Satan being limited, prohibited, removed, and prevented from harming others, but Scripture presents us with a paradox.

A Surprising Paradox
Jesus and the saints possessed authority, but their authority didn't always work itself out in the way we might expect. If we turn through the photo album of the Bible, we see some unusual snapshots.

Bible Snapshots

Snapshot 1—The same Jesus who said, " 'Away from me, Satan!' " (Matt. 4:10) is the same Jesus who allowed the devil to hang around 40 days and then set Jesus on the pinnacle of the temple (Matt. 4:5).

Snapshot 2—The same Jesus who cast a legion of demons out of a man (Mark 5:8) is the same Jesus who allowed that legion of demons to kill 2,000 pigs (Mark 5:13).

Snapshot 3—The same Jesus who healed a girl from severe demon-possession (Matt. 15:28) was the same Jesus who granted Satan permission to sift the disciples (Luke 22:31).

Snapshot 4—The same God who built a hedge of protection around Job (Job 1:10) was the same God who granted permission for it to be removed (Job 1:12).

Snapshot 5—The same God who promised to deliver one church from the trial coming on the whole earth and make those who are a synagogue of Satan bow at their feet (Rev. 3:9-10) is the same God who warned another church that the devil would persecute them and throw them into prison (Rev. 2:10).

Snapshot 6—The same Paul who cast out a spirit (Acts 16:18) is the same Paul who was given a messenger of Satan to torment him the rest of his life (2 Cor. 12:7).

Snapshot 7—Often demonic presences were immediately removed, but occasionally demonic presence continued to be present for an extended time such as the possessed slave girl following Paul (Acts 16:18).

Snapshot 8—Sometimes deliverance was immediate; other times saints were required to endure (Rom. 16:20; 1 Pet. 5:8-10; Rev. 13:10).

How can we explain this paradox? Why was Satan's presence immediately removed at times but at others people were required to endure?

Check one or more of the implications of the paradox.

❑ The people involved had weak faith or they didn't understand how to use their authority. Some problem lay with them.

❑ I don't know why things worked out that way, but it doesn't really matter much. I shouldn't try to figure it out.

❑ Authority does not always guarantee the immediate removal of Satan's presence and activity in my life.

❑ A Christian must understand a biblical view of authority in order to respond to God correctly.

Which answers did you choose? Jesus' experience in the wilderness rules out the first answer. He neither had a spiritual problem nor was His faith weak. The ostrich approach of burying your head in the sand in answer two could prove fatal in spiritual battles. Hopefully you marked the last two. What is the biblical view of authority?

The Purpose of Authority Is to Execute God's Will

The secret lies in understanding the nature of authority. Jesus made a revealing statement about His life in John 10:18. Jesus did not view authority as the right to use the power of God any way He wanted. He could not decide on a plan, then claim that the Father was obligated to do His will. Instead, He believed that only the Father had the right to determine how His authority would be exercised. Jesus understood three truths about authority and the implications for His life.

First, authority is derived, not inherent. The authority for having authority comes from God. We are not born with it. Authority begins with God and flows toward humanity. Implication: We do not have the right to choose how we will exercise authority.

Second, authority is subservient, not independent. Jesus knew He could not set a direction different from His Father's. Whenever an ambassador represents the king, he knows that his decisions and actions cannot violate the purposes of his king. He is free to make decisions, but they must always be in harmony with the desires of his king. Jesus did not view authority as the right to set His own agenda. Implication: The use of authority must always be in keeping with God's purposes.

Third, authority is shared, not separate. Jesus recognized that He shared His Father's authority as long as He did His Father's will. This principle works in a similar way in business. Although a boss delegates authority for an employee to handle the company finances, the employee is not granted unlimited freedom. If the employee were to embezzle or mismanage funds, the boss can call for accountability because he still retains ultimate authority. The employee's authority remains operative only as long as he functions in harmony with his boss' wishes. Implication: Authority is effective only as we are in line with the will of God.

These truths explain the paradox. Obviously, the immediate removal of Satan is not always the will of the Father. Unfortunately,

" 'No one takes it from me, but I lay it down of my own accord. I have authority to lay it down and authority to take it up again. This command I received from my Father.' "
—John 10:18

" 'He has given him authority to judge because he is the Son of Man. … By myself I can do nothing; I judge only as I hear, and my judgment is just, for I seek not to please myself but him who sent me.' "
—John 5:27,30

" 'I did not speak of my own accord, but the Father who sent me commanded me what to say and how to say it.' "
—John 12:49

" 'Don't you believe that I am in the Father, and that the Father is in me? The words I say to you are not just my own. Rather, it is the Father, living in me, who is doing his work.' "
—John 14:10

many Christians have misunderstood authority as the right to exercise power over the devil whenever and however they decide. By grasping only half the truth, many Christians mistakenly assume that

- victory in warfare always means the immediate removal of Satan or squelching his plans;
- Christians are immune from warfare;
- when warfare occurs, Christians can always rebuke/bind/cast out Satan to get relief;
- when warfare does not immediately stop, the Christian is to blame. It's his or her spiritual problem.

The biblical view of authority is that believers respond to God by cooperating with Him. The focus of a Christian's authority is not over Satan but with and under God. Sometimes God's purposes require the demonic to be immediately removed, but other times God allows warfare to continue. Christians are not immune, nor does authority guarantee immediate relief. Victory is a result of obeying God.

Day 2 examines the two purposes of our authority. Today, focus on God's purposes in your life.

Are you in a season of spiritual warfare? If so, describe it in the margin. If not, identify other ways God is building your character. Write your response in the margin.

DAY TWO

TWO APPLICATIONS OF OUR AUTHORITY

God has all authority in heaven and earth. Why should He share it?

AUTHORITY
"It is the uniform witness of the Bible that all authority is located in God. People possess authority only as the Lord gives it (Rom. 13:1). Religious authority derives from the authority of the Father, as that authority is revealed in the Son, manifested by the Holy Spirit, and given in and through the Bible to the church and the world."[1]

Imagine standing before God and requesting that He give you the authority to bring about something on earth. What arguments would you give to persuade Him to agree with you?
- ❏ I really want this to happen.
- ❏ I think it would be a good idea.
- ❏ It will make me happy.
- ❏ You love me and want to bless me.
- ❏ I want the same thing You want. I'll be responsible to exercise authority in keeping with Your purposes.

Authority is powerful. God will not indiscriminately let it be used by us in any way we see fit. He first requires that we understand the purpose for authority: it is not for our own desires, but rather for doing His will. His will always includes two primary considerations. Understanding these two truths explains the paradoxes from day 1. By applying these principles, you can exercise authority wisely.

The Edification of Others

The first truth is that authority is to be used to edify others. To edify is to instruct or improve spiritually. Notice in 2 Corinthians 13:10 Paul assumed that a primary use of authority was for building others up. He didn't claim authority so he could get his way or bend things to his advantage. He knew that God grants authority for the purpose of executing whatever is in the best interests of fellow Christians. Sometimes that meant he confronted sin (2 Cor. 13:2); sometimes that meant he was gentle (1 Thess. 2:7; Philem. 1:8-9). The bottom line for Paul was that edification determined when and how he exercised authority.

"This is why I write these things when I am absent, that when I come I may not have to be harsh in my use of authority—the authority the Lord gave me for building you up, not for tearing you down."
—2 Corinthians 13:10

An Example from the Life of Jesus

Since Jesus is God, we can study Jesus' actions to know how to respond. In Mark 9 Jesus returned from the mount of transfiguration and found the waiting crowd in chaos. The disciples couldn't cast a demon from a boy. The amazed crowd ran to meet Jesus. The father cried out for help. Jesus said, " 'Bring the boy to me.' " By that statement Jesus announced His intention to do battle with Satan. Here is an unmistakably clear picture of how God wants His authority exercised.

When the demon saw Jesus, it had a violent reaction to His presence. It immediately threw the boy into a convulsion so that he wallowed on the ground, foaming at the mouth. Question—if you were the King of kings and Lord of lords, the Almighty God with the power to do anything, and you have just announced You are going to take care of this situation, what do you do next? Think of it—this boy is your very own creation. You formed him with your very own hands. You have loved him with an everlasting love. Now this demonic being who has tried to kill him since childhood has the audacity to throw him into a seizure in your very presence.

If you had been Jesus in this situation, what would you have done next?

_____

Logically, one would assume that Jesus would cast out the demon, but instead He strikes up a conversation with the father. " 'How long has he been like this?' " Jesus' question is astounding. While the demon was in the middle of throwing the boy into something like an epileptic fit, Jesus decided to let it go on a while and talk to the dad! There was no binding, no rebuking, no deliverance. Why would Jesus delay?

Can a perfect God ever fail to take a perfect course of action? No. The father's response revealed Jesus' motive. Hear the agony in the man's voice as he recounted the helpless struggle of the boy's life. He begged Jesus to take pity on them if He could. Jesus looked at him with those piercing eyes and exclaimed, "What!? If I can? All things are possible for him who believes!" (Mark 9:23, author's paraphrase). The father suddenly realized his faith had faltered and exclaimed, "I do believe. Help my unbelief!" Jesus then cast out the demon.

Why did Jesus delay? What was He seeking to accomplish in the life of the father? Respond in the margin.

From Jesus' perspective what was more important: exorcism or faith? Obviously Jesus wanted to deliver the boy because He called him into His presence for that very purpose. However, Jesus did not cast out the demon until He had first cast out unbelief. He knew that the man's greatest need was faith because without faith it is impossible to please God (Heb. 11:6). Therefore, His exercise of authority was based on what would edify everyone involved.

The boy did eventually get delivered, but first the father had his relationship with God strengthened. Jesus knew what, when, and how to exercise authority because He responded to the purposes of His Father, not the presence of Satan. The Christian life is not about doing battle with Satan but about knowing God and doing His will. Correctly handling warfare is tied to understanding God and His purposes.

The Advance of the Kingdom

The second truth about the exercise of authority is that it must relate to the advance of God's kingdom. In examining the life of Jesus and His disciples, we see this pattern at work.

Why the Father Gave Authority to the Son

Have you ever wondered why Jesus waited until He was 30 years old to begin His ministry? Jesus Himself gave us at least one reason in His first hometown sermon. Read what He said in Luke 4:18-19.

In other words Jesus was saying, *Do you recognize God's timing? Interpret my preaching, teaching, healing, and deliverance ministry as the time of God's favor. My actions show His goodness to you so that you will return to Him. It's God's signal that now is your invitation to be restored. Therefore, take courage. Come and repent, for He desires to bless you.*

Jesus began performing miracles when the Father's timing determined the year He would draw His people back to Himself. Jesus never lost sight of the purpose of authority. He refused to perform miracles at the whim of the Pharisees or the crowd but immediately used miracles when they validated His message, drew people to Him, or encouraged faith.

For what purpose did the Father grant authority to Jesus?

_____

Why the Son Gave Authority to the Disciples

Did God's pattern for granting authority hold true for Jesus' disciples? Three times the Bible records that Jesus granted authority to the disciples.

First, in Matthew 10:1 Jesus gave the twelve authority over unclean spirits. Immediately prior to this verse, He had commanded them to ask the Lord of the harvest to send out workers. Immediately after this command, they were to go out and preach to the nation of Israel.

> *" 'The Spirit of the Lord is on me,*
> *because he has anointed me*
> *to preach good news to the poor.*
> *He has sent me to proclaim freedom for the prisoners*
> *and recovery of sight for the blind,*
> *to release the oppressed,*
> *to proclaim the year of the Lord's favor.' "*
> —*Luke 4:18-19*

Second, in Luke 10:17 the 72 came back from preaching and remarked that the demons submitted to them in the name of Jesus.

Third, Jesus stated that all authority had been given to Him; we are to go into all the world and make disciples of all nations (Matt. 28:18-19).

For what purpose did Jesus grant authority to His

disciples? _____

Why the Son Gave Authority to the Church

Three examples from Acts reveal why evil spirits were cast out. **First,** Philip preached the gospel in Samaria, performed miracles, and evil spirits left with a loud voice. As a result, people paid close attention to what he said (Acts 8:4-8).

Second, Paul cast out a spirit. The girl's irate masters threw Paul and Silas in jail. God sent an earthquake, and, as a result of their release, the jailer's entire family was converted (16:18-34).

Third, God was doing extraordinary miracles through Paul, including driving out evil spirits. Some non-believers tried to exorcise a demon in the name of Christ; instead, the demon beat them up. As a result, the name of Jesus was held in high honor, and new believers confessed their sins publicly and burned witchcraft books (19:11-20).

For what purpose did God grant authority to the early

church? _____

Learning the Right Use of Authority

Did you notice the common denominator? The Father gave the Son authority when it was time to call Israel back to Himself. Jesus gave authority in the context of sending His disciples to proclaim the good news. In Acts the authority to cast out demons revolved around Jesus' being honored and conversions occurring. The context of authority was being on mission with God. Do you need to add to or change your answers to the questions above?

How does learning to use authority help us in spiritual warfare? We must spend time understanding from God's perspective what edifies others and advances the kingdom. Sometimes believers are most bene-fited by the instant removal of Satan's presence. Other times we must endure testing for a season. When something of kingdom significance is at stake, be confident that God will grant the exercise of His authority.

AUTHORITY
"The church and its ministry possess genuine religious authority only as they serve the mission of Jesus in faithfulness to the Bible and in building up of the church (Matt. 28:18-20). The Christian accepts the truth of Scripture as authoritative by faith, and the command of Scripture as authoritative in obedience, and so demonstrates love for the Lord."[2]

DAY THREE

CHARACTER THROUGH WARFARE

Last week's studies revealed that God wants us to be conformed to the image of His Son. When God wills something for your life, how determined does He have to be to bring it about? How much energy and diligence will God expend? To what lengths might He go to conform you to His image? Will He miss any opportunity? Will He fail to use any means necessary?

Mark with an X on the scale the degree to which God is determined to conform you to the image of His Son.

mildly interested   very determined

Today we will explore the major aspect of Christ's image that He develops in us—character. God so strongly desires to develop character that He will not waste any opportunity or means to do it. Although He primarily uses the Holy Spirit, the Word of God, and other believers in the process, He does not overlook the use of Satan.

Temptations Occur for Our Development

Read Matthew 4:1-11, Jesus' first recorded encounter with spiritual warfare during His ministry. Surprisingly, the Holy Spirit led Jesus into the wilderness for the express purpose of His being tempted by the devil. Jesus did not go there for a prayer time, only to have Satan unexpectedly interrupt it. Instead, it was a prearranged rendezvous. God's Spirit insisted so strongly that Mark 1:12 records that the Spirit drove Him. The Spirit of God did not suggest to Jesus that He go there to be tempted but rather left Him no alternative.

The record grows stranger by looking at Luke's account. Upon His arrival, the temptations became constant. Scripture only records three of those temptations, but Luke 4:2 says "for forty days he was tempted by the devil." Jesus didn't spend 39 days in prayer and 1 day resisting temptations. He was constantly, habitually resisting the devil.

Why do you think the Holy Spirit led Jesus into a situation of testing? Write your response in the margin.

Part of the answer concerns the timing. Each Gospel records that the temptation occurred at the beginning of Jesus' public ministry. The Father knew the types of temptations that Jesus would encounter later. If He could win the private victory in the desert, then when the same type of temptation happened later in His public ministry, His initial response would have already been settled. God wanted to strengthen the righteous character of Jesus by giving Him a greater resolve to obey.

Admittedly, the idea that Jesus' character could be developed may sound strange because He was already sinless. However, Hebrews 5:8-9 confirms that His character was developed. The Greek word for *perfect* does not address Jesus' performance or sinlessness, but His character. *Perfect* means mature, complete, growing to full stature. According to this verse, in order for Jesus' character to be developed to the fullest, it

"Although he was a son, he learned obedience from what he suffered and, once made perfect, he became the source of eternal salvation for all who obey him."

—*Hebrews 5:8-9*

had to come through suffering trials like the desert temptations. Just as Jesus could grow in wisdom and stature and in favor with God and man (Luke 2:52), He could also mature in character.

For clarity's sake, we are not saying that Jesus ever sinned or that He wasn't fully God. We are saying what the Scripture says: His character was fully matured through the trials He endured. Jesus passed the test, and His strength to do righteousness increased all the more. He learned obedience because the Father used Satan as a tool.

If the Father developed character in His Son, then He will do the same in your life. (Check one.) ❑ True ❑ False

Allow me (John) to give a personal illustration from a pivotal time in my own life. When I was 18 years old, my godly grandfather died. God's presence was so real through that experience that I decided, *If God is that good, I want to get to know Him better.* Immediately, I entered the greatest crisis of my life. I no longer had peace about whether I was saved. I knew all the right answers, was active in my church, and even served as a youth director, but I just couldn't get any certainty.

The constant anxiety hounded me relentlessly. Outwardly, nothing appeared wrong, but inwardly a daily, consuming fear plagued me—fear when I woke, fear throughout the day, fear when I went to bed. I was churning internally and for five years tried everything I knew to rid myself of this affliction. I rewalked the aisle, was rebaptized, spent whole days in prayer and fasting, and sought professional counseling. In my desperation I had even enrolled in seminary to do nothing but study what it meant to be saved. Finally, in the second year of seminary God graciously pulled back the dark curtains of doubt and let me see into the spiritual realm. One day He supernaturally revealed my dark night of the soul was caused by five years of constant demonic attack.

If God loved me, why would He grant Satan permission to afflict me? In hindsight I discovered He did it precisely because He loved me. Several things about my character hindered me from having a dynamic love relationship with God. As I discovered, I was saved—but spiritual immaturity, complacency, and laziness prevented me from pursuing Him.

Before those five years, I had been occasional about spiritual things. However, the constant inner turmoil became a steady motivator to earnestly seek Him. The pain spurred me to the daily habit of prayer and Bible study. Now the pain is gone, but that practice became part of my character that remains to this day. Without the encouragement of trouble, I never would have known what it means to have a love relationship with God, and I would have missed out on so many blessings He has given me as a result. God used Satan to develop some foundational character qualities I needed to know and obey God more.

God didn't stop there. Even after the turning point, I still struggled with doubt for three more years. God continued maturing several other aspects of my character. I became more compassionate toward people with problems. I learned the benefits of transparency and admitting weakness. I discovered what it means to walk by faith even when no answer appears on the horizon. I learned perseverance. God did not instantly remove the demonic attack because many of the qualities had not become part of my character to the degree He wanted. (I am not under the mistaken assumption that I've arrived, but without that trial I would have much further to go.) All of the blessings I received would not have been possible without God using Satan for my benefit.

How does John's story impact your response in warfare?
- ❏ I would still want the warfare removed immediately.
- ❏ There is nothing wrong with my character.
- ❏ I would patiently ask God to show me what He wants in my life.
- ❏ I would direct God to my neighbor down the street who could use a little correcting.

As a disciple of Christ, you are a student being taught by the Master. His school requires rigorous discipline. Do you desire Christ's character? Are you willing to endure whatever it may take to be like the Master?

Character Development Is a Process

Can you wave a magic wand and immediately produce character? Unfortunately not. James 1:2-4 and Romans 5:3-4 explain that character development is a process. Peter highlights the order of the process in 1 Peter 5:8-10 as it relates to spiritual warfare.

Read these passages in the margin. Peter spiritually instructed his readers how to interpret their warfare.

Number Peter's thought pattern in these verses.
___ After a season of suffering God will perfect, establish, strengthen, and settle you.
___ Resist Satan because you know fellow Christians are suffering just as you are.
___ Satan is seeking someone to devour.

"Consider it pure joy, my brothers, whenever you face trials of many kinds, because you know that the testing of your faith develops perseverance. Perseverance must finish its work so that you may be mature and complete, not lacking anything."

–James 1:2-4

"Not only so, but we also rejoice in our sufferings, because we know that suffering produces perseverance; perseverance, character; and character, hope."

–Romans 5:3-4

"Be sober, be vigilant; because your adversary the devil walks about like a roaring lion, seeking whom he may devour. Resist him, steadfast in the faith, knowing that the same sufferings are experienced by your brotherhood in the world. But may the God of all grace, who called us to His eternal glory by Christ Jesus, after you have suffered a while, perfect, establish, strengthen, and settle you."

—1 Peter 5:8-10 (NKJV)

The order is important. **First,** Satan seeks to destroy Christians. **Second,** believers are to resist him. In this particular case Peter encouraged them by the example of other Christians' faithfulness in the midst of persecution. **Third,** he reminded them that their trials would produce gains in Christlike character. He assumed the church's character would rise to a whole new level as a result.

Notice the crux of warfare occurs at the point of reaction. Believers all over the world were experiencing the same trials. Peter called for them to resist, to stand firm. In warfare the battle is won or lost at the point of response, not attack.

Character Development Results in God's Blessing

God always wants us focused on Him, not warfare. Staying focused on God and His purposes causes us not to give in to Satan. Afterwards, we enjoy the "peaceable fruit of righteousness" (Heb. 12:11, KJV). Character produces many benefits.

First, character produces freedom. Freedom doesn't come by the mental function of believing but by abiding in the Word, incorporating it in our lifestyle until it becomes a part of our character. When our character changes, we can understand truth and experience freedom. The freest people are those who have the inner strength to do the right thing regardless of the temptation or consequences. The ability to obey produces peace.

Second, the degree of the character determines the degree to which God will use us. Just as earthly parents don't give car keys to an eight-year-old, so our heavenly Father will not give us responsibility without character. The more we become like Jesus, the more He can entrust to us (Matt. 25:21). God will not give us more responsibility than we can handle.

Third, character will impact our future life in heaven. Although very little is known about the next life, Paul did imply that a connection exists between the earthly life and the life to come (1 Tim. 4:8). Although Paul didn't specify whether this value is in the form of rewards, authority, honor, or responsibility, some type of greater blessing will be experienced in heaven based on our obedience on earth.

Isn't it exciting to know that earthly suffering produces benefits greater than the suffering? Nothing is pointless or just a call to endure. Instead, believers have hope that God has His plans, and He can be trusted. Jesus endured the cross by focusing on the joy set before Him (Heb. 12:2). Paul persevered because he considered his troubles as light and momentary, but they were working for him an eternal weight of glory (2 Cor. 4:17). "In all these things we are more than conquerors through him who loved us" (Rom. 8:37).

Can you thank God for your troubles and sufferings, in the knowledge that they have purpose and will benefit you in eternity? ❏ Yes   ❏ No

If not, ask God to give you an obedient heart and a willing spirit to trust His purposes.

> **CHARACTER DEVELOPMENT RESULTS IN GOD'S BLESSING**
> * *Character produces freedom.*
> * *The degree of character determines the degree to which God will use us.*
> * *Character will impact our future life in heaven.*

> *"Physical training is of some value, but godliness has value for all things, holding promise for both the present life and the life to come."*
> —*1 Timothy 4:8*

DAY FOUR

CHARACTER THROUGH ENDURANCE

Spiritual warfare can be painful. When you encounter pain, what do you do? I (John) know what I did during my trial—I tried to get rid of it! I went to seminary, sought counseling, talked with others who had had the same experience, reserved days of prayer, and pled with God. It hurt, and I wanted relief. The problem, however, was that relief didn't come—at least not for years.

While I was in the middle of the warfare, I tried the standard advice of rebuking the devil, claiming the blood, and getting power over Satan, but to no avail. Then came my turning point. In my desperation, I promised God that I would read the Bible an hour a day and pray an hour a day. The prayer time was as miserable, unproductive, and useless as talking to a wall. The Word of God, however, changed my life. I began to understand the ways of God and to see His perspective. I realized there are times of immediate victory, but when God wants to develop character, He will not remove the warfare. Character development requires endurance.

Biblical Examples of This Principle

This truth is wonderfully illustrated in the life of Joseph (Gen. 37–50). His brothers betrayed him by selling him into slavery. While he was in slavery, his master's wife falsely accused him of attempted rape and had him thrown into prison. In prison he was forgotten by Pharaoh's cup-bearer and stayed imprisoned two more years.

God did not deliver Joseph from becoming a slave, being falsely sentenced to prison, or spending extra time in prison. Instead, He required perseverance. Why would God allow such a thing in the life of someone He loved? Because He was letting endurance have its perfect work so Joseph would be mature, complete, and lacking nothing. If God had delivered him prematurely, his character would have been stunted.

Joseph's 13 years of testing reflect the pattern Paul recorded in Romans 5:3-4. Joseph had trials; he endured by not losing faith in God; and the result was a magnanimous character—one of the greatest in all the Bible. When his brothers finally did show up in Egypt, Joseph not only spared their lives but treated them most graciously. Joseph's trials became the hammer and chisels that carved his character.

"Not only so, but we also rejoice in our sufferings, because we know that suffering produces perseverance; perseverance, character; and character, hope."
–Romans 5:3-4

Based on the outcome of Joseph's life, circle the letter beside the statement that best represents his mindset:
a. Joseph focused on what he lost—the injustices, the wasted years, and failures of others.
b. Joseph didn't lose faith in God but adopted a victim mentality of just suffering through.
c. Joseph sat down and did nothing until God delivered him.
d. Joseph embraced the character development the trials brought because he knew God had a purpose for his life.

Job is another example of someone who had to endure suffering for character development. Although the Bible never explicitly says why God allowed warfare in Job's life, it does give a clear picture of how Job's character changed. In the midst of the trial Elihu quoted Job accusing God of being unjust in afflicting him and declared that Job was purer than God (Job 33:9-11; 34:5-6; 35:2).

When God revealed Himself in the last chapters, Job recognized his sinfulness in accusing God of evil (Job 40:3-5; 42:5-6). At the end of the warfare, he gained a proper perspective of his righteousness, and his character changed to trust God's righteousness.

"So I have been allotted months of futility, and wearisome nights have been appointed to me. ... Oh, that I were as in months past, as in the days when God watched over me."
—Job 7:3; 29:2

Mark *T* **(true) or** *F* **(false) by the following statements:**

___ Character development does not require enduring trials.

___ I should expect some seasons of warfare that God will not immediately remove.

___ I should be confident during the trial that God is in control, and He will use the trial for multiple benefits.

Character Development Follows a Cyclical Process

God's Spirit constantly conforms His children into the image of Christ. In order to take believers to the next level of character development, the Spirit of God routinely leads them through a cyclical process that will be repeated many times throughout life. The end of the process is that God takes believers to new levels of maturity.

Understanding this four-fold process should encourage believers when God chooses not to remove a trial. **First,** when God wants to develop character, He does not deliver us from trials but through them. The Lord's Prayer (Matt. 6:13) has an unusual phrase: " 'lead us not into temptation, but deliver us from the evil one.' " The phrase is not unusual because of what it says, but because of the way it plays itself out in the life of Jesus, the disciples, and the rest of the Bible characters. Jesus was specifically led into temptation in the desert; in addition, the Spirit directed Him to Jerusalem knowing Satan was scheming through Judas and the chief priests.

In John 17:15 Jesus prayed for His disciples that the Father " 'protect them from the evil one.' " Yet tradition holds that all the disciples except John were martyred. Revelation 13:7 records, "He was given power to make war against the saints and to conquer them." Obviously, Jesus, the disciples, and Christians were not delivered from evil if deliverance is defined as not experiencing warfare. Then to what kind of deliverance did Jesus refer?

The pattern of Scripture gives a clear picture. When persons in Scripture successfully handled warfare, they were not delivered from the experience of evil but rather from yielding to the temptation to sin. They never were overcome in their spirits. They did not cave in to discouragement, violate God's ways, or disobey Him. Jesus did not turn from the cross. Satan could not dissuade Paul from being obedient to the heavenly vision. The devil could persecute the church even to the point of death, but he who overcame would not be hurt by the second death (Rev. 2:10).

When developing character, God does not promise to deliver us from the experience of warfare, but He does promise to deliver us from the danger to sin when in the trial. Oddly enough, deliverance is actually found by going through the trial, not around it. Therefore, instead of focusing on how to remove it, a Christian ought to focus on God's preserving activity in the process. Please note—we are not saying you should put up with all trials. If you can change your situation through wise choices, you probably should. No glory exists in needless suffering. Also, we are not saying all trials are spiritual warfare. Trouble comes in our lives for a variety of reasons. What we are saying is that God will

THE PROCESS OF
CHARACTER DEVELOPMENT
1. *God does not deliver us from trials but through them.*
2. *God provides a way for believers to endure.*
3. *Warfare is for a season.*
4. *After a trial, expect rest and blessing.*

"No temptation has overtaken you except what is common to humanity. God is faithful and He will not allow you to be tempted beyond what you are able, but with the temptation He will also provide a way of escape, so that you are able to bear it."
—*1 Corinthians 10:13 (HCSB®)*

"The other criminal rebuked him. 'Don't you fear God,' he said, 'since you are under the same sentence? We are punished justly, for we are getting what our deeds deserve. But this man has done nothing wrong.' Then he said, 'Jesus, remember me when you come into your kingdom.' Jesus answered him, 'I tell you the truth, today you will be with me in paradise.' "
—*Luke 23:40-43*

use warfare for character development. Understanding this truth helps us respond correctly when it happens.

Recall an experience when God did not deliver you from a trial but delivered you from sinning during the trial. Thank God for your deliverance.

A **second** step in the cyclical process is that God provides a way during the test for believers to endure it. First Corinthians 10:13 does not mean that every time Christians encounter a temptation, God is going to make an exit door. This thinking creates a false expectation that could lead to disillusionment. The "way of escape" in the verse is not the removal of a trial but the ability to bear it.

When Satan tested Jesus on the cross to save Himself (Luke 23:35-39), how did the Father "provide a way of escape" that the Son was "able to bear it"? Read Luke 23:40-43.

Notice that the second criminal suddenly had a change of heart. He rebuked the first, acknowledged that he was getting justice, and declared Jesus innocent. Even more amazing was his statement in verse 42. What could possibly cause him to look at the form of a naked, helpless, beaten, despised man dying alone on a cruel, Roman cross and conclude that He was coming into His kingdom? In effect the thief said, *I believe you are the Messiah. Let me be in paradise with You.*

Jesus said in John 6:44: " 'No one can come to me unless the Father who sent me draws him.' " This criminal could not have believed had the Father not opened his eyes. As Satan's evil arsenal pounded Jesus with the temptation to focus on self and forget God's plan, God reminded Him of the purpose of His life. The Father's action shouted encouragement. *Stay focused, Son. Don't forget why You came. This man serves as a reminder that I will accomplish salvation through Your suffering.* No doubt Jesus quickly recognized the activity of His Father and drew strength from His encouragement. He confidently proclaimed to the thief: " 'Today you will be with me in paradise' " (Luke 23:43).

This is what it means to "provide a way of escape, so that you are able to bear it" (1 Cor. 10:13, HCSB®). When you are in the middle of warfare, expect God to encourage you, remind you, correct you, and do anything else to help you stay faithful. Although God does instantly remove some trials, those are the easy tests. The harder ones demand that we stay faithful during the refining process.

A **third** phase of the cycle is that warfare is for a season. When God has accomplished His will, He delivers His children. God never does anything without a purpose. Recall 1 Peter 5:8-10. Peter understood that warfare often comes in seasons. He refused to speculate when it would end, but he was confident that it would. He fully believed God would perfect, establish, and strengthen them as a result. This expectation reveals that God delivers when He has accomplished His purposes.

The **fourth** phase of the cycle is a time of rest. After Paul was converted, Acts 9:31 says: "Then the church throughout Judea, Galilee and Samaria enjoyed a time of peace. It was strengthened; and encouraged by the Holy Spirit, it grew in numbers, living in the fear of the Lord." Similarly, Job's suffering had an end. The cross did not last forever. Paul had seasons of rest in Antioch and Ephesus. God's purpose in warfare is not warfare for warfare's sake. He uses warfare as a springboard to develop character. Once He accomplishes His purpose, believers can expect a season of rest and blessing.

Those Who Endure Will Be Blessed

Read James 1:12 and 5:11. James reminded us that God always gives back more than the suffering of the trial. Job received double from the Lord (Job 42:10-16). Daniel, Shadrach, Meshach, and Abednego were all promoted by refusing to compromise their integrity (Dan. 3). Joseph became second in command in Egypt (Gen. 41:38-43). David received a throne (2 Sam. 2:1-7).

God did not limit their blessing to just temporal things or their life-times. Their examples have also been the means God has used to encourage people for thousands of years. In heaven they will carry throughout eternity the honor of persevering. Isn't it encouraging to know that God never wastes any of our suffering, nor is it ever point-less? These four truths mentally arm us with the strength to face difficult seasons in life.

"Blessed is the man who perseveres under trial, because when he has stood the test, he will receive the crown of life that God has promised to those who love him."
—James 1:12

"As you know, we consider blessed those who have persevered. You have heard of Job's perseverance and have seen what the Lord finally brought about. The Lord is full of compassion and mercy."
—James 5:11

Label the four steps around the circle with the stages in the cyclical process of character development. If you need help, refer to the margin of page 39.

1. _____ 2. _____

_____ _____

4. _____ 3. _____

_____ _____

DAY FIVE

GOD USES SATAN TO DISCIPLINE WAYWARD BELIEVERS

What does God do when a believer adopts a disobedient lifestyle? Will He look down from heaven and hand-wring in despair, paralyzed and indecisive because He's at a loss for what to do? Will apathy overtake Him as He lazily yawns and drifts off to sleep? Will He become an indulgent, look-the-other-way, laissez-faire Father? Of course not! God will discipline those whom He loves. Interestingly, sometimes God chooses Satan to be one of those ways.

"Luther points out that the devil is God's tool, like a hoe that is used to cultivate God's garden. Though the hoe might take pleasure in destroying the weeds, it can never move out of God's hands, nor weed where He does not wish, nor thwart His purpose of building a beautiful garden. Thus the devil always does God's work. Even today, God uses Satan to discipline the disobedient."[3]

—ERWIN LUTZER

God May Give Satan Access to a Disobedient Person's Life

In 1 Corinthians 5 Paul addressed a problem in the church. One of the church members was having sexual relations with his father's wife—either his mother or stepmother. According to verse 2, the church was puffed up about it—proud of the whole situation for some reason. The Bible does not say why. Perhaps they thought his actions magnified the complete victory of the cross to cover sin, and the more this man sinned, the more God's glory in forgiveness was shown. Perhaps they thought forgiveness and freedom in Christ meant no consequences or accountability. Whatever the case, Paul was not happy, to say the least, and he gave some shocking advice on how to handle the situation. He actually commanded the church to turn this man over to Satan so that his flesh might be destroyed but his soul saved.

In a second example, Paul counseled Timothy in 1 Timothy 1:18-20 about how to wage "the good fight." He encouraged him to have faith and a good conscience. In contrast, he noted some had rejected these things, specifically Hymenaeus and Alexander, and their faith had suffered shipwreck. Consequently, Paul turned these two men over to Satan to teach them not to blaspheme. This action was a severe form of church discipline! Why would Paul give such advice to the Corinthians and mention such a solution to Timothy?

With which answer do you agree? (Check one.)
- ❑ Paul was just trying to scare them. He was exaggerating to make a point.
- ❑ Paul assumed that God could turn a wayward believer over to Satan in order to deal with his sin.

Obviously, Paul would not recommend what he did not believe about God. Therefore, Paul must have assumed that God could deal with sin by turning a wayward believer over to Satan.

Do you think most Christians realize that God may use Satan as a means of accountability and discipline?
❑ Yes   ❑ No

Do you think this truth might lead disobedient Christians to repent? ❑ Yes   ❑ No

Unfortunately, many Christians are ignorant of the fear of God. A disturbing number can sin with no sense of accountability or awareness that God will discipline them. Too many mistakenly believe forgiveness means they can comfortably cling to sinful lifestyles, and God is obligated to exempt them from disciplinary consequences. Christians need to be warned that a very real possibility of being turned over to Satan exists if they live in iniquity. Understanding the fear of God would cure many vices among church members. It would diminish cheating on taxes, committing adultery, gossiping, and a host of other sins. If more believers realized it is not a question of *if* there will be accountability but *when* there will be accountability, then fewer Christians would tempt God.

Discipline Is Designed to Lead to Repentance

The fear and the warning can fortunately be balanced with God's intent. When God grants Satan access to an unrepentant Christian, He is after repentance. God's goal in discipline is not getting even. He's not exacting some type of sadistic satisfaction in watching one of His children squirm. Instead, He seeks to restore fellowship and mold character in the process. Once a Christian repents, God immediately comforts and reaffirms His acceptance of that person.

Paul understood this principle. In 2 Corinthians 2:5-11 he spoke of a church member who was in danger of being swallowed up by too much sorrow as a result of church discipline. Since the only one Paul recommended for church discipline was the man who had his father's wife, we can logically assume it was he. Because the man was crushed and repentant over his sin, Paul instantly changed gears. No longer did he give harsh advice but instead urged the church to reaffirm their love for this brother lest he be swallowed up by too much sorrow. The goal had been achieved. Therefore he was to be restored.

> **Mark each statement *T* (true) or *F* (false). God uses Satan to discipline**
> ___ when He is getting even;
> ___ whenever we sin;
> ___ when He is trying to break us of sin so that we will return to a love relationship with Him.

The realization that God may use Satan as a means of disciplinary action can raise unwarranted fear in some people's minds. Some mistakenly believe that every time they sin God will unleash Satan in their lives. This belief does not square with God's intent. God's use of Satan is determined by our love relationship with God, not reprisal. Pain is not God's goal—molding character is. False impressions can lead to neurotic Christianity whereby a Christian continually lives in fear. Instead we can draw confidence from God's heart. Since He loves us and since He is perfect, His use of Satan in the life of a believer is the very best thing that could happen to a believer. God uses Satan to break a believer of sin so that the love relationship with God may be restored.

God uses Satan to break a believer of sin so that the love relationship with God may be restored.

This Discipline Usually Follows Persistent Rebellion

Understanding the context in which God uses Satan to discipline also proves helpful. Typically when God used Satan to discipline, the people were in a state of disobedience. They had not committed an occasional sin but were very contentedly continuing in their sin. The thought of repentance wasn't even a stop on their joy ride. The man living with his father's wife was proud about it. Alexander and Hymaneus were blaspheming. These examples reveal that their hearts had become so dull to hearing God that radical means were needed to get their attention.

God's intent also tells us how long and how severe the discipline will be. The degree of discipline depends on the willingness to respond. If someone is stubborn and resistant, he or she can expect it to get worse. God's holiness means uncompromising opposition to a believer in sin. In the case in Corinth, had the man persisted in disobedience, it would have ultimately resulted in Satan destroying his life. This explains why in the Bible the Lord rarely speaks encouragingly to the unrepentant. Conversely, the Lord never had a harsh message for the truly broken and contrite. Whenever the unrepentant became repentant, His favor returned. This pattern can be seen time and again in Judges when the Lord delivered His people from the enemy after repentance. Therefore, we can expect heart contrition to be the factor that determines God's actions.

Repentance Is the Only Thing That Will Remove Satan

Wouldn't it be foolish for a Christian to try to bind, rebuke, or cast out Satan if God is using Satan to discipline a person? If the Lord hands a person over to Satan, then what authority does anyone have to reverse it? What good would it have done for anyone in the Corinthian church to rebuke Satan on the behalf of the man who had his father's wife? Could Hymenaeus and Alexander have come against Satan while they continued to blaspheme? Obviously not! The only solution for these three was to get on their knees before a holy God and repent.

Victory in spiritual warfare never comes from formulas but from a right relationship with God. His presence and favor are the foundations required for Satan's removal. No Christian under discipline can expect relief any other way.

How might this truth affect the way you pray for a disobedient believer under spiritual attack? (Check one.)
- ❑ I would try to use my authority in Christ to stop the devil, or I would ask God to remove the warfare.
- ❑ I would adopt the attitude that they are getting what they deserve and wait until they come back to God.
- ❑ I would sincerely pray for their restoration and seek to be available if God would open a door for me to be involved.

This week's studies have explored God's ways and purposes in authority and character. Pray for yourself in four ways:
- You will focus on God, not Satan.
- You will better know how to work with or respond to God when warfare is in process.
- You will understand why the paradoxes of immediate victory versus endurance exist in Scripture.
- You will not be disillusioned if victory doesn't turn out to be easy or immediate.

[1]Trent C. Butler, *Holman Bible Dictionary* (Nashville: Holman Bible Publishers, 1991), 133.
[2]Ibid.
[3]Erwin W. Lutzer, *The Serpent of Paradise* (Chicago: Moody, 1996), 113.

VIEWER GUIDE

1. Biblical _____ is the right to carry out the will of God in our lives.

2. Through the wilderness temptations, Jesus essentially said to the devil, I am going to do it the way of the _____.

3. Jesus' authority was directly tied to the _____ He had received from His Father.

4. It is not always the immediate will of God to have the presence of

   _____ removed.

5. One of the reasons for authority is _____ of others.

6. Another purpose of authority is kingdom _____.

7. We are called to defend ourselves against the enemy. We can do that only in the

   authority of _____.

8. Disobedience creates a foothold for the devil. The solution is not for me to get rid

   of the devil. The solution is for me to _____.

9. We do not respond to the presence of Satan.

   We respond to the _____ of God.

Schemes for Individuals

SPIRITUAL
WARFARE

CASE STUDY

Do you remember the daily briefings of the battles in the Persian Gulf war? Every day in this brief war, one of the American generals gave a televised report of the progress of the American and allied troops. With the help of these reports and continual media coverage, we watched this war unfold.

What we were privileged to see, though, were only the results of a fully developed strategic plan to liberate Kuwait from the Iraqi forces. We knew a strategy existed, but that information was classified. The generals typically gave reports of past events rather than of future plans. All we knew was that they had a strategic plan and that plan was working.

The information we need to win spiritual battles, however, is not so classified. The Bible tells us how Satan works and how we should respond to the enemy's tactics. With that information, we have no reason not to win the battles of spiritual warfare.

DAY ONE

HE USES THE SINFUL NATURE

This week we will study specific ways Satan attacks individual believers. Knowing his wiles helps to keep us from falling into his traps. Understanding potential dangers can prevent us from being blindsided. Day 1 will uncover Satan's most dangerous ally. The following days will describe how Satan distorts the Word of God, tempts us to sin, promotes bitterness and anger, and seeks to get our focus off of God.

Who is your worst enemy? Many Christians mistakenly identify Satan as their greatest adversary. To be sure, we ought not to underestimate him, but James 1:14-15 outlines the process of how individuals are led into sin. "Each one is tempted when, by his own evil desire, he is dragged away and enticed. Then, after desire has conceived, it gives birth to sin; and sin, when it is full-grown, gives birth to death." Notice that James' primary concern is not the devil, but rather the individual's

own internal desires. Evidently, James was more concerned with the evil bent of the heart than with Satan.

Read Romans 7:15-23. Paul identified the inner struggle we experience. In verse 20 Paul observed, "Now if I do what I do not want to do, it is no longer I who do it, but it is sin living in me that does it." The Bible teaches that one of the consequences of the fall is that our innocent nature was corrupted, and now we have a nature that inherently sins. It cannot do right and, what's more, it eventually does wrong.

Of course, when Christ saved us, He gave us His nature and freed us from slavery to sin, but that sinful nature—the old human nature, or "the flesh" as different translations call it—remains a constant presence for the rest of our lives. The greatest threat to your walk with God is to underestimate its ability to defeat you.

To prove just how dangerous the sinful nature is, let's see who it defeated in the Bible. Draw lines to match the following outstanding people to the outcome of their temptation.

PERSON	OUTCOME OF TEMPTATION
David, the man after God's own heart	Judges 16:16-20
Moses, the most humble man	2 Samuel 11:1-5
Samson, the strongest man	1 Kings 11:9-11
Solomon, the wisest man	Numbers 20:9-12

"I do not understand what I do. For what I want to do I do not do, but what I hate I do. And if I do what I do not want to do, I agree that the law is good. As it is, it is no longer I myself who do it, but it is sin living in me. I know that nothing good lives in me, that is, in my sinful nature. For I have the desire to do what is good, but I cannot carry it out. For what I do is not the good I want to do; no, the evil I do not want to do —this I keep on doing. Now if I do what I do not want to do, it is no longer I who do it, but it is sin living in me that does it. So I find this law at work: When I want to do good, evil is right there with me. For in my inner being I delight in God's law; but I see another law at work in the members of my body, waging war against the law of my mind and making me a prisoner of the law of sin at work within my members."

—Romans 7:15-23

Do you see how powerful sin is? It defeated all these men with all these outstanding qualities. Samson's great strength was no match for his internal enemy. Moses' humility eventually failed. David had a sincere desire for God but abandoned it in a moment of passion. Solomon's great wisdom meant he knew better, but he did not have the moral strength to resist the temptations around him.

The enemy—our sinful nature—proves more dangerous than Satan. He and his minions cannot be everywhere at once. They are not omnipresent. However, in each person resides this powerful enemy against whom no one can win, and this enemy is always present. No wonder Paul looked at this reality and praised God for the freedom only Jesus can give. He knew that without the Lord he would be overcome as well, but in Christ he would have victory. Therefore, he said in Romans 7:24, "What a wretched man I am! Who will rescue me from this body of death? Thanks be to God—through Jesus Christ our Lord!"

The Sinful Nature Seeks Self First

The sinful nature has many manifestations but one common denominator. All sin springs from a desire to seek self's interests first, regardless of God's will. This nature focuses on gratifying self, exalting self, serving self, pleasing self, and meeting the needs of self. It relegates God and others to a secondary position. It willingly compromises integrity, truth, justice, honor, faithfulness to God, or any other virtue when it believes an alternative is in its best interests.

All sin springs from a desire to seek self's interests first, regardless of God's will.

Satan Stirs Up Those Desires Against Us

What is the relationship between Satan and our sin nature? How does he manipulate this enemy within us? Satan cannot make anybody do anything (except in the case of demon possession), but he can stir up the inherently sinful tendencies in us. He will use circumstances good or bad, persuasion pleasant or unpleasant, suggestions at our point of weakness or strength, and any other means at his disposal to awaken desires in us that will lead to sin.

Examine how this principle worked in Peter's life on the night he betrayed the Lord. What was it that led him to deny Christ? How could he have walked three years with Jesus yet have forsaken the Lord on the night of His greatest trial? The answer may surprise you. We often think Peter's failure was solely a matter of fear—fear for his life and the lives of others he might implicate. When we more closely examine the events of the evening, we find that Satan actually laid the foundation by capitalizing on Peter's desire for status and prestige—for self to be exalted.

The gospels record several times when Jesus had to teach His disciples that greatness in the kingdom comes through humility and service, not being a ruler and lording it over people (such as Matt. 20:26-28). Interestingly enough, the disciples never argued over who was going to be the greatest until they believed Jesus was the Christ. Why? Because it dawned on them that if Christ were indeed the Messiah—the King—then the King had to have a cabinet with different ranks of importance. From that moment on, they constantly jockeyed for position. Luke 22:24 records that at the supper table on the night of the Lord's betrayal, they argued over who was the greatest.

In verses 25-34 Jesus corrected them again, but for the first time He talked about their position in the kingdom. They would sit with Him on thrones judging Israel. That declaration was music to their itching ears, but the very next thing Jesus said must have horrified Peter. We miss the full effect in English since we can't tell when *you* is singular or plural, but Jesus actually said, "Simon, Simon! Indeed, Satan has asked for you all, that he may sift you all as wheat. But I have prayed for you, that your faith should not fail; and when you have returned to Me, strengthen your brethren" [author's translation]. Do you realize what Jesus announced for everyone to hear? He emphatically said that all the disciples would be sifted, but Peter would fail the test.

What would that kind of statement from your boss in front of your coworkers mean to you?
❏ I'll never get promoted!
❏ I've just blown the biggest deal in company history!
❏ I think I'll be looking for a new job!

The threat to his future aspirations was not lost on Peter. Immediately he swore his allegiance—"Lord, I am ready to go with you to prison and to death" (v. 33). After that, he had something to prove.

Do you see the condition of Peter's heart? He had already lost the warfare before he ever entered it. His and all the disciple's inherent self-desire for status prevented them from comprehending Jesus when He taught about the humility and servanthood the cross represented. Since they couldn't hear the Lord with their hearts, and since their desires were on their own interests, they were unable to respond correctly when it came to being tested.

No wonder Peter began swinging a sword when Judas showed up in the garden with soldiers (John 18:10). Jesus' refusal to defend Himself surely must have bewildered Peter and caused him to forget everything that the Lord had predicted a few hours earlier. In this state of confusion Peter had no defenses for the sifting that was coming upon him. Fear quickly overtook him, but Satan ultimately won the victory when he used Peter's preexisting desire for self-exaltation to disorient him from Jesus.

The contrast to Peter, of course, was the Lord. Jesus withstood an infinitely worse test than Peter's, but before His trial He alluded to His victory in John 14:30-31 (NKJV). He declared that " 'the ruler of this world is coming, and he has nothing in Me. But that the world may know that I love the Father, and as the Father gave Me commandment, so I do.' " The reason that Satan could not defeat Jesus was because Satan had nothing inherent in Jesus with which to work. Jesus didn't lust for position; He wasn't motivated by materialism; He wasn't even concerned with saving His own life. His singular desire was the will of His Father. Thus, Satan couldn't "best" Him. Peter loved Jesus and wanted the best for Him, but he also craved recognition. Unfortunately, Peter's self-focus led to his downfall. Jesus' God-focus led to His victory.

Satan knows the areas of sinful nature over which we have not gained mastery. If it is materialism, we will have plenty of opportunities to get entangled by money or things. If someone is preoccupied with sex, temptation will be common. An individual who is excited about gossip will have no lack of people sharing the latest tidbits. Christians must know their own inherent weaknesses and guard themselves.

Peter's self-focus led to his downfall. Jesus' God-focus led to His victory.

What are your inherent areas of weakness in the sinful nature? Underline or write them in the space provided.

Pride	Gossip	Unforgiving spirit	Critical spirit
Unbelief	Alcohol/drugs	Discouragement	Gluttony
Lust	Anger	Creating division	Procrastination
Laziness	Envy	Feelings of worthlessness	

other?_____

Satan seldom works successfully in areas that individuals have mastered.

Satan seldom works successfully in areas that individuals have mastered. That fact raises another issue. Why would God allow Satan to test us at the very points where we are most likely to fail? Wouldn't God want to protect us most at those points? Your authors believe He allows it for four reasons. We will relate these reasons to how they were manifested in Peter's life.

First, God wants to free us from the dominion of sin. Peter's denial broke him from seeking to exalt self. Evidently he was so grateful just to be forgiven and included that he no longer had a need to focus on Peter; instead, he just wanted to serve Jesus from a heart of gratitude.

Second, God wants to develop character in the area of temptation so that we become like Christ. After his bout with self-exaltation, Peter finally understood servanthood and grew in the likeness of the Lord. In his letter to the scattered believers, Peter wrote, "live as servants of God" (1 Pet. 2:16).

Third, God wants to prepare us for greater kingdom service. Several months before the denial, Jesus had already told Peter that He would give him the keys to the kingdom of heaven (Matt. 16:19). However, Peter didn't become the leader of the early church until God changed him. Peter was unfit to be entrusted with the responsibility God had for him until he learned to lay down his life as Jesus did.

Fourth, believers are reminded of their dependence on God. Peter's denial broke him from self-reliance. Prior to the cross, he was so sure his way was right that he actually rebuked Jesus when He prophesied His death on the cross. In the garden Peter asked whether he should strike with the sword, but didn't wait for the answer. Instead, he took matters in his own hands and began swinging. Peter's life after the denial was characterized by relying on God. The Book of Acts recounts several instances when Peter could have been imprisoned for his faith but courageously placed his life in God's care. (See Acts 4:18-22; 5:40-41.)

In what areas are you currently being tempted?

_____

_____

Explain how the Lord might use the temptation to bless you according to the four reasons given.

1. _____

2. _____

3. _____

4. _____

Develop a Game Plan for Victory

The only way to overcome any area of temptation is to recognize our weakness against it and turn to the Lord in dependence. We trust that He will deliver us from the attraction of that sin and will grant the power to overcome it because of our desire for Him.

We need to have a game plan ahead of time that helps us deal with these areas. Memorizing Scriptures such as 1 Corinthians 10:13 and Philippians 4:13 reminds us of what God has said. Pray these Scriptures back to the Lord when tempted.

Remember that in your life Satan will use circumstances and opportunities to stir up those desires in you that are contrary to the Lord. The key to victory is to be aware and armed with the Word of God so that when Satan tempts you, you will be able to stand.

Many methods can help believers stay faithful, but one common denominator exists. Day 2 will reveal the secret and identify methods to help us stay true.

Write a prayer asking God to alert you to Satan's schemes through your areas of temptation.

_____

_____

DAY TWO

HE DISTORTS THE WORD OF GOD

To uncover Satan's schemes against individuals, we need to study Satan's two most obvious attacks on people in the Bible: Satan's approach to Adam and Eve in the garden of Eden (Gen. 3:1-7) and his schemes against Jesus in His wilderness temptation (Matt. 4:1-11). Satan's plan of action in both cases involved attacking the Word of God.

The Presupposition—The Word Is Life-changing

Before examining how Satan seeks to distort God's Word, we need to understand why he tries to do so. The Word of God is powerful, "living and active" (Heb. 4:12), and life-changing; if the enemy can entice us to question the Word, we no longer trust the very message of God.

Read the following Scriptures, and match the description of God's Word on the right with the biblical text on the left. As you read the texts, meditate on the power of God's Word to change your life.

1. _____ Hebrews 4:12

2. _____ Psalm 119:105

3. _____ John 17:7-8

4. _____ Genesis 1:3

a. At God's Word, creation came into being.

b. God's Word judges our intentions and attitudes.

c. The Word lights our paths and gives direction.

d. God's truth sets us apart and makes us holy.

"All Scripture is God-breathed and is useful for teaching, rebuking, correcting and training in righteousness."
—2 Timothy 3:16

Read 2 Timothy 3:16 in the margin. God's Word is inspired ("God-breathed") and useful for teaching (the source for doctrine), rebuking (exposes doctrinal error and personal wrongs), correcting (guides believers to restoration after wrong), and training in righteousness (shows us how to live disciplined, holy lives). If God's Word so powerfully affects us, Satan would want to attack the Word. He would not want us to trust God's Word.

Did God Really Say ...

"The Lord God commanded the man, "You are free to eat from any tree in the garden; but you must not eat from the tree of the knowledge of good and evil, for when you eat of it you will surely die."
—Genesis 2:16-17

Read Genesis 2:16-17. This text is often read only as a prohibition, but we need to see God's provision and blessing in it as well. As Creator of the garden and of humanity, God knew what would be best for Adam and Eve. He graciously offered them all of the trees of the garden with only one exception. In fact, even His warning of the possibility of death reflected God's goodness—He told them the consequences of disobedience to encourage them toward obedience. What was at stake at that point was not whether God was good, but whether Adam and Eve would trust God's Word.

The serpent came as Satan's instrument. Read Genesis 3:1-7. What was the serpent's strategy in his question to Eve?

_____

Interestingly, the serpent apparently spoke only twice, but his words were designed to cause doubt concerning God's Word. "Did God really say ... ?" must have been the first words Adam and Eve ever heard that questioned God. Subtly, the serpent led them also to question God.

The serpent's question probably was intended to question the character of God as well as His Word. Remember, God had graciously given Adam and Eve access to all but one of the trees of the garden, but the serpent focused only on the prohibition. *What kind of God would have placed such restrictions on Adam and Eve?* he suggested. And, *if He were a God who unfairly restricted them, why should they trust Him or His Word?*

The serpent's second statement, "You will not surely die" (v. 4), was a half-truth. When they ate from the tree, Adam and Eve did not immediately die physically, though they did eventually die (Gen. 5:5). Satan's goal was achieved: maybe God didn't really mean what He said. In fact, the serpent implied that God gave the warning of death only because He selfishly didn't want Adam and Eve to be like Him. Maybe God's Word couldn't be trusted because God Himself couldn't be trusted.

In the end, Adam and Eve questioned God and His Word to the point that they gave in to the temptations of the serpent. We often betray our confidence in God's Word when we sin.

Mark the following statements *T* (true) or *F* (false). Then read the indicated verses to help inform your choices.

____ Sometimes I convince myself that I can get away with my sin. After all, no one will ever find out (1 Cor. 4:5; 2 Cor. 5:10).

____ I'm not sure that I will reap what I sow. The consequences aren't always so bad—at least not immediately (Gal. 6:7-8).

____ God loves me so much that I don't think He will make me answer for my lifestyle. After all, I'm a Christian (1 Cor. 3:10-15).

____ I can always turn from my sin tomorrow. One more day of fun won't hurt me (Luke 12:13-20).

Satan Quotes Scripture

Jesus Himself was not immune from Satan's attacks. Read Matthew 4:1-11. This text records a blatant attempt of the devil to lead Jesus into sin. Note specifically Satan's usage of Scripture in the temptation event.

Based on Matthew 4:1-11, answer the following questions.

During which specific temptation did the devil clearly quote Scripture? (Check one.) ❑ First ❑ Second ❑ Third

Which Scripture did he quote?

_____

_____

What was Jesus' response to this specific temptation?

_____

_____

The temptation in Matthew's account was the second of three temptations. The devil took Jesus to a high point of the temple and challenged Him to throw Himself down. As he tempted Jesus, he quoted Psalm 91:11-12, daring Him to trust God to fulfill the psalmist's promise of protection when He jumped.

Some debate exists concerning the interpretation of this temptation, but clearly the devil was tempting Jesus to put God to the test—to force God to keep His promises of protection. However, Jesus knew well that tempting God was itself sinful, and He responded to the devil's temptation by quoting Deuteronomy 6:16.

We can draw at least two conclusions. **First,** the devil himself can quote Scripture, and he will do so to try to mislead and deceive us. If he did so to Jesus, shouldn't we assume he will probably misuse Scripture with us as well? Sometimes Satan easily deceives us because he knows more about God's Word than we do. He knows enough to be dangerous.

Second, like Jesus, we must know God's Word sufficiently to respond to the devil's attacks. In addition to the content, we should also know how to interpret the Word properly. For example, look again at how Jesus responded to the devil's use of Psalm 91. He didn't deny the promises in Psalm 91, but He did recognize that the promises didn't give Him permission deliberately to test those promises. He knew that Deuteronomy 6:16 expressly forbade Him from testing God. Thus, He didn't follow the devil's application of Psalm 91 because He knew that that application contradicted another clear biblical mandate. He allowed the clear biblical passage to guide His interpretation of another passage.

The principles for Bible interpretation included in the sidebar on this page will help you as you study and interpret Scripture.

BASIC PRINCIPLES FOR BIBLE INTERPRETATION
1. *Read the text.*
2. *Using appropriate study tools, study the cultural and historical background of the passage.*
3. *Understand the type of writing studied (gospel, letter, prophecy, and so forth).*
4. *Look for the author's intended meaning.*
5. *Read the passage in its context in the specific biblical book and in the Bible as a whole.*
6. *Allow more clearly and more frequently stated teachings to inform obscure passages.*

As you conclude today's lesson, mark each of the following goals that you would like to adopt. Talk with your group at the next session to determine specific steps to take toward achieving these goals.
- ❏ I want to begin a systematic, consistent Bible study plan so that I can be prepared to defend against the enemy.
- ❏ I read the Bible daily, but I'm not sure how best to interpret it. I want to study more about Bible interpretation.
- ❏ I'm not even sure that I fully trust God and His Word. I would like to talk with someone about these issues.
- ❏ I read God's Word sporadically, but it really hasn't changed my life much. I would like to enlist an accountability partner who will help me read and apply the Word.
- ❏ I am faithful in my daily Bible reading, and I think I'm learning how to interpret the Word.
- ❏ I recommit myself to continue the daily discipline of Bible study.

DAY THREE

HE TEMPTS US TO SIN

It's probably not surprising that one of Satan's primary schemes is tempting Christians to sin. We are battling three enemies: the world, the flesh, and the devil (Eph. 2:1-2). When the world itself is distorted by sin and when people have a natural inclination to sin, it is no wonder that the devil seeks to capitalize on these issues. Day 3 helps prepare us to fight against temptations.

The Word Is Critical

As day 2 noted, the Word of God is critical to fighting temptation. It is a light to our path (Ps. 119:105). We need to know God's Word to know how to live fruitful Christian lives.

Read Psalm 119:11 in the margin. What does keeping God's Word in our hearts help us avoid?

_____

"Your word is a lamp to my feet and a light for my path."
—*Psalm 119:105*

"I have hidden your word in my heart that I might not sin against you."
—*Psalm 119:11*

The phrase "hidden your word in my heart" includes believing the Word, memorizing the Word, and living in accordance with the Word. Satan may try to distort God's Word, but Christians can be prepared to defend against his schemes. Remember that knowing and living God's Word helps us to wage successful battles against the devil who works through three steps in the process of temptation.

Step 1—The Enemy Engages Us in Conversation

Review Genesis 3:1-7 and think again about how the serpent lured Eve into sin. Though we don't know for certain how much Eve knew about the serpent's crafty ways, with hindsight we can agree that her first mistake was to enter a conversation with the devil. Although we don't verbally speak with the serpent as Eve did, we often carry on the same kind of conversation when temptation comes:

- Satan: "Go ahead, the sin won't hurt you just this once."
- Believer: "But I shouldn't do it … although it probably won't hurt me. At least it will hurt only me, if anybody."
- Satan: "That's right. And besides, no one will know."
- Believer: "I probably can hide it."
- Satan: "And think about the pleasure it will bring you."
- Believer: "Yeah, it would be fun."
- Satan: "Just think what you'll be missing."

On and on the conversation goes, until we decide to give in to the temptation. Take note of this truth: the longer we debate the temptation, the more likely it is that we will give in and sin. We will convince ourselves that the sin doesn't matter if we rationalize the sin long enough.

Take note of this truth: the longer we debate the temptation, the more likely it is that we will give in and sin.

Check each of the following excuses that you have used to convince yourself to give in to temptation:

❑ "God really wouldn't want me to miss out on this fun."

❑ "If I commit this sin, nobody else will get hurt."

❑ "Nobody else will find out about the sin. I'll keep it hidden."

❑ "I can always turn from my sin (repent) tomorrow. Just one more time won't hurt."

❑ "I know God loves me, and He will forgive me again."

❑ "Maybe it's not really a sin anyway. Maybe I'm just being too legalistic."

If we Christians are prone to rationalizing our way into sin, what should be our best response to temptation?

Read the following verses and circle any words that tell us what to do when temptation comes.

"Flee from sexual immorality" (1 Cor. 6:18).

"Submit yourselves, then, to God. Resist the devil, and he will flee from you" (Jas. 4:7).

" 'Watch and pray so that you will not fall into temptation' " (Matt. 26:41).

You probably circled the words *flee, submit, resist,* and *watch and pray.* When temptation comes, it is best NOT to enter into conversation with the enemy. Rather, submit to God, pray, resist the devil, and run from the temptation. Any lingering will probably bring trouble.

Step 2—The Enemy Focuses on What We Are Missing

God had given Adam and Eve access to all of the trees of the garden, warning them, however, not to eat of the tree of knowledge of good and evil. He made more than adequate provision for them, but the serpent directed them to what they thought they were missing. God, he said, was only keeping the tree from them because He didn't want them to be like Him.

When we focus our attention on what we don't have, we place ourselves in a dangerous place of temptation. We are so afraid of missing some of the temporary fun that the world offers that we give in to the temptations. We don't have what others have, so we greedily covet (Ex. 20:17). Likewise, lust is driven by a desire for someone rather than something. Worry is a similar sin. We get so caught up in what we cannot control that we lose our focus on God's provision (Matt. 6:25-34). If we would simply remember that the Father makes adequate provision for all of our needs, we needn't focus on what we're missing and we would be less susceptible to many temptations.

" 'You will not surely die,' the serpent said to the woman. 'For God knows that when you eat of it your eyes will be opened, and you will be like God, knowing good and evil.' "
—Genesis 3:4-5

Step 3—*The Enemy Makes Sin Look Good*

Read again Matthew 4:1-11. Note below any evidence of Satan's power in the verses listed:

Verse 5 _____

Verse 8 _____

Satan was powerful enough that he not only transported Jesus to the temple but "showed him all the kingdoms of the world and their splendor" (v. 8). Luke's gospel records that Satan gave this kingdom display in "an instant" (Luke 4:5). While the Spirit of God was in control of this entire event (Matt. 4:1; Luke 4:1), Satan's power was nevertheless clear. He offered the world to Jesus.

By comparison, the temptation to Adam and Eve may seem minimal, but it, too, was powerful. The forbidden fruit looked "good for food and pleasing to the eye, and also desirable for gaining wisdom" (Gen. 3:6). The fruit appealed to their physical desires, looked inviting, and seemingly offered knowledge they did not have. The "lust of the flesh and the lust of the eyes and the boastful pride of life" (1 John 2:16, NASB) caught Adam and Eve—not unlike the ways individuals today are trapped by the same desires.

Let's be honest: most of the time, we sin because sin looks good to us. Like a hunter who lures with bait that hides the deadly consequences of taking the bait, Satan makes sin look pleasurable. In fact, sin usually is fun—but only for a time (see Heb. 11:25). The prodigal son must have been lured by the exciting prospects of living a life of luxury, and he probably had a good time as he "squandered his wealth in wild living" (Luke 15:13). In the end, though, he found himself a hired servant in a pigpen (v. 15).

The problem is a focus on the temporary while ignoring the long-term consequences of sin. Satan offers the world, but he wants us to ignore the cost of worshipping him (Matt. 4:8-9). Because sin looks so inviting, we are often easy prey for the enemy.

Before concluding today's study, determine several action plans you will take this week to help you win the battles of temptation.

Because knowing the Word is critical in temptation, I will _____

_____

When I am tempted to enter into a dialogue with the enemy

concerning temptation, I will _____

_____

HOW DO I RESPOND TO TEMPTATION?
1. *Run to God. When the devil wants you to enter into conversation with him, choose instead to talk to God.*
2. *Focus on God's goodness and blessings. When the devil entices you to see what you're missing, remember the blessings of God. Take time to think about all that God has done for you.*
3. *Remember the consequences of sin. The enemy makes sin look inviting, but the consequences are devastating. Think past the temporary pleasure to recognize the long-term pain of disobedience.*
4. *Be sure to thank God for protecting you when He has given you strength to defeat the enemy.*

When sin looks inviting to me this week, I will _____

_____

DAY FOUR

HE PROMOTES BITTERNESS AND ANGER

Have you come across biblical texts that made you so uncomfortable that you wished the texts weren't in the Bible? For example, all of us are challenged by the difficult standards Jesus set for us in the Sermon on the Mount, such as "rejoice" when you are persecuted (Matt. 5:12), "love your enemies" (Matt. 5:44), and "do not worry about tomorrow" (Matt. 6:34). Although we love and respect the Word of God, often we find ourselves squirming as we try to apply the Scriptures to our lives.

Today as you read about another of Satan's schemes against individuals, you may find yourself challenged more than you want to be. Take a moment to ask God to speak to you and open your heart to Him as we focus on one of Satan's strongest strategies to keep us defeated.

A Difficult Word: We Must Forgive Others

Read Matthew 6:14-15, and then check each of the statements that reflects your feelings.
- ❏ I have forgiven everyone, so these words don't apply to me.
- ❏ These verses frighten me because I have not forgiven certain persons.
- ❏ I know these words are speaking to me, but I'm just not ready to deal with forgiving this person.
- ❏ I think I have forgiven everyone, but I need this reminder about the seriousness of not forgiving others.
- ❏ I need to forgive some persons, and I want God to help me to let go of my bitterness.

> " 'If you forgive men when they sin against you, your heavenly Father will also forgive you. But if you do not forgive men their sins, your Father will not forgive your sins.' "
> —*Matthew 6:14-15*

If you are struggling with unforgiveness, perhaps this lesson will help you learn to forgive. If you have no present need to forgive someone, perhaps this study will help you guard continually against an unforgiving spirit. Our main purpose for approaching this subject is its relationship to spiritual warfare.

Many of us struggle with forgiving others for past or present wrongs. In some cases, the bitterness is justified, and humanly speaking, we see no logical reason for forgiveness. Nevertheless, Matthew's word is clear: God doesn't forgive His children if they don't forgive others. Believers aren't ready to receive God's forgiveness as long as they themselves remain unforgiving.

This issue of forgiveness is especially relevant today. With the break-down of the home, some people know little other than emotional pain. At the same time, society has fostered an attitude of blame among "victims" of that pain—"I can't help the way I am; I'm a product of my upbringing." While we should not deny the reality of hurt or the influence of our upbringing, we still need this warning: when the world is full of pain and people have learned only to blame others for their hurt, they find it increasingly easy to hold onto bitterness. Forgiveness is then not an acceptable option, for forgiving means taking personal responsibility for our choices and lifestyle—regardless of what circumstances have influenced us. It may seem easier to stay angry and bitter.

Why is this issue a matter of spiritual warfare? **First,** Satan wants us to live disobediently, and unforgiveness is disobedience. Godly obedience demands forgiving others, even when we don't "feel" like being obedient. **Second,** forgiving others is a mark of persons who themselves have been forgiven much (see Matt. 18:21-35). We model God's love—and thus weaken Satan's influence—when we forgive as He forgives.

Why is unforgiveness a matter of spiritual warfare?

Third, our witness through relationships is weakened when we choose not to forgive. Godly relationships are a testimony to God's work in our lives. For example, the world will know that we belong to God by the way that we love one another (John 13:35). Marriage relationships model Christ's love for His church (Eph. 5:22-33). We honor God by bearing one another's burdens (Gal. 6:2). Obviously, bitterness that harms a relationship also hinders the Christian witness of that relationship. Satan, of course, is pleased when that happens.

Finally, bitterness and anger can control us; that is, we may live in bondage to our pain and never fully experience the freedom that Jesus offers. If Satan can direct our attention to our pain and anger, we take our eyes off God. Directing our attention away from Him is never good.

Use the following letters to evaluate yourself regarding forgiveness: *A* **(agree),** *U* **(uncertain), or** *D* **(disagree).**

_____ a. Regarding forgiving others who have hurt me, I am living obediently before God.
_____ b. I know I need to forgive someone, but I just don't feel like it right now.
_____ c. God has forgiven me much, but I have been unwilling to offer that same kind of forgiveness to others.
_____ d. I have modeled God's love by forgiving others.
_____ e. If I am honest, bitterness and anger are controlling my life; I am not focused on God.

Maybe you aren't sure if you need to forgive someone. The following questions are not a perfect guide, but they might help you to determine if you still need to forgive someone who has hurt you. Take a minute to review these questions, and ask God to help you to be honest with yourself as you respond.

How Do I Know if I Need To Forgive?

- Do I think often about the pain?
- Do I experience physical symptoms (stomach problems, lack of appetite, overeating, insomnia, and so forth) when I think of the pain?
- Do I want the person to hurt as I did before I offer forgiveness?
- Can I pray for the person?
- Will I rejoice if God blesses the person?

How Do I Begin the Process of Forgiving?

If you need to forgive someone for wrong, the following steps may help:

- Ask two or three prayer partners to pray with you about the matter. Because Satan doesn't want believers to forgive, he will fight strongly against you. Enlisting prayer partners may provide the added strength to face and to win this spiritual battle.
- Dwell on God's forgiveness of you. When you consider God's grace toward you, you will find it easier to offer grace to others. God forgives you repeatedly. Shouldn't you be willing to forgive others?
- Remember that forgiving does not justify the wrong, nor does it give permission for the offender to hurt you again. God forgives His children for their wrongs, but He still holds them accountable for the sin. Even as He forgives you, He says, " 'Go now and leave your life of sin' " (John 8:11).
- Determine either to forgive or to be disobedient to God. If God demands that we forgive others, to do anything less is to be disobedient. Disobedience never brings joy or peace with God; thus, an unforgiving, disobedient spirit will only bring more pain.
- Make the decision to forgive, regardless of any feelings. Love is seldom divorced from emotions, but making loving choices is not dependent upon emotions.You may not "feel" like forgiving, but you can still make the intellectual decision to do so in obedience to God. God changes hearts as we follow Him faithfully.
- Pray for the other person. Again, Jesus is our model as He prayed even for those who crucified Him, " 'Father, forgive them' " (Luke 23:34). When we pray for God to extend His grace toward those who have hurt us, we begin to lose our animosity and anger. Satan's hold on our lives is then weakened as we become increasingly like Christ.
- Be accountable to your prayer partners. Even after the offender has been forgiven, the enemy may try to refocus you on yesterday's pain. He so much wants us to live in defeat that he will recurrently try to bring up the pain. Keep in touch with your prayer partners—and seek their prayer support when the enemy strikes.

Conclude day 4 by praying for someone who needs your forgiveness. Write your prayer in the space provided on the next page. If there is no one to forgive, ask God to guard you against becoming bitter and unforgiving.

"Lord, help me _____

_____

_____."

DAY FIVE

HE TEMPTS US TO LOSE FOCUS

Read Matthew 6:22-23 in the margin. At first glance these verses may not make sense. The King James version literally translates the Greek into English. The eye isn't usually referred to as being single or evil. Upon further meditation, however, Jesus' meaning becomes clear.

Jesus wanted to communicate the spiritual truth that a single eye, a sole look, a solitary gaze, a lone focal point is what causes light. Anything else causes evil and darkness. Keeping our eyes fixed on the Lord is the key to victory. Having any focus other than the Lord spells disaster. If your light comes from another source, the light in you will be darkness. How does this truth apply to spiritual warfare? Jesus said, *If your focus is right, you'll make it. If your focus is wrong, you're in big trouble!*

Satan Will Try To Distract Your Focus from the Lord

Satan knows that if he alters a believer's focus, that person will be unable to function spiritually. Remember that in Luke 22:31 Jesus specifically forewarned the disciples, and especially Peter, that they would be sifted by Satan. The rest of chapter 22 identifies Satan's ways, techniques, and use of circumstances that led Peter to misfocus.

Read Luke 22:54-62. At this point Jesus had been arrested and led to the house of Caiaphas for a mock trial. Peter followed at a distance and managed to work his way into the courtyard. Whether he was thinking of how to free Jesus or perhaps just concerned about how they were treating Him, Peter found himself in a hostile environment. A servant girl looked intently at him. Put yourself in Peter's position. If you were in enemy territory, you would be nervous. As you warmed yourself by the fire, what would a penetrating gaze do to you? Perhaps this slave girl skirted the campfire and angled up to Peter with that deadly stare. Then to his horror she identified him and exposed his identity in front of everyone.

When Satan sifts, isn't he clever? All those previous centuries of practice and understanding human nature were directly employed against Peter with deadly effect. Oh, the concealed shudder that must have racked Peter's body. Oh, the cold chill that must have run up his spine. What could he do but quickly absolve himself of any suspicion by emphatically renouncing any association with Jesus? He denied Him the first time.

" 'The light of the body is the eye: if therefore thine eye be single, thy whole body shall be full of light. But if thine eye be evil, thy whole body shall be full of darkness. If therefore the light that is in thee be darkness, how great is that darkness!' "
—Matthew 6:22-23

> "The Bible is clear that Satan has a powerful kingdom that Christians must reckon with at every turn. And we are living in the midst of it—in enemy territory. ... In our day, we need to be taught the enemy's strategy if we are to be prepared for battle."[1]

BETH NETHERY FEIA

Consider what Satan does next. Verse 58 notes that after a little while Peter was accused by another person. Satan let Peter stew in his own fears before he came out for round two. Have you ever been scared at night? Have you ever noticed that the longer you wait the more noises you hear and the worse things you imagine? The passing time magnifies fears. Surely this must have happened to Peter. Most likely Satan was encouraging thoughts in Peter's mind, such as, *I don't think that slave girl bought it. I think they know. I wonder what she's whispering to the man over there. I'd better be careful. Don't blow it.* The time lapse certainly must have caused the fears to magnify.

Satan also had another strategy. Luke recorded that a man accused him the second time, but Mark stated that the same servant girl accused him again. Matthew reported that another girl accused Peter. John pulled all of these accounts together by saying "they" accused him. Evidently the servant girl began to talk and stir up the others (Mark 14:69). Finally those who were suspicious all began to accuse him. Satan now had ganged up on Peter. Several people were in on it. They applied pressure to Peter. Surely by this time he must have been extremely worried.

Again Satan let Peter simmer in his fears. Luke recorded that after about an hour had passed another person confidently affirmed that Peter had been with Jesus. No doubt the hour had seemed one of the longest in Peter's life, and his fears had magnified. Peter surely must have been scared for his own life by this point. The clamor of accusing voices had risen again, and the tide turned against him. People were not just suspicious; now they were confident of Peter's guilt. At this moment Satan went for the jugular. Not only did the bystanders point to hard evidence that he was from Galilee, but John recorded that the relative of the man whose ear Peter cut off accused him (John 18:26). He said in effect, *Yeah, you were the one in the garden, weren't you?*

Poor Peter. Satan had amassed quite an array of brilliant tactics against him, all designed to take his focus off of God and onto self. Peter quickly crumbled the third time, denying his Lord. He had forgotten the warnings at the last supper and the garden of Gethsemane. Satan disoriented him from God and turned his mind toward himself. Only Luke recorded it, but while the words were still in his mouth, and while the rooster was still crowing, the Lord turned and looked directly at Peter (Luke 22:61). Suddenly the gaze of Jesus snapped him out of it. His piercing eyes jarred his focus back to where it should be, but it was too late. He had already denied the Lord three times.

This account helps us see how Satan sifted Peter. All his tactics were designed to get Peter's eyes off Jesus. The devil knows whatever we focus on will determine whether we stand or fall.

What Tactics Does He Use?

What tactics will Satan use in your life? According to the biblical picture, Satan's tactics vary. You will probably never experience a replica of Peter's denial. Satan does not repeat the same scenario, just as God never repeats the exact same scenario.

Let's look at this truth from the lives of people in the Bible. Match the following people with the tactic used.

PERSON(S)	TACTIC
Eve (Gen. 3:6)	pleasure
Job (Job 34:5)	money
Judas (Matt. 26:15)	gossip
Jesus (Matt. 4:1-11)	hunger
Ananias/Sapphira (Acts 5:3)	praise of others
Younger widows (1 Tim. 5:13-15)	self-righteousness

Satan uses a myriad of tactics to get us to take our focus off of God, including causing us to focus on past failures, past offenses, busyness, pleasure, our rights, distractions, good instead of the best, and others' wishes.

Satan uses a myriad of tactics to get us to take our focus off of God.

What Brings Victory?

Victory comes from the flipside of the coin: Do whatever is necessary to focus on God. The solution is simple but requires work. Recognize that everything in life works against maintaining focus on God. Staying focused requires effort and concentration. It requires lifestyle changes.

Ways to Focus on God

- Saturate your mind with Scripture—Jesus answered Satan, " 'It is written' " (Matt. 4:4). Scriptures are the pure and undefiled thoughts of God. In them we find how God thinks—His focus, His perspective. By saturating our minds with Scripture, we are less susceptible to forgetting.
- Develop a daily time with God—Meeting daily with God orients us to Him. It helps us focus on who He is and His purposes. No great saint ever lived who did not spend consistent time with God. Judas knew where to find Jesus because He often went to the garden of Gethsemane "as He was accustomed" (Luke 22:39, NKJV).
- Create an environment of godliness—What messages surround your life? What music do you listen to in the car? With what group of people do you spend the majority of your time? What television programs play in your house? What literature do you read? We don't want to so insulate ourselves that we live in a bubble, but we must make sure that our major influences are from God.
- Ask the right questions—To focus on God, ask the right questions about your actions and activities. Here are four that prove helpful:
  - Will it bring glory to God?
  - Will it advance the kingdom?
  - Will it help or hinder my becoming like Christ?
  - Does it edify everybody involved?

What positive changes do you need to make in your life to help you stay focused on God?

_____

_____

Is anything in your life causing your focus to be off of God? If so, write it below.

1. _____

2. _____

3. _____

Whenever we adjust our lives to obey God, He has tremendous blessings in store. Today, if you have decided to make changes, you are on the front end of tremendous blessings from God. You may want to conclude today by thanking Him for the blessings He will give as a result of these changes.

"Dear Father, _____

_____

_____."

---

[1] Beth Nethery Feia, *Daily Strength for the Battle* (Ann Arbor: Servant Publications, 1999), 27.

VIEWER GUIDE

1. In Scripture we have a worse enemy than Satan, our _____ nature.

2. The enemy targets our _____.

3. A more subtle tactic of Satan is to get us at our _____.

4. At the point of temptation, ask:

   1) How did I _____ _____ ?

   2) What am I _____ _____ ?

5. If Satan can get me to hold on to my _____ and _____

   toward other people, then he effectively undercuts my relationship with God.

6. If Satan can get us to stay bitter, angry, and unforgiving, then ultimately our

   effectiveness in the _____ is hindered.

7. When we don't forgive, we end up being the ones in _____.

8. What is the basis for our hope?

   1) Find some _____ partners.

   2) Our hope for victory is based on the _____.

   3) Choose _____.

What Satan Really Wants

CASE STUDY

My (Chuck's) questions seemed simple ones: *Where does Satan most often attack us? Where are we most vulnerable?* Somewhat to my surprise, though, the young adults with whom I was working gave several different responses.

"I think he hits us hardest through our relationships. Bad relationships open us up to his attacks."

"No, he gets me most by keeping me from reading my Bible and praying."

"I'm usually most in trouble when I watch worldly movies. He gets me through the media."

"That's simple—he attacks us where we most often give in to temptation. If we weren't weak there, he wouldn't come after us."

While all of these answers have elements of truth, they miss the main site of Satan's arrows. Where do you think Satan most often attacks us? Where are you most vulnerable to him? How would you have answered my questions?

DAY ONE

SATAN WANTS YOUR MIND

In war generals seek to identify the key objective that will most limit their enemy's ability to fight. Experienced generals do not randomly attack their foes. They want to capture or destroy the vital area that determines the opposing army's capacity to wage war. In World War II the Allies staged incredibly dangerous air raids on a key Romanian oil field because they knew that crippling Hitler's gasoline output would greatly paralyze war material production and supply.

This worldly pattern sheds light on a spiritual reality. Imagine sitting in Satan's command and control center as he strategizes with top demons. What would be their key objective? More than anything else, what would they target to cripple your ability to wage war? You might safely assume that most efforts would be directed toward this area of

vulnerability. Your victory or defeat would be determined by how well you defended this strategic point.

Read these Scriptures and write Satan's point of attack on these persons/groups.

Acts 14:2 _____

2 Corinthians 4:4 _____

2 Corinthians 11:3 _____

Satan knows the value of capturing the mind. No other single factor has more impact on how we respond to God. Paul's writings reveal that he recognized this reality. He used some form of the words *mind, knowledge* and *understanding* over one hundred times in his letters. He warned, encouraged, admonished, and counseled about the mind. He viewed the mind as so significant that over 40% of his intercessory prayers were petitions for God to impact a function of the mind! Obviously, there must be a reason he prayed this way. Today we will explore six functions of the mind that show its importance and why Satan so desperately wants it.

1. The Heart Is Changed by the Mind

Jesus said, " 'Follow Me and I will make you become fishers of men' " (Mark 1:17, NKJV). By that statement He declared He would lead them through a process of change. The Gospels reveal Jesus' discipleship methods.

Read the verses in the margin and underline Jesus' discipleship method.

Jesus sought to change the disciples by enlightening their understanding. He turned every circumstance into a teaching opportunity. The question of eating food with unwashed hands became a springboard for teaching on the heart. When they had no bread, He taught them to beware of the yeast of the Pharisees. A moment alone with them became an occasion to teach about how people respond to the

" 'Are you still so dull?' Jesus asked them. 'Don't you see that whatever enters the mouth goes into the stomach and then out of the body?' "
—Matthew 15:16-17

" 'Do you still not understand? Don't you remember the five loaves for the five thousand, and how many basketfuls you gathered?' "
—Matthew 16:9

" 'How is it you don't understand that I was not talking to you about bread? But be on your guard against the yeast of the Pharisees and Sadducees.' "
—Matthew 16:11

"Then Jesus said to them, 'Don't you understand this parable? How then will you understand any parable?' "
—Mark 4:13

Word of God. In every instance, Jesus did not just command rote behavior but gave the reasons for His teachings and actions. Since the mind is the gateway to the transformation of the heart, Jesus never wasted an opportunity to challenge the disciples' belief systems.

Paul reflected this truth in Romans 12:2. Again he said in Ephesians 4:23, "and be renewed in the spirit of your mind" (NKJV). Conversely, Satan seeks perverted understanding in order to retain hearts. Jesus said in Matthew 13:19, "When anyone hears the message about the kingdom and does not understand it, the evil one comes and snatches away what was sown in his heart." Satan retains control by blinding our minds.

Both Jesus and Satan continually seek to influence our hearts by influencing our minds. Although Jesus has won the ultimate victory, Satan surely wins daily skirmishes when we give in to his influence.

Name one way Jesus has changed your heart (transformed you) by changing your understanding. Consider areas such as your use of money, establishing priorities, or relating to others.

_____

_____

How is He seeking to transform you in a specific way now?

_____

_____

> *"Do not be conformed to this world, but be transformed by the renewing of your mind, that you may prove what is that good and acceptable and perfect will of God."*
> —Romans 12:2

2. The Mind Perceives Truth and the Will of God

Jesus sought to change His disciples through touching their minds. For example, Luke 24:44-45 records that Jesus wanted His followers to understand the truth of Scripture through their understanding. Romans 12:2 tells us our ability to know God's will comes from a transformed mind.

When Satan attacked biblical characters, his main tactic was to subvert their minds. He tried to deceive, to cause people to misunderstand, to come to the wrong conclusion about truth, to forget, or to misfocus. People who won the victory against Satan had trained their minds in the truth of God. Satan knows that if he can corrupt your mind, you will be unable to perceive the will of God.

How do you guard your mind against Satan's influences?

_____

_____

> *"Then He said to them, 'These are the words which I spoke to you while I was still with you, that all things must be fulfilled which were written in the Law of Moses and the Prophets and the Psalms concerning Me.' And He opened their understanding, that they might comprehend the Scriptures."*
> —Luke 24:44-45 (NKJV)

Is anything hindering your mind from knowing the will of God? If so, list it below.

_____

3. *Your Belief System Determines Direction, Actions, and Responses*

In the Gospels the disciples often missed the mark. In the margin, read the disciples' wrong reactions to events in their lives.

Why did they so often respond incorrectly? They reacted according to their preexisting belief systems. Peter could not fathom that the Messiah must die; therefore, he tried to correct Jesus when He announced His death. The disciples thought Jesus was too important to bother with children; therefore, when parents brought them to Jesus, the disciples tried to stop it. John believed anyone not in their group would undercut Jesus' ministry; therefore, he proudly announced that he stopped the man casting out demons. What they believed determined ahead of time their actions and responses.

Satan knows the victory for most temptations is not won at the point of the temptation because whether or not we stand usually is settled long before the situation arises. For example, if we believe in taking revenge, then we will exact revenge when we are offended. The moment of the offense is not the battlefield for victory or defeat. The battle occurs much earlier over what we believe. That's why Jesus sought to tear down the disciples' strongholds of false thinking. He knew the direction of their lives was determined by their belief systems.

Should a Christian expect God to routinely challenge his or her false patterns of thinking? Why or why not?

_____

_____

"Peter took him aside and began to rebuke him. 'Never, Lord!' he said. 'This shall never happen to you!'"
—**Matthew 16:22**

"Then little children were brought to Jesus for him to place his hands on them and pray for them. But the disciples rebuked those who brought them."
—**Matthew 19:13**

"Master," said John, "we saw a man driving out demons in your name and we tried to stop him, because he is not one of us."
—**Luke 9:49**

4. *Unity with God/Other Christians Requires the Mind*

In John 15:15 Jesus noted a relationship change between Himself and the disciples. Now they could experience the intimacy of friendship. Friends know each other's business; they understand each other. As the disciples learned Jesus' true nature, His character, they became increasingly transformed into His image.

In the Gospels, division over who would be greatest marked the disciple's lives, but in Acts they were in "one accord" (Acts 2:1). Why the transformation? Because their understanding of God and His ways changed. Paul also understood this principle. When the church in Corinth was split four ways, Paul begged them to have unity in the way they thought. Then he did not immediately tell them what to do, but spent the first four chapters of 1 Corinthians telling them how to think. After this foundation, he began to make application to behavior.

"I no longer call you servants, because a servant does not know his master's business. Instead, I have called you friends, for everything that I learned from my Father I have made known to you."
—**John 15:15**

"I appeal to you, brothers, in the name of our Lord Jesus Christ, that all of you agree with one another so that there may be no divisions among you and that you may be perfectly united in mind and thought."
—**1 Corinthians 1:10**

"All Scripture is God-breathed and is useful for teaching, rebuking, correcting and training in righteousness."
—2 Timothy 3:16

Satan knows if he can cause differing opinions on important matters, then church conflict will result. Both Jesus and Paul worked to build unity by dealing with false doctrine.

What approach should Christians take when they conflict over differing opinions? Support your answer with Scripture.

_____

_____

5. A Corrupted Mind Will Block Your Usefulness to God in the Kingdom

"I fear, lest somehow, as the serpent deceived Eve by his craftiness, so your minds may be corrupted from the simplicity that is in Christ."
—2 Corinthians 11:3 (NKJV)

Paul expressed a concern for the Corinthian church in 2 Corinthians 11:3. Did you notice he used the word *corrupted*? The Corinthians were originally doing well, but Paul feared they would easily be led astray.

Even if we understand the truth, Satan may at some point in the future turn us aside from the right way. The result is a state of disobedience in which we lose our usefulness in extending the kingdom of God. Perhaps this fact explains Jesus' diligence with the apostles. When they were in error, He immediately corrected them.

6. The Mind Is the Battlefield for Bondage or Freedom

"Evidently some people are throwing you into confusion and are trying to pervert the gospel of Christ."
—Galatians 1:7

"You foolish Galatians! Who has bewitched you?"
—Galatians 3:1

"Those people are zealous to win you over, but for no good. What they want is to alienate you from us, so that you may be zealous for them."
—Galatians 4:17

"That kind of persuasion does not come from the one who calls you."
—Galatians 5:8

The church in Galatia tried to live their Christian lives under the law. Paul reacted as violently to this abuse as anything else in his writings. Paul made four bold statements. Read them in the margin.

Paul vividly saw the danger of the church buying into this false belief system. He said in Galatians 5:1, "Stand fast therefore in the liberty by which Christ has made us free, and do not be entangled again with a yoke of bondage" (NKJV). Paul knew that what they believed would lead them to freedom or bondage.

Satan knows that if he can deceive us, we will be enslaved. Christ knows if we continue in His Word, we will know the truth and the truth will set us free (John 8:32). Bondage and freedom originate from our belief systems.

Do you see the mind's importance for spiritual warfare?
❑ Yes   ❑ No

Explain why Satan wants your mind.

_____

_____

No wonder Satan so desperately wants your mind. It determines your intimacy with God, your effectiveness as a Christian, and your relationships with other believers. In days 2-5 you will study the mind's role in spiritual warfare.

DAY TWO

STRONGHOLDS OF FALSE THINKING

Let's review the six functions of the mind from day 1. Fill in the blanks that explain why Satan wants your mind. See pages 67-70 if you need help in listing them.

1. The _____ is changed by the mind.

2. The mind perceives _____ and the will of God.

3. Your belief system determines _____, actions,

   and _____.

4. _____ with God/other Christians requires the

   _____.

5. A _____ mind will block your usefulness to

   God in the _____.

6. The mind is the battlefield for _____ or _____.

Consider how thinking processes influence your actions. Are you aware of how Satan tries to capitalize on the way you think? The goal of this week's remaining lessons is to help you live in victory over the enemy's attacks on your mind.

As you read today's lesson, pause for prayer and ask God to help you identify Satan's schemes against your mind.

The Nature of Strongholds—Wrong Thinking

Read 2 Corinthians 10:3-5 in the margin. In this text the apostle Paul defended himself against false teachers in the city of Corinth. Paul recognized their accusations against him as a spiritual battle, and he responded with spiritual weapons (vv. 3-4).

Specifically, the apostle claimed his weapons had "divine power to demolish strongholds" (v. 4). The text suggests that strongholds were human reasoning and arguments opposing the truth of the gospel. That is, strongholds are ideas and thought patterns that oppose God and that hold persons in bondage. Our response, according to Paul, is to "take captive every thought to make it obedient to Christ" (v. 5).

"Though we live in the world, we do not wage war as the world does. The weapons we fight with are not the weapons of the world. On the contrary, they have divine power to demolish strongholds. We demolish arguments and every pretension that sets itself up against the knowledge of God, and we take captive every thought to make it obedient to Christ."
—2 Corinthians 10:3-5

"An entrenched pattern of thought, an ideology, value, or behavior that is contrary to the word and will of God."[1]

"A mind-set impregnated with hope-lessness that causes us to accept as unchangeable, situations that we know are contrary to the will of God."[2]

In the margin read the two definitions for a *stronghold*. Both definitions, given by contemporary spiritual warfare writers, use similar wording. Underline the words in both definitions that seem most significant to you.

Maybe you underlined such words as *entrenched, hopelessness,* and *contrary to the will of God.* Let's combine the concepts into a single definition: a *stronghold* is an entrenched pattern of thinking and acting that we believe cannot change, even though we know that such thoughts and actions are contrary to God's will. If a Christian believes that nothing will change—that even God apparently can't change a situation—then he gives up hope. He stops fighting the battles when he thinks to himself, *It's no use. I'm not going to change anyway.*

Do you have a stronghold, a pattern of thinking and acting that you believe won't change? (Circle one.)   Yes   No

Obviously, the enemy has won when we give up the battle. In fact, sometimes the devil has so captured us that we don't even realize that our thinking has become distorted. Two particular strongholds of wrong thinking often take us captive.

Strongholds of Poor Self-Worth

Maybe you've heard these kinds of messages over the years: *You're no good; You never did live up to our expectations; Your brother (or sister) was always better than you; I knew you wouldn't amount to much.* Perhaps repeated failures have only confirmed these messages. If so, you know that these words are not only painful, but they are also seemingly impossible to overcome. When we hear these messages so much that we internalize them, poor self-worth results.

In some respects, these words of condemnation reflect our human condition before Christ saves us and gives us a new identity. As unbelievers, we are "dead in … transgressions and sins" (Eph. 2:1). None is good apart from God (Matt. 19:17). What righteousness we do have is only as "filthy rags" (Isa. 64:6). Even when we become believers, we are saved by grace through faith—not by works (Eph. 2:8-9). There is no room for pride in the Christian life.

Nevertheless, if you are a Christian, understand that God has chosen you and made you one of His children (Eph. 1:4-8; John 1:12). We are "co-heirs with Christ" (Rom. 8:17), members of His body (1 Cor. 12:27), sons of God (Gal. 4:7), citizens of heaven (Phil. 3:20), and "a people belonging to God" (1 Pet. 2:9). We mean so much to God that He sent His Son to die for us (1 John 2:1-2).

We can know intellectually that we are special to God, but Satan continually reminds us of the negative messages of the past. The old tapes we play in our heads become his messages— "You're not good enough for God to use you." "You'll never overcome your rotten past." "God didn't really forgive you for your sins." "You just think you've changed—give it some time, and you'll return to your old habits."

When we reach the point that it seems we'll never overcome the negative messages, strongholds develop. We give up the spiritual battle.

Most often, false thinking leads to inappropriate behavior. We will do whatever it takes to make ourselves feel better. Often, feeling better is a brief experience followed by negative consequences.

Put an "X" on the scale to evaluate your attitude about your self-worth. If you struggle here, ask God to help you win the battle against poor self-worth.

I struggle with poor self-esteem all the time.

I sometimes struggle with messages of poor self-worth, but I'm learning to counter them with God's truth.

I'm OK here. I don't struggle with messages of poor self-worth.

Strongholds of Pride

At the other end of the stronghold of poor self-worth is the stronghold of pride. Believers are less inclined to admit this hold in their lives. We might say Christians are too proud and too self-righteous to admit that they are proud and self-righteous!

This stronghold, too, is an issue of the mind. When we think too highly of ourselves, pride affects our attitudes and actions toward God and others. Consider Jesus' story about the tax collector and the sinner praying in the temple.

Read the story in Luke 18:9-14, and place an "X" by each of the following statements that describes the Pharisee.
_____ 1. He could not even look toward heaven.
_____ 2. Compared to others, he was better than them.
_____ 3. He reminded God of how good he was.
_____ 4. He confessed his wrong to God.
_____ 5. He stood as he prayed, apparently in a posture of arrogance.
_____ 6. He sought God's mercy.

Pharisees were religious persons who assumed they deserved God's blessing because of their outward obedience to God's laws. Their attempts at perfection—keeping the smallest points of the Mosaic law—led them to think of themselves as better than others. While few of us would be as blatantly arrogant as this man, sometimes we, too, compare ourselves to others and remind God of how good we are. Sometimes we arrogantly assume that God, His work, and His church cannot go on without us. The Pharisee was characterized by 2, 3, and 5.

How, then, is pride a stronghold? A stronghold of pride develops when we know pride is wrong, but either (1) we are unwilling to admit

"Pride goes before destruction, And a haughty spirit before stumbling."
—**Proverbs 16:18 (NASB)**

"When pride comes, then comes dishonor, But with the humble is wisdom."
—**Proverbs 11:2 (NASB)**

that pride is the problem, or (2) we fight against God's breaking our pride, believing instead that our "goodness" deserves better treatment from Him. Wrong thinking convinces us that God owes us something.

In that sense, this type of stronghold may be the most deceptive. Many Christians see pride in others, teach against such pride, and sometimes wonder if other prideful people will change—all the while not seeing the same issues in their own lives. Or they see the problem, but remain so caught in pride that they are not willing to confess and turn from that sin. The situation is "unchangeable" because they really don't want it to change. In either case, the enemy has a stronghold.

On page 71 you asked God to help you identify Satan's schemes in your life. Trusting Him to guide you now, check each statement that might reflect a pride issue in your life. Ask God to break any potential stronghold that might be developing. If none of the statements applies, seek His continual protection against pride.

❏ I try not to be prideful, but sometimes I do wonder how my church would get along without me.
❏ I do at times compare myself to others, then determine that I am better than most people.
❏ I am tempted sometimes in my praying to remind God of how faithful I have been.
❏ I think I am more spiritual than most people; in fact, that's one of the reasons I am taking this course.
❏ I think God wants to break the pride in me, but I'm not ready for that painful process.

Take some time to thank God for loving you and dying for you "while we were still sinners" (Rom. 5:8). Thank Him for giving you the privilege of serving Him even though we, like John the Baptist, are not worthy even to untie His sandals (John 1:26-27). Your humble gratitude today will weaken the enemy's influence in your life.

DAY THREE

STRONGHOLDS OF SIN

Fill in the words to complete our proposed definition for a *stronghold* from day 2. Refer to page 72 if necessary.

A *stronghold* is "an entrenched _____ of

thinking and _____ that we believe cannot

_____, even though we know that such

thoughts and actions are contrary to God's _____."

Today's lesson focuses on patterns of entrenched sins in our lives. Pause again to pray, asking God to help you identify your sin strongholds.

The Start of the Pattern: A Foothold Is Evident

Read Ephesians 4:25-27. In the context of warning against harboring unresolved anger, Paul made this statement: "Do not give the devil a foothold" (v. 27). The word *foothold*, also translated as opportunity (NASB) or place (KJV), literally means "space." Hence, Christians are to be careful not to give the devil any space in their lives. When he gets any opening at all, he seeks to influence individuals as much as possible. (Do you recall Eve's first mistake from last week's study? She entered into a conversation with the serpent.)

How do we give "space" to the devil? The process is deceptively simple: we give him opportunities to attack any time we move in his direction—and moving in his direction always begins in the mind. For example, a believer prone to lust places himself under attack if he watches movies that entice his lusts; in fact, his mind is already headed in the wrong direction. If pornography is a struggle, he should avoid any literature that could even remotely stir wrong thoughts. Because his actions are undeniably tied to his thinking, he must discipline his mind to pure thoughts.

The more we place ourselves in the way of temptation—the more space we give to the devil—the more likely it is we will lose a spiritual battle. Based on lies the enemy plants in our minds, we decide to move in Satan's direction. And the foothold may well lead to a stronghold.

Consider the sin issues in your own life. While we are not asking you to state the specific sins with which you wrestle, you should be aware of how you might give the devil a foothold.

Check each of the following ways you might be giving the devil a foothold or add other ways not listed here. If none of these ways applies in your life, be sure to thank God for His gracious protection.

❑ I watch media that lead me in the wrong direction.
❑ The music I listen to sometimes leads me more toward the devil than to God.
❑ The places where I go are not always God-honoring places.
❑ I read literature that doesn't always direct me toward God.
❑ Maybe because I don't always faithfully attend church, I often focus in the enemy's direction.
❑ I am easily swayed by friends and seldom take a stand for my Christian beliefs.
❑ I probably don't study God's Word enough to be prepared for spiritual battles.
❑ I spend too little time praying, giving too little attention to God.

❑ Other: _____

"Therefore each of you must put off falsehood and speak truthfully to his neighbor, for we are all members of one body. 'In your anger do not sin': Do not let the sun go down while you are still angry, and do not give the devil a foothold."
—*Ephesians 4:25-27*

" 'The light of the body is the eye: if therefore thine eye be single, thy whole body shall be full of light. But if thine eye be evil, thy whole body shall be full of darkness. If therefore the light that is in thee be darkness, how great is that darkness!' "
—*Matthew 6:22-23*

Notice again how these footholds begin in the mind with a decision. As the old cliché says, "Put garbage in, and you will get garbage out."

The Process Continues: A Foothold Becomes a Stronghold

A stronghold seldom, if ever, develops overnight. Rather, the process begins when we give the devil a foothold, then fail in the accompanying temptations, and experience guilt and shame over our ensuing failures. Satan attacks not only in the temptation itself but also in the accusations after the sin (see Rev. 12:10). The enemy who lured us with bait then accuses us after we've taken the very bait that he offered.

Recall that Satan wants us to give up, to believe that patterns of sin can never be changed. Have you heard the accuser say any of these words after you've fallen into sin?

- "I told you that you would fall again."
- "God probably won't forgive you this time."
- "There's no way that God will ever use you again now."
- "You're so easy to deceive and mislead. You're not even a challenge anymore."
- "You'll never overcome this sin. Why do you even try?"

When we believe that we cannot change, we stop trying to change—and the stronghold becomes apparent. The following diagram will help you understand Satan's process:

THE DEVELOPMENT OF A STRONGHOLD

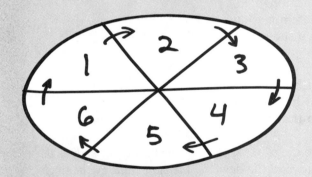

1. We place ourselves in the way of temptation.
2. Satan entices us to give in to temptation.
3. We fail, and Satan strikes with accusations.
4. We listen to the accusations, assuming we cannot change.
5. We lose our hope.
6. Having lost our hope, we again place ourselves in the way of temptation—and lose the battles.

Recognize how thinking processes influence this pattern. Temptations most often begin in the mind. Particularly if we have heard the past negative messages of poor self-worth, we might seek to hide those messages through the pleasure of sin. On the other hand, sometimes our ego sets us up for failure. In either case, we convince ourselves through our thought processes to succumb to the temptation. Satan accuses us again, and we hear his words of accusation in our minds. With no hope, we continually open our minds to further temptation—and, ultimately, to defeat.

How, then, do we know when a stronghold of sin has developed? No 100 percent accurate way determines the presence of a sin stronghold, but answering yes to any or all of the following questions may suggest that a stronghold is developing.

- Has the sin become habitual? That is, do I continually commit the sin, even though I know that God is displeased?
- Have I given up fighting the sin? Am I close to saying, "What's the point of trying? I just can't overcome this sin"?
- Do I continue placing myself in the way of temptation? Though I know that temptation—and probably failure—await, do I still move in the devil's direction?
- With regard to my sin, is it hard for me to believe Bible promises such as "When you are tempted, he will also provide a way out so that you can stand up under it" (1 Cor. 10:13)?
- Have I stopped spending time with God, reading His Word and praying, because I am so overwhelmed by the guilt of my sin?

Confess any sin strongholds to God. If you are unaware of sin strongholds, thank God for His grace in your life.

Ending this lesson at this point may leave you somewhat in despair. Be aware, though, that the next two lessons provide direction and insights for overcoming strongholds in our lives. For now, confess any strongholds in your life, and spend some time meditating on the promise of 1 John 1:9 found in the margin. Thank God that He is willing to forgive you and make you clean.

"If we confess our sins, he is faithful and just and will forgive us our sins and purify us from all unrighteousness."

—1 John 1:9

TRUTH BREAKS STRONGHOLDS

Mark each statement true (T), false (F), or uncertain (U). The answers are provided at the end of this lesson.

_____ 1. Satan is more interested in what we do than what we think.

_____ 2. Strongholds are usually related to our thinking.

_____ 3. Strongholds are not related to our actions.

_____ 4. After we become Christians, Satan can no longer affect our minds.

_____ 5. Our new birth in Christ guarantees that we will never again wrestle with negative messages from the past.

_____ 6. Satan wants us to give up when we are tempted, to assume that we can never really overcome temptations.

Having reviewed the concepts we have been studying this week, consider the question left unanswered in the previous lessons: if Satan attacks the mind and builds strongholds in thoughts and actions, how do we break the strongholds?

Truth Encounters Versus Power Encounters

Some warfare writers differentiate between these two distinct ways to counter strongholds. A power encounter is a visible display of God's power, such as physical healings or exorcisms. A truth encounter is the intentional application of biblical truth to life so that we might overcome the lies and power of the enemy. This latter approach most readily brings freedom from strongholds in the mind.

To see this point more clearly, read the following verses from the Gospel of John. As you fill in the blanks, think about the power of the truth of God.

" 'Then you will know the truth, and the truth will _____

_____ _____.' " —John 8:32

"Jesus answered, 'I am the way and the _____ and the

_____. No one comes to the Father except through

_____.' " —John 14:6

" 'When he, the Spirit of truth, comes, he will guide _____ into

all _____.' " —John 16:13

" '_____ them by the truth; your word is truth.' "

—John 17:17

John's point is clear. Jesus is the truth (14:6), and He sends the Spirit of truth who leads believers into all truth (16:13). God's truth ultimately sanctifies (17:17) and sets His children free (8:32). Through God's Word, incarnate in Jesus and written in the Scriptures, Christians experience freedom—including freedom from strongholds.

Needless to say, countering strongholds through God's truth assumes that an individual knows Jesus personally and knows God's written Word well enough to use it as a weapon (see Eph. 6:17). If you aren't certain that you have met Jesus personally as the One who saves you from your sin, review the "Steps to Salvation" on page 182. Talk with your pastor, group leader, a Christian friend, or a church staff member about your desire to follow Christ. If you want to break the strongholds in your life, affirm your relationship with Him first.

Jesus: Our Model for Living the Truth

Often Jesus displayed His power in overcoming Satan. Indeed, He often cast out demons and healed the sick as He proclaimed the message of the kingdom (see Matt. 4:23-25; 8:16-17; 9:35). But He also used truth encounters to defeat Satan.

Jesus did not have strongholds in His life that demanded removal. He was a perfect Savior who was "tempted in every way, just as we are—yet [who] was without sin" (Heb. 4:15). Nevertheless, Jesus' response to the devil in the wilderness reveals the effectiveness of using the truth of God's Word to respond to the enemy. Take the time now to read again Matthew's account of the temptation (Matt. 4:1-11). Several truths are pertinent to today's study.

1. Satan blatantly attacked Jesus.

If he was brazen enough to take on Jesus, how much more willing is he to attack us? Believers are obviously easier prey for him. Although he couldn't defeat Jesus, he can still defeat Jesus' followers. He wants us to live defeated lives marked by strongholds. Thus, it is imperative that we learn how to defend ourselves against him.

2. Jesus responded to each temptation with the Word of God.

Three times, Jesus quoted the Book of Deuteronomy (8:3; 6:13,16), and the Old Testament Word served as His sword against the devil (see Eph. 6:17). Though the devil didn't give up easily, the Word of God was powerful enough to drive him away (Matt. 4:11). Jesus' encounter with the devil was both a truth encounter and a power encounter.

> "When Jesus Christ was assailed by Satan in the wilderness, He had a great choice of weapons with which to fight Satan, but he took none but this sword of the Spirit: 'It is written.' This is our battle-ax and weapon of war. A spiritual kingdom must be set up and supported by spiritual means only."[3]
>
> CHARLES SPURGEON
> 19TH CENTURY
> ENGLISH PREACHER

Why Memorizing the Word Is Important

- Hiding His Word in our hearts helps us to guard against sin (Ps. 119:11).
- Knowing His Word helps us to think about things that are honoring to God (Phil. 4:8).
- The Word, quoted out of a life of holiness, causes the devil to flee—at least for a little while (Luke 4:13).
- The truth sets us free (John 8:32).
- What we put into our minds affects how we live.
- We don't always have access to a Bible when we face spiritual attacks.
- Even when we have access to a Bible, we can't always immediately locate needed texts.

3. Jesus not only quoted the Word, but He also lived it out.

Satan tempted Jesus to turn stones to bread, placing His own needs above trusting the Father to provide (Matt. 4:3). He also tempted Him to test the Father's care and protection (4:5-6), followed by a temptation to gain the world through a shortcut (4:8)—He could rule the world without enduring the cross. Jesus, though, would have no part in Satan's schemes, either on the mountain of temptation or in the years following. He continually placed the Father's will over His own, ultimately enduring the obedience of the cross (see Matt. 26:36-45; Phil. 2:5-8). Simply quoting the Word in some formulaic way was not Jesus' intent; He quoted it, but His commitment to the Word was as evident in His daily living as it was in His words.

Jesus is the model for overcoming the enemy: know the truth, trust the truth, memorize the truth, and live the truth.

Jesus was the Truth living out the truth. He is the model for overcoming the enemy: know the truth, trust the truth, memorize the truth, and live the truth. His mind was centered on God and His Word, and His actions reflected the focus of His thinking.

One way that Christians can break strongholds is to meditate on and memorize the Word of God—then to be faithful to the truths learned. These suggestions will guide you as you reflect on God's Word.

Suggestions for Bible Study

- Read a passage of Scripture.
- Thank God for any promises apparent in the text.
- Think about the teachings in the passage, focusing on their application to your life.
- If you recognize wrong in your life, confess it and turn from it. As God challenges you to live a more godly life, commit yourself to it.
- Write down any commitments that you make.
- Consider memorizing any passage that God brings to your attention.

In day 5 we will apply biblical truths to the battles Christians face. Conclude this lesson by reacting to these statements: In a single sentence, strongholds are broken when Christ lives in us and we know and follow His Word. In a single word, strongholds are broken when we choose in His power to be *obedient* to His revealed truth.

Check any of the following statements that reflect your feelings about breaking strongholds.
- ❏ "I'm disappointed. I was looking for a quick-fix solution to breaking my strongholds."
- ❏ "This process sounds like I have some work to do. Obedience is never easy."
- ❏ "Why can't I just pray against the spirits that hold me in bondage?"
- ❏ "I'm not surprised that obedience is necessary. I just need God's help to stay obedient when I'm under attack."
- ❏ "I need to know God's Word better and follow Him more faithfully if I want to experience freedom in Christ."
- ❏ "I am committing myself today to know God's Word, trust God's Word, memorize God's Word, and live God's Word."

(answers to day 4 activity p. 77: 1. F; 2. T; 3. F; 4. F; 5. F; 6. T.)

DAY FIVE

APPLYING TRUTH

Obedience to God is an ongoing, never-changing requirement that demands that we take up our crosses and follow Him daily (Luke 9:23).

If we hope to win spiritual battles, we must learn to apply the truths of God's Word to all areas of our lives each day. The goal of today's study is to guide you to make this kind of daily application.

Taking Thoughts Captive—Daily Submission of the Mind

Recall from previous lessons that a *stronghold* is defined as "an entrenched pattern of thinking and acting that we believe cannot change, even though we know that such thoughts and actions are contrary to God's will." In 2 Corinthians 10:4, strongholds more specifically referred to ideas and thought patterns that oppose God and that hold persons in bondage. Spiritual weapons were needed to overcome the strongholds, and those weapons had "divine power" to "demolish" the strongholds (v. 4).

In the margin read how Paul concluded the passage (2 Cor. 10:4-5).

Focus specifically on Paul's statement: "We take captive every thought to make it obedient to Christ." The word translated *thought* in this verse may also be understood as *mind*. In fact, Paul used the same word in 2 Corinthians to speak of the Israelites' hardened minds in the wilderness (3:14), the blinded minds of unbelievers (4:4), and the potentially deceived minds of the Corinthian believers (11:3).

The image in 2 Corinthians 10:5 depicts a military invading force, seeking to capture minds that are opposed to God and to conform their thinking to obedience to Christ. The implications of this image are at least two-fold.

First, conforming the mind to obedience to God is not always easy; in fact, it may be a battle. Because the mind so influences all that humans do, it should not surprise us that the devil works hard to maintain his influence there. He fights with great fervor to direct our thinking away from God. Spiritual weapons are indeed powerful enough to demolish the strongholds, but the battle is nevertheless real. Daily, we struggle to keep our minds pure before God and obedient to Him.

Consider the process of breaking (and avoiding) strongholds through daily submitting to God.

1. Study God's Word each day—know the truth.
2. Believe and accept the truths of God's Word.
3. Daily reject the lies that the enemy sends—claim the truths against the lies.
4. Practice the truth—live in obedience.
5. Daily ask for God's guidance and protection.

A second implication of 2 Corinthians 10:3-5 is that our battles are fought on behalf of others so that their minds might be freed from the enemy's lies. Paul fought against the strongholds of false thinking so that some might come to know Christ. As one Bible scholar stated, "Christ's prisoners who have been snatched from Satan's clutches can take the offensive and capture others for the gospel."4 Future lessons will look more closely at how believers take the offensive through proclaiming and evangelizing on behalf of others who are not believers.

"The weapons we fight with are not the weapons of the world. On the contrary, they have divine power to demolish strongholds. We demolish arguments and every pretension that sets itself up against the knowledge of God, and we take captive every thought to make it obedient to Christ."
—2 Corinthians 10:4-5

How "captured" is your mind for Christ? Place an "X" on the following scale to indicate your evaluation.

My mind is regularly disobedient to Christ.	I am learning to be obedient, but I have a long way to go.	My mind is consistently captured for Christ.

In the margin, write one action step you can take (something you will do, or perhaps something you will stop doing) that may help bring your thoughts into captivity to Christ.

Taking Thoughts Captive—Thinking About Good Things

Capturing thoughts is more than just deciding not to think about things that are displeasing to God. Rather, believers take thoughts captive by thinking about things that are pleasing to God—and then by living disciplined Christian lives built upon that Christian thinking (Phil. 4:8-9).

Christians are more likely to break spiritual strongholds when they think and act on the truths of God's Word. For example, you may struggle with the issue of poor self-worth. If you or someone you know struggles with this issue, review these truths about who believers are in Christ.

Fill in the blanks. We have used the personal pronoun "*I*" to place yourself in these texts.

- John 15:15: I am a _____ of Christ.

- Romans 6:22: I have been _____ _____ from sin.

- 2 Corinthians 5:17: I am a _____ creation.

- Colossians 3:12: I am one of God's chosen, holy and dearly

  _____.

- 1 Thessalonians 5:5: I am a son of the _____.

To keep your focus on God rather than yourself, thank Him for graciously applying these truths in your life.

While these texts reflect only a few biblical truths regarding believers, they do help us think good thoughts. Believers are Christ's friends (John 15:15), set free from sin (Rom. 6:22), and made new creations (2 Cor. 5:17). They are holy and dearly loved (Col. 3:12), sons of the light and of the day (1 Thess. 5:5). Thinking about these truths will help us capture our thoughts in obedience to Christ.

> Faith is not merely an intellectual belief or theory. Of course, faith includes what you believe, but faith never stops at mere intellectual assent and belief. Faith is always practical. Faith always applies the truth.[5]
>
> ### D. MARTYN LLOYD-JONES

Meditate on the following truths. Place a check beside each one that specifically gives you encouragement about overcoming your sin strongholds.

- ❏ "God is faithful; he will not let you be tempted beyond what you can bear. But when you are tempted, he will also provide a way out so that you can stand up under it."—1 Corinthians 10:13
- ❏ "If we confess our sins, he is faithful and just and will forgive us our sins and purify us from all unrighteousness."—1 John 1:9
- ❏ "I can do everything through him who gives me strength."—Philippians 4:13
- ❏ "We do not have a high priest who is unable to sympathize with our weaknesses, but we have one who has been tempted in every way, just as we are—yet was without sin."—Hebrews 4:15
- ❏ "I write this to you so that you will not sin. But if anybody does sin, we have one who speaks to the Father in our defense—Jesus Christ, the Righteous One."—1 John 2:1

Thank God for each truth. Ask Him to give you faith to trust these promises. Consider writing these verses on a card and refer to them when you need a reminder to capture your thoughts for Christ.

Living Out God's Truths: Examples of Faith

Hebrews 11, the "faith chapter," lists several heroes of faith. Among these heroes are persons who trusted God even in difficult circumstances, believing that He would be faithful to His Word. Though their stories don't explicitly address spiritual warfare, they do provide examples of persons who lived by God's promises—persons whose right thinking led to obedient living in spite of struggles.

Abraham (Heb. 11:8-12,17-19) left his homeland, believing that God would lead him to his promised land. He was also willing to slay his son because he believed that God would resurrect the son and keep His promise of offspring through him. Later, Moses so believed in God's leading that he chose disgrace among the people of God rather than the riches of Egypt (11:24-26). Still others remained faithful even unto death, trusting the promise of resurrection (11:35). In each of these cases, belief in God—even when their thinking made little sense from the world's perspective—produced obedient living. Faith was evident in actions.

Review the remainder of Hebrews 11, listing below any other heroes whose beliefs were evidenced in their faithful living.

_____

_____

_____

_____

Like other persons of faith, we cannot allow the enemy to hinder our trust in God and His promises. As we conclude this week's lessons, ask God to make you a person of faith. Ask Him to help you trust His Word, live out His truths, and thus demolish the strongholds in your life.

[1]Tom White, *Breaking Strongholds* (Ann Arbor, MI: Servant Publications, 1993), 24.
[2]Ed Silvoso, *That None Should Perish* (Ventura, CA: Regal Books, 1994), 155.
[3]Charles Spurgeon, *Spiritual Warfare in a Believer's Life*, ed. Robert Hall (Lynnwood, WA: Emerald Books, 1993), 73.
[4]David Garland, *Corinthians,* vol. 29 in *The New American Commentary* (Nashville: Broadman & Holman, 1999) 437.
[5]D.M. Lloyd-Jones, *The Christian Soldier* (Grand Rapids: Baker Book House, 1977), 305.
[6]Charles Lawless, "Preaching About Spiritual Warfare," *Proclaim!,* Summer 2000, 17-20.

——— DECLARING A WAR ALREADY WON ———

The narratives of the temptation of Christ (Matt. 4:1-11; Mark 1:12-13; Luke 4:1-13) provide general truths for understanding the biblical portrait of spiritual warfare.

While many would rightly contend that the current interest in spiritual warfare has created an unhealthy fascination with the demonic, we must recognize that we daily face a literal enemy. For Jesus, the tempter was as real as the temptations themselves. Nowhere is there an indication that Jesus viewed Satan as only an impersonal force or a mythological explanation for evil. Clearly, He recognized Satan as a literal enemy, and He responded forcefully to him.

We who are fallen, yet redeemed, seldom recognize Satan as readily as Jesus did. We are too often easy prey for the "roaring lion, seeking someone to devour" (1 Pet. 5:8, NASB). We too frequently choose to follow the "angel of light" into disobedience, especially when we fail to recognize Satan's schemes (2 Cor. 2:11; 11:14). The temptation narratives, though, call us to recognize our enemy. Satan is real, cunning, and deceptive. He who deliberately challenged the Son of God will certainly challenge us, and we are biblically negligent to ignore his reality.

Satan is not, however, the focus of the temptation narratives. The focus of the narratives, indeed, of the Bible, is God. It was the Son of God who fought and won the battle on the mountain of temptation. It was the Word of God that served as the primary weapon of battle.

It was the angels of God who ministered to Jesus (Matt. 4:11). In fact, it was the Spirit of God who led Jesus to the place of temptation in the first place (4:1).

The Spirit did not tempt Christ (see Jas. 1:13), but He did compel Jesus to go to the wilderness to be tempted by the devil. He had divine purposes for leading Jesus to the place where the enemy would tempt Him.

The sovereignty of God in the temptation establishes the proper focus for any study of spiritual warfare: God the victor rather than Satan the tempter. Hence, the primary task of the spiritual warrior is not to know Satan well—it is to know God so intimately that Satan's counterfeit becomes obvious in comparison.

The message of victory through the cross must be the focus of our teaching about present spiritual warfare; that is, we cannot fully appreciate Jesus' victory at the mount of temptation until we place that event in the shadow of Jesus' victory on Mt. Calvary. Our foe is a defeated one, and his final destruction has been assured (Rev. 12:7-9; 20:10).

The battle nevertheless remains a real one, and we have the assurance that God will sustain us. Our victory gained in the cross is evidenced by the resurrected Lord who now intercedes for us (Heb. 7:25). Principalities and powers cannot separate us from the love of God (see Eph. 6:12, Rom. 8:38-39). Thus, from a position of victory we declare the war already won.[6]

VIEWER GUIDE

1. Why does Satan attack the mind?

   1) Our _____ come out of our hearts and minds.

   2) Our mind is _____.

2. We give Satan access by opening our minds to the _____,

   the _____, and the _____.

3. A stronghold is accepting as unchangeable that which I know is

   _____ to God.

4. The mind is the command and control center of our _____ lives.

5. What you believe in your mind will determine ahead of time how you will

   _____ to God.

6. If I have a stronghold in my life, I must

   1) find _____ support.

   2) be accountable to someone.

   3) know the truth of the _____ in my heart.

Schemes for Churches

CASE STUDY

The leaders in the local church didn't know what to do. No matter what they tried, nothing seemed to work. The church had been divided over several issues for some time. The pastor and the deacons seldom agreed on anything. Every business meeting ended in turmoil. No one was inviting friends to the church, and the few visitors who did attend didn't return.

Another church in the same town wasn't experiencing the turmoil of the first church. In fact, their numbers were increasing slightly. However, this church was teaching that God provides means of salvation other than through a personal relationship with Jesus.

Which of these churches might be experiencing spiritual warfare? The first church? the second church? both churches? How do we know when a church is facing spiritual warfare? How does Satan attempt to derail churches? This week's lessons seek to answer these questions.

DAY ONE

WARFARE IN THE CHURCH

Read the statements concerning a recent survey. Mark whether you believe each statement is true (T) or false (F).

_____ Church growth experts maintain that at least 80 percent of the churches in America are plateaued or declining.[1]

_____ Seventy percent of American adult Christians believe there are no absolute moral or ethical standards that apply to everybody.[2]

_____ Only 20 percent of them state that living a life according to God's will is the single most important thing in their lives.[3]

Regrettably, each of these statements is true. One cause is spiritual warfare. Satan has plotted against the church, and he has in many ways

succeeded in American churches. Our goal in this week's studies is to analyze the devil's specific schemes against the church. In so doing, we want to help our churches prepare for and respond to the reality of spiritual warfare.

Why Does Satan Attack the Church?

Read Ephesians 6:11 in the margin. The word translated *schemes* may be understood as "strategies" or "methods," and the connotation of the word is typically "deceit." The devil is crafty, cunning, and lying in wait to deceive God's own.

In Ephesians 6 each individual believer is expected to be prepared for the fight, but the context is corporate—that is, believers put on the armor and fight battles most effectively in the context of the church. As we will see throughout this week, Satan has specific strategies to weaken the church. Let's consider why the enemy attacks the church.

First, the church is called to preach the gospel to the world. Read Matthew 28:18-20. You know these verses as the Great Commission, but have you considered the responsibility that Jesus gave to His followers?

List the tasks of the church according to this text:

_____

_____

Jesus called His followers, including us, to make disciples of all the world. We are to teach people the gospel, baptize new converts, and continue to teach them as they become disciples of Christ. Remarkably, Jesus gave the church—and only the church—this responsibility.

Do you see why Satan attacks a church committed to this task? He doesn't want the church preaching the gospel. He doesn't want to lose the unsaved persons who are held in his kingdom (Col. 1:13). If he can sidetrack the church from fulfilling the Great Commission, he holds his captives longer. He attacks the church in order to direct their focus away from their mission.

Second, the unity of the church is a witness to Christ's love. Read John 13:34-35 and 17:22-23 in the margin on the next page.

"Put on the full armor of God so that you can take your stand against the devil's schemes."
—Ephesians 6:11

"Then Jesus came to them and said, 'All authority in heaven and on earth has been given to me. Therefore go and make disciples of all nations, baptizing them in the name of the Father and of the Son and of the Holy Spirit, and teaching them to obey everything I have commanded you. And surely I am with you always, to the very end of the age.' "
—Matthew 28:18-20

WHY SATAN ATTACKS
THE CHURCH
1. *It is called to preach the gospel.*
2. *The unity of the church is a witness to Christ's love.*
3. *The church teaches the life-changing Word of God.*

"A new command I give you: Love one another. As I have loved you, so you must love one another. By this all men will know that you are my disciples, if you love one another.'"
—*John 13:34-35*

" 'I have given them the glory that you gave me, that they may be one as we are one: I in them and you in me. May they be brought to complete unity to let the world know that you sent me and have loved them even as you have loved me.'"
—*John 17:22-23*

"I appeal to you, brothers, in the name of our Lord Jesus Christ, that all of you agree with one another so that there may be no divisions among you and that you may be perfectly united in mind and thought. My brothers, some from Chloe's household have informed me that there are quarrels among you. What I mean is this: One of you says, 'I follow Paul'; another, 'I follow Apollos'; and another, 'I follow Cehas'; still another, 'I follow Christ.'"

"Is Christ divided? Was Paul crucified for you? Were you baptized into the name of Paul?"
—*1 Corinthians 1:10-13*

According to these verses, how will the world recognize Jesus' followers?

_____

The world recognizes Jesus' followers by their love for one another and their unity in spirit. If that's the case, Satan would want to create disharmony and division in the church to counter the church's witness. During this week, we'll see how the enemy worked in the church in Corinth. Read 1 Corinthians 1:10-13.

Why do you think Paul was so concerned about the divisions taking place in the church?

_____

_____

Third, the church teaches the life-changing Word of God. God's Word is a powerful weapon to defend against the enemy. If Satan can entice the church to ignore, neglect, or distort the Word, he will have weakened the church overall. In fact, Paul warned Timothy that some in the church would follow "deceiving spirits and things taught by demons" (1 Tim. 4:1). The demons themselves weren't teaching, but their power stood behind false teachers who distorted the Word of God and deceived others. When the truth is not proclaimed, how can anyone be freed from the lies of the enemy?

On the other hand, the devil knows that he cannot stand against the Word of God (see Matt. 4:1-11). He knows that the truth sets people free (John 8:32). Consequently, he attempts to keep the church from teaching the Word.

Using the following possible responses, evaluate your church with regard to Satan's strategies:

A = agree   D = disagree   U = uncertain

_____ Our church is united; the enemy has little access to us through division.

_____ Our church leaders consistently teach the Word of God.

_____ The focus of our church is evangelism, both in our local context and around the world.

_____ Our community knows by our church's unity and our love that God is working among us.

_____ Most of our church members love and follow the Word of God.

_____ Our church is focused on the Great Commission.

_____ Satan has been ineffective in His strategies against our church.

What Is the Relationship Between Warfare for Individuals and Warfare for Churches?

Distinguishing individual warfare from church warfare is difficult because of the nature of the church—the church consists of individuals, but it is also a corporate body.

How do these verses reflect the corporate nature of the church?

1 Corinthians 12:12-27 _____

_____

1 Peter 2:9-10 _____

_____

As the church, we are the body of Christ and the chosen people of God. We are individual members but interrelated (1 Cor. 12:27).

God has so designed the church that when one member of the body suffers, all members suffer (v. 26). Likewise, spiritual warfare in the lives of individual members affects the entire church, even though other members may not be aware of the specific battles. A member who consistently loses spiritual battles ultimately affects the entire church. We most successfully stand firm against the enemy (Eph. 6:11,13) when we realize that Christian brothers and sisters are standing alongside us.

Consider the following stories. A man in the church in Corinth succumbed to incest, and the whole church arrogantly flaunted the sin (1 Cor. 5:1-2). Satan enticed Ananias and Sapphira to lie about their income (Acts 5:3), and great fear fell upon the entire church when God judged the liars (Acts 5:11). A demonic man attacked the sons of Sceva in Ephesus, yet the believers in that city turned from their sin as a result (Acts 19:11-19). In each case, individual battles affected others as well.

Satan also strikes the corporate church hoping to harm individuals. He sends false teachers so that individuals may be deceived—one by one. He seeks to create division, with the goal of wounding individual relationships. He fights the church's evangelistic efforts so that lost persons might remain blinded to the truth (2 Cor. 4:3-4).

The diagram below shows how intertwined warfare is for individuals and churches. Because the enemy strives to weaken the church through its members, we must pray for one another.

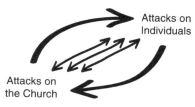

Attacks on Individuals

Attacks on the Church

Pray for the concerns listed in the margin.

PRAYER CONCERNS
- Pray for your church leaders as they direct your church.
- Pray that God will help the leaders to recognize any lack of organization or strategy that might open the door for the devil.
- Pray that your church would strive to grow believers whose faithful lives glorify God.
- Pray that your heart would be right with God.
- Pray that this week's lessons will help you as a church member to guard against the enemy's influence in your church.

DAY TWO

TO CREATE DIVISION

Jesus made a startling statement in Matthew 12:25—" 'Every kingdom divided against itself will be ruined, and every city or household divided against itself will not stand.' " Jesus did not say, *might have difficulty, be a little tougher,* or *have to work twice as hard.* He said, "will not stand."

THE FRONTS OF SPIRITUAL WARFARE THAT AFFECT A CHURCH'S SPIRITUAL BATTLES
1. The **personal** front: our participation in the internal battles of daily life and the foundation for all other fronts.
2. The **interpersonal** front: our efforts to help others who are under attack; the ways we can challenge and encourage them such as one-to-one counseling or small-group ministry.
3. The **local church** front: centered in an individual or a small group of people but impacting the whole church.
4. The **systemic** front: the struggle against the domination systems that make up our societies—cultural, political, economic, and religious systems.
5. The **cosmic** front: the unseen front of warfare in which angels and demons engage each other in conflict under God's sovereign control.[4]

Based on Jesus' statement, what is the likelihood that your church will stand if you have unresolved conflict? (check)

❏ 100%   ❏ 75%   ❏ 50%   ❏ 25%   ❏ 0%

Have you ever seen a church in the middle of a conflict grow, launch dynamic new programs, start new initiatives to the community, or gain a better reputation?

What results when church members fight? Anger, hurt feelings, destroyed friendships, bitterness, loss of membership, loss of finances, and a host of other problems generally surface. The tree of a house divided produces bitter fruit. Churches in that condition cannot stand. Wouldn't it make sense, then, that one of Satan's major goals would be to create division in the church?

What Creates Division?

If different opinions created division, no church could hope for unity, for no two people will ever see things exactly alike. Paul understood and allowed room for disputable matters (Rom. 14:1). Instead, division occurs because Christians relate and react inappropriately. Today's lesson examines four common reasons churches experience division.

First, division occurs when believers sin against each other. Ephesians 4:25-32 explains how church members should relate to one another. Paul told them to speak truthfully, be kind, forgive one another, and rid themselves of all bitterness, rage, and anger. In the middle of this passage he reminded them not to give the devil an opportunity. When Christians wrong and harm one another, when someone remains offended, when the church doesn't immediately deal with conflict, trouble can walk through the door.

In verse 26 Paul counseled, "Do not let the sun go down while you are still angry." In other words, deal with anger immediately. Don't let it fester. If you do, you're inviting problems. The devil then has something to work with. He can capitalize on hurt feelings, encourage someone to start talking about another, convince people to take up somebody else's cause, draw lines, take sides, create gossip and slander, and so on—all the things that lead to division. Paul said, "Make every effort to keep the unity of the Spirit through the bond of peace" (4:3). That's how you avoid giving Satan a foothold.

Reread Ephesians 4:25-32. Underline each statement below that your church members consistently practice.

seek reconciliation quickly
wait for the other person to admit blame
blame others whether or not they have the facts
spread gossip, slander, and rumor

hang on to hurt
speak kindly
forgive
build others up

Based on your findings, does Satan have an opportunity to gain a foothold in your church?

❑ Yes ❑ No

If you are aware of unresolved conflict in your church, what role can you play? Be prepared to discuss your answer with your group.

_____

_____

"Therefore each of you must put off falsehood and speak truthfully to his neighbor, for we are all members of one body. 'In your anger do not sin': Do not let the sun go down while you are still angry, and do not give the devil a foothold. He who has been stealing must steal no longer, but must work, doing something useful with his own hands, that he may have something to share with those in need. Do not let any unwholesome talk come out of your mouths, but only what is helpful for building others up according to their needs, that it may benefit those who listen. And do not grieve the Holy Spirit of God, with whom you were sealed for the day of redemption.
—*Ephesians. 4:25-30*

Second, division occurs through loss of love for one another. Paul counseled the Colossian church, "And over all these virtues put on love, which binds them all together in perfect unity" (Col. 3:14). The bond that unites us is love. Perfect unity comes from church members whose hearts are fervent toward one another. No storm, no trial, no disaster can separate members who truly care for each other. Conversely, if our love for our brothers cools, we can tolerate disunity. If allowed to go unchecked, a waning heart will eventually justify division.

The Corinthian church was at just such a fork in the road. Read 2 Corinthians 2:6-11. A church member had undergone church discipline. Obviously, the man was repentant and sorrowful. Upon realizing his change of heart, Paul counseled the church to reaffirm their love, forgive, and comfort him, so that Satan might not take advantage of them. Paul knew the man was in danger of discouragement; the church had not yet reached out in love to restore him. They were at a point of crisis because Satan had a situation he could exploit. Paul knew the devil's scheme would be undercut if church members reestablished their unity through affirming their love for this brother.

"The punishment inflicted on him by the majority is sufficient for him. Now instead, you ought to forgive and comfort him, so that he will not be overwhelmed by excessive sorrow. I urge you, therefore, to reaffirm your love for him. The reason I wrote you was to see if you would stand the test and be obedient in everything. If you forgive anyone, I also forgive him. And what I have forgiven—if there was anything to forgive—I have forgiven in the sight of Christ for your sake, in order that Satan might not outwit us. For we are not unaware of his schemes."
—*2 Corinthians 2:6-11*

Answer these questions from your knowledge and experience. Compare your responses to those of others at your next group session.
How does your church respond if members begin missing regularly?

_____

How does your church reach out to restore fallen members?

_____

Do church members routinely fellowship with each other outside of regularly scheduled church events? ❑ Yes ❑ No
Can a church fervent in love be easily divided? ❑ Yes ❑ No

"Such 'wisdom' does not come down from heaven but is earthly, unspiritual, of the devil. For where you have envy and selfish ambition, there you find disorder and every evil practice."

—James 3:15-16

Third, division occurs when members seek self-interest instead of the interests of others. James identified the devil as the source of envy and selfish ambition. Self-seekers engage in demonic thinking. The Christians to whom James wrote had unfortunately bought into the devil's wisdom.

Paul also admonished believers not to look out for their own interests first, but to put others first. In particular, six times he warned the Corinthian church against being "puffed up" about themselves. Arrogance apparently caused them to focus only on self and ignore others' needs.

Not surprisingly, Paul found the church in the middle of a four-way split. Paul knew they were under spiritual warfare and had already lost. He told them, "The very fact that you have lawsuits among you means you have been completely defeated already" (1 Cor. 6:7). Perhaps this is why he spent so much time talking about spiritual warfare to this church (see 1 Cor. 6:7; 10:20; 2 Cor 2:11; 6:15; 10:5; 11:3,14). Unfortunately, they seemed unaware that Satan had defeated them.

No wonder Paul warned them that when he came he would use his authority to tear down the strongholds of false thinking that Satan had built in their minds. He expressly stated that he would deal with any "contentions, jealousies, outbursts of wrath, selfish ambitions, backbitings, whisperings, conceits, tumults" (2 Cor. 12:20, NKJV) that result from serving self-interests.

Fourth, division occurs when a church does not see as God sees. Paul pointed out in 1 Corinthians 3:1-3 that the presence of divisions indicated they were still carnal, thinking and acting as the world does. Paul knew it would be spiritually impossible for the church to see as God sees and remain divided. How did he deal with this problem?

Paul warned them not to be wise in their own eyes but rather to look to God's wisdom (1 Cor. 3:18-23). Churches that take time to seek the mind of God will find they cannot be divided and be in His will.

FOUR REASONS CHURCHES EXPERIENCE DIVISION

1.

2.

3.

4.

In the margin write four reasons for division.

One Deadly Consequence of Division

Jesus taught that unity plays a vital role in evangelism. In John 17:20-21 He pled with the Father to restore unity among believers as a prerequisite for the world knowing that the Father sent Jesus. When the world sees true oneness—love for one another despite our differences—the unity stands so starkly in contrast to their experience in the world that they see something they want. Conversely, when believers bicker and fight, non-believers show little interest in being a part of the church. They can stay at home without feeling like a hypocrite. Christians ought to recognize the preciousness of unity and diligently guard against the devil's schemes to divide us.

" 'My prayer is not for them alone. I pray also for those who will believe in me through their message, that all of them may be one, Father, just as you are in me and I am in you. May they also be in us so that the world may believe that you have sent me.' "

—John 17:20-21

Evaluate the degree to which you contribute to the unity of your church.

source of disunity   source of unity

DAY THREE

TO SPREAD FALSE DOCTRINE

If your church proudly proclaimed, *Come join us for an exciting doctrine study starting this fall!* how much interest would this announcement generate in the community? Unfortunately, many Christians believe "exciting doctrine" is an oxymoron. The word *doctrine* is more likely to be associated with a cure for insomnia than with an exhilarating, life-changing experience. That's unfortunate. Scripture reveals a church's very life depends on its knowing sound doctrine.

God Places Importance on Sound Doctrine.

Sound doctrine is critical in God's design for the church. In fact, He inspired the Bible as a resource for teaching true doctrine, for refuting false doctrine, and for guiding proper living (2 Tim. 3:16). These verses underscore the importance of true doctrine, or teaching.

- "Then they understood that he was not telling them to guard against the yeast used in bread, but against the teaching of the Pharisees and Sadducees." —Matthew 16:12
- "Then we will no longer be infants, tossed back and forth by the waves, and blown here and there by every wind of teaching and by the cunning and craftiness of men in their deceitful scheming." —Ephesians 4:14
- "The Spirit clearly says that in later times some will abandon the faith and follow deceiving spirits and things taught by demons." —1 Timothy 4:1
- "Nevertheless, I have a few things against you: You have people there who hold to the teaching of Balaam, who taught Balak to entice the Israelites to sin by eating food sacrificed to idols and by committing sexual immorality. Likewise you also have those who hold to the teaching of the Nicolaitans. Repent therefore! Otherwise, I will soon come to you and will fight against them with the sword of my mouth."—Revelation 2:14-16

What do these verses reveal about the importance of doctrine?

_____

_____

Scripture puts a high premium on true doctrine. Ten times the New Testament commands believers not to be deceived (Matt. 24:4; Mark 13:5; Luke 21:8; 1 Cor. 3:18; 6:9; 15:33; Gal. 6:7; Eph. 5:6; 2 Thess. 2:3; Jas. 1:16). On at least 20 other occasions people or Satan are pictured as aggressively trying to deceive others; we are warned to be on guard against this form of spiritual warfare. Deception is one of Satan's main strategies.

Warnings

" 'For many will come in my name, claiming, "I am the Christ," and will deceive many.' " —Matthew 24:5

" 'False Christs and false prophets will appear and perform signs and miracles to deceive the elect—if that were possible.' " —Mark 13:22

"Such people are not serving our Lord Christ, but their own appetites. By smooth talk and flattery they deceive the minds of naive people."—Romans 16:18

"Such men are false apostles, deceitful workmen, masquerading as apostles of Christ."—2 Corinthians 11:13

"I tell you this so that no one may deceive you by fine-sounding arguments."—Colossians 2:4

"The Spirit clearly says that in later times some will abandon the faith and follow deceiving spirits and things taught by demons." —1 Timothy 4:1

"Evil men and impostors will go from bad to worse, deceiving and being deceived."—2 Timothy 3:13

"Many deceivers, who do not acknowledge Jesus Christ as coming in the flesh, have gone out into the world. Any such person is the deceiver and the antichrist."—2 John 1:7

Commands

"Jesus said to them: 'Watch out that no one deceives you.' " —Mark 13:5

"He replied: 'Watch out that you are not deceived. For many will come in my name, claiming, "I am he," and, "The time is near." Do not follow them.' " —Luke 21:8

"Do you not know that the wicked will not inherit the kingdom of God? Do not be deceived: Neither the sexually immoral nor idolaters nor adulterers nor male prostitutes nor homosexual offenders."—1 Corinthians 6:9

"Let no one deceive you with empty words, for because of such things God's wrath comes on those who are disobedience." —Ephesians 5:6

"Don't let anyone deceive you in any way, for that day will not come until the rebellion occurs and the man of lawlessness is revealed, the man doomed to destruction."—2 Thessalonians 2:3

Why Doctrine Is Important

If God is that concerned about doctrine, why does the word *doctrine* conjure up images of stuffy lectures on points of religion that don't really matter? Unfortunately, the teaching of doctrine has often been devoid of application to real-life issues. As a result, once-eager students have gained head knowledge without understanding how that information impacts daily life.

Doctrine is the sum of our beliefs, values, and teaching about who God is, how He acts, how we relate to Him, and how the truth works itself out in everyday life. Everything about it has practical application for living. When the Word of God is applied in such a way as to be irrelevant, the teacher has perverted the nature of Scripture.

How do you view doctrine? Write how these doctrines impact your everyday life.

Doctrine of lordship: Jesus is Lord and Master over all. _____

_____

Doctrine of salvation: Jesus offers eternal life by grace not works:

_____

Doctrine of sovereignty: God is in control of all things. _____

_____

Because doctrine is so relevant, Satan tries to pervert it for at least three reasons. **First,** doctrine shapes or determines our actions and lifestyles. Doctrine creates our beliefs about God. What we believe will determine what we do. The doctrine of the sovereignty of God frees us from worry so we can do whatever our hands find to do with all our might. If we believe salvation is by works, we will act one way. If we believe salvation is by faith, we will act another.

Second, doctrine gives us a filter for evaluating truth. The world is full of conflicting messages and beliefs. People take opposite stands on abortion. Some affirm that God views homosexuality as sin, while others declare that God created some people different from birth. A popular belief is that no absolute truth exists, while tradition holds that absolutes do exist. Who is right? How will you decide? Every person must have some means of evaluating truth claims that they hear. By searching the Scripture, the doctrines we learn become filters for discerning the truth.

Third, doctrine is necessary for usefulness in God's kingdom. The Pharisees were very religious but missed the promised Messiah. Their doctrine of how the Sabbath ought to be kept caused them to oppose Jesus (Mark 2:23-28). Similarly, the Nicolaitans perverted sexuality, and church members in Smyrna were deceived and began practicing acts

WHY SATAN
PERVERTS DOCTRINE
1. *Doctrine shapes or determines our actions.*
2. *Doctrine gives us a filter for evaluating truth.*
3. *Doctrine is necessary for usefulness in God's kingdom.*

abominable to God (Rev. 2:15). Jesus said He would come and fight against them. The purer we are in understanding the God of the Bible, the purer our actions will be. The purer our actions are, the greater God works through us.

How Does Satan Try to Pervert Doctrine?

It should not come as a surprise that Satan seeks to pervert doctrine. Because doctrine is so critical, the question is not *will someone try to deceive me with false doctrine?* The question is *when someone tries to deceive me with false doctrine, will I recognize it?* The whole of Scripture reveals a constant supply of those who were false prophets. Indeed, Jesus told the church that many would come for the express purpose of deceiving. In light of this fact, the tendency to downplay doctrine in our day is disturbing. Many Christians through their carelessness have set themselves up for deception. Interestingly, identifying Satan's major deceptions is not that difficult.

Satan tries to twist doctrine in one of four major ways. **First,** Satan seeks to call into question the divinity or the humanity of Christ. He will deny that Christ is fully God, or he will deny Christ is fully man. One of these errors can be seen in the teachings of the first century sect called the Gnostics. The Gnostics did not believe Jesus came in the flesh but rather only appeared to be a man.[5] A few centuries later, a man named Arius taught that Christ was not fully divine.[6] Popular modern-day cults such as Mormonism, Jehovah's Witnesses, or the Unification Church all call into question the deity of Christ.

Second, Satan causes us to question our basis of salvation. Typically, cults teach that salvation comes by works, or it comes by faith plus works. The believer must do something to aid in his or her salvation. Cults also downplay or deny the need for Jesus to offer a blood sacrifice for atonement of sin.

Third, Satan encourages beliefs that lead to immorality. Tradition holds that the Nicolaitans were antinomians—individuals who believed it did not matter what behavior was practiced since we are under grace and not the law. They twisted Scripture to justify a lifestyle of immoral sexual practices. When someone adopts an immoral lifestyle and believes it is acceptable, some biblical doctrine has been perverted.

Fourth, Satan nurtures viewpoints that lead to division. Satan uses differing beliefs of Christians against them. In Romans 14:1-7 Paul mentioned Christians with different doctrinal convictions. For example, one person may believe God wants us to be vegetarians; another may think it's acceptable to eat meat. One person may believe Sunday is extra special; another may think every day is equal. Paul offered a definite opinion on the vegetarian/meat issue (v. 14), but counseled believers not to let disputable matters become a basis for division. When Christians divide over issues that have nothing to do with the nature of Christ or salvation, they fall prey to Satan. While it is appropriate to hold convictions, we need not separate ourselves from those from whom God has not separated Himself. What God has not made an issue of fellowship should not be an issue for us either.

WAYS SATAN TWISTS DOCTRINE
1. Satan seeks to call into question the divinity or the humanity of Christ.
2. Satan causes us to question our basis of salvation.
3. Satan encourages beliefs that lead to immorality.
4. Satan nurtures viewpoints that lead to division.

How Are Christians Deceived?

First, you can be deceived on the basis of ignorance. The universal characteristic of all those deceived is that they never knew they were deceived. If churches do not know what the Bible says but instead rely only on church leaders' interpretation, then they are ripe for deception.

Since ignorance is the basis of all deception, the solution is simple. To guard against being deceived, we must arm ourselves with the Word of God. Knowing His Word will guard us from lies. Where we have believed lies, the truth will expose them. Therefore, the solution is to stay in the Word of God so that we will respond correctly.

Second, deception comes from not comparing and analyzing a teaching in light of the whole counsel of God. Satan's temptations often have strong logic. When Satan told Jesus to jump off the temple and the angels would catch Him, He was absolutely right.

The only way Jesus recognized his deception was by comparing it to the whole counsel of God. He answered, " 'It is also written. ...' " By analyzing Satan's logic, Jesus saw that Satan was technically right, but his advice violated other Scripture. Therefore, Jesus was not deceived.

Jesus sent believers the Holy Spirit to teach us the truth—to guard us against false doctrine (John 16:13). Ultimately, we must learn to depend upon the Spirit and not our own intellect or Bible study skills. Ask the Spirit to be your Guide daily as you walk in truth.

DAY FOUR

TO ATTACK LEADERSHIP

God requires His church to spend time understanding Him and His ways so that we will respond appropriately when in warfare. We should not expect to be shielded from all attacks, but rather we should stay focused on Him so that we will stand the test.

God expects our standing to be a team effort. We're not unrelated parts who only care for ourselves but rather a body that zealously seeks the good of other members. Church leaders have greater responsibility in that process because how they respond has greater potential for good or bad. Today we will examine why Satan wants leaders to fail, ways he tempts them, and how leaders and followers should respond.

Why Satan Wants Leaders to Fail

First, when a leader fails, those under his leadership are negatively affected. Most of King David's actions greatly benefited the nation of Israel. On other occasions, his sin had tremendous negative consequences. In 1 Chronicles 21:1-14 Satan incited David to take a census. Although his general warned him not to do it, David caved in to the temptation. Scripture records God's reaction: it was "evil in the sight of God" (v. 7). As a result, God sent a plague in which 70,000 people died. Because of the leader's sin, everyone was impacted.

The same holds true in all of life. If a company goes bankrupt because the CEO is convicted of falsifying tax records, others lose their jobs as well. If the pastor yields to temptation (whether or not the church knows), his actions will negatively affect the whole church.

How often do you pray for your pastor?
❏ never   ❏ once a week   ❏ once a month   ❏ daily

Ask God if your prayer life for your pastor is adequate. When you have heard His answer, respond in obedience.

Second, when a leader compromises, others go astray (Matt. 16:22; Gal. 2:11-13). We find this pattern in the life of Peter. In order to prepare His people for the gospel going to the Gentiles, God began to alert His church, and especially Peter, to what He was doing. God took Peter to the house of a Gentile so that Peter would realize that God doesn't show partiality (Acts 10:34-35,44-48).

In spite of this, Paul recounted in Galatians 2:11-13 a surprising confrontation he had with Peter. Why would Peter do an about-face? These men were from James, the half-brother of Jesus, a very influential church figure. It would appear Peter yielded to peer pressure. When Peter compromised, others began to follow his example. Even Barnabas, who had been on a missionary journey to the Gentiles, joined in the hypocrisy. Peter's status as a leader had enormous influence on others under him. Had it not been for Paul, he could have led the whole church to disassociate with Gentiles at the very moment God was moving to extend the gospel to the Gentiles.

How important it is for leadership to base its decisions on the will of God instead of opinions of men! How important it is for church members to be grounded in Scripture so they can help leaders to be true to God! Like Paul, they can encourage leaders who waver.

Third, when a leader is untried, he is prone to arrogance, which leads to judgment (1 Tim. 3:6). Many people jokingly remark how much smarter their parents became after they themselves entered their 20s. They experience a few hard knocks, and the ego deflates just a little bit. The testing of life has a wonderful effect of bringing about wisdom and humility. In the same way, Paul counseled that a church ought not install someone who is new at Christianity. He feared that their inexperience would lead to arrogance that God would have to judge. No church can expect much positive to happen in the immediate future if God is about to discipline their leader. Therefore, Paul strongly counseled Timothy against making such a mistake.

Satan, for his part, would love to create a scenario that would set up a church for failure. A congregation, however, need not experience this trap if they are careful to test the maturity level of those they appoint as leaders. Age does not have to be the overarching factor, but the maturity level of the leader does.

Fourth, when a leader is self-centered, he will take advantage of those under him. Whenever God appoints a shepherd, he requires that

"When Peter came to Antioch, I opposed him to his face, because he was clearly in the wrong. Before certain men came from James, he used to eat with the Gentiles. But when they arrived, he began to draw back and separate himself from the Gentiles because he was afraid of those who belonged to the circumcision group. The other Jews joined him in his hypocrisy, so that by their hypocrisy even Barnabas was led astray."
—Galatians 2:11-13

he be willing to lay down his life for his flock. God's Word pictures the behavior of a self-centered leader in Ezekiel 34:1-6.

List the actions of the shepherds in verses 2-4:

_____

_____

List the results of the shepherds' behavior:

_____

_____

If a pastor, deacon, Sunday School teacher, or any other church leader acted this way, what would be the result? The church would be full of hurting people who didn't find help from fellow Christians. Others would feel taken advantage of and would leave, never to come back. Others might turn to another source for leadership, becoming vulnerable to false teaching or perhaps cults. Satan knows if he can place a self-centered leader in a church position, he will trouble the flock.

How can churches guard against this trap? Jesus specifically taught that recognition of false leaders comes by inspecting their lifestyles (Matt. 7:15-20). He focused attention on their actions. They were known by their fruit. How many pulpit committees would benefit by doing a background check on a prospective pastor instead of judging him only by his sermons!

How Satan Especially Tests Leaders

Although the following temptations are common to everyone, they are especially prevalent in leadership. The higher one climbs the ladder to success, the easier it is to fall into these traps.

Ego—The position, power, status, honor, compliments, and other benefits that come with leadership can subtly whisper the message that the leader is of primary importance. Ego exerts a pull toward self-focus. Mature leadership knows how to resist this pull by staying in the presence of God so that life falls into its proper perspective. Otherwise, adulation can generate pride and an inflated ego.

Abuse of power—You've probably heard the phrase "absolute power corrupts absolutely." With authority comes an inherent advantage to use the rules or shape the circumstances in such a way as to benefit self. Satan would like nothing better than to encourage leaders to use their positions for personal gain. An element of proven character that God requires includes using position for the benefit of others, not for self-seeking.

Immorality—Samson and David represent some of the notable Bible characters who fell because they yielded to sexual temptation. Solomon allowed idolatry to infect his kingdom.

> *"Demas, because he loved this world, has deserted me and has gone to Thessalonica."*
> —2 Timothy 4:10

Money—Jesus knew that the love of money would exert a powerful influence. Leaders must guard against materialism, lest their lives and witness shipwreck on its dangerous rocks.

Dissipation of focus—Leaders have to juggle several balls at once. They can easily lose focus in their activities.

Bad counsel—If Satan can get the leader to listen to the wrong crowd, mistakes will follow shortly. A leader must surround himself with those who have godly wisdom.

How Leaders and Followers Can Help Each Other

The way to help leaders is really the same way we help any person under spiritual warfare attack. **First,** challenge each other to respond in such a way as to stay faithful to God. For example, Jesus forewarned Peter and the others that they were to be sifted by Satan. When they fell asleep in the garden of Gethsemane, He told them to rise and pray lest they entered into temptation. Jesus reminded the soldiers, the chief priests, and Pilate of the truth and the evil of their actions in the trial before His crucifixion.

Paul intended his Roman letter to help the people be wise about what is good and remain innocent about evil; God would soon crush Satan under their feet (Rom. 16:19-20). He reminded the Corinthians of God's standards that they could not partake of the table of demons and the table of the Lord (1 Cor. 10:21). Paul boldly told the Galatians that their desire to return to the law was not from the Lord but from another source (Gal. 5:8).

Second, always pray in a way that will help others to stand the test. Jesus prayed for His disciples and those who would believe throughout history (John 17). Paul prayed for the churches he had helped birth.

HOW TO HELP THOSE UNDER SPIRITUAL WARFARE ATTACK
• Stay faithful to God.
• Pray for others to stand the test.
• Focus on the people of God, not Satan.

Third, focus on the people of God, not Satan. One would be hard pressed to find Paul, Peter, or other saints seeking to rebuke, bind, or remove the presence of Satan. Instead, they focused on how to help others stay faithful to God, a fact that makes sense for two reasons. First, to seek victory on the basis of the removal of Satan is to disallow personal accountability for the one under attack. Second, victory based only on Satan's absence overlooks the presence of the Spirit in a believer's life. Christians ought to learn to let the Holy Spirit strengthen them to the point that they can handle tougher assignments.

Today's lesson has explored why Satan wants to attack leaders. Tomorrow's study will look at another scheme he has against the church.

DAY FIVE

TO PROMOTE A BAD REPUTATION

Once our nation's leaders inscribed Scripture on government buildings, allowed the teaching of the Bible in schools, and hung the Ten Commandments on courtroom walls. Now influential sectors of society rise to systematically stamp out any vestige of our Christian heritage. Even more ominous, the Judeo/Christian values of the past have been cast aside in favor of moral relativism. Since the 60s, Christians have lost in every arena of battle—in the courts, schools, and value systems of American minds. We no longer have the influence Christ intended to affect our society as salt and light. In short, our culture is not listening to us. Part of the reason may be found in this fourth trap of Satan.

A Bad Name Is One of Satan's Primary Goals

As an old man, Paul wrote two letters of advice to a young man. He was concerned that his protegee would "know how people ought to conduct themselves in God's household" (1 Tim. 3:15). His advice addressed an aspect of spiritual warfare for three groups of people.

Pastors (1 Tim. 3:7)

Read 1 Timothy 3:1-7. Paul addressed the qualifications for the office of overseer, or pastor. An overseer must have good character, know how to manage people, not be untried, and have a good reputation with out-siders. Paul specifically tied the fourth requirement to spiritual warfare. He noted that a bad reputation with unbelievers is a trap of the devil.

Why is a pastor's bad reputation a trap of the devil?

_____

_____

Deacons (1 Tim. 3:8-10)

While Paul did not expressly spell out deacon qualifications in light of spiritual warfare, he did use the word *likewise*. What was true for the pastor must also be true for the deacon. Paul must have believed that a deacon with a bad reputation would have been a trap of the devil, as well as a pastor with a sullied name.

Why is a deacon's bad reputation a trap of the devil?

_____

_____

Widows (1 Tim. 5:13-15)

The membership, specifically widows in these verses, can succumb to Satan's traps. Some women were still young when their husbands died. They promised not to marry again because they wanted to serve Christ for the rest of their lives without distraction. Paul noted two problems, however. First, the desire to remarry was too great and many widows broke their promises. Second, many of them went from house to house, wasting time and gossiping. Therefore, Paul counseled the younger widows to remarry and put themselves to work raising children so that the enemy would have no opportunity for slander. Paul called this "turning away to follow Satan."

"Here is a trustworthy saying: If anyone sets his heart on being an overseer, he desires a noble task. Now the overseer must be above reproach, the husband of but one wife, temperate, self-controlled, respectable, hospitable, able to teach, not given to drunkenness, not violent but gentle, not quarrelsome, not a lover of money. He must manage his own family well and see that his children obey him with proper respect. (If anyone does not know how to manage his own family, how can he take care of God's church?) He must not be a recent convert, or he may become conceited and fall under the same judgment as the devil. He must also have a good reputation with out-siders, so that he will not fall into disgrace and into the devil's trap."
—1 Timothy 3:1-7

"Deacons, likewise, are to be men worthy of respect, sincere, not indulging in much wine, and not pursuing dishonest gain. They must keep hold of the deep truths of the faith with a clear conscience. They must first be tested; and then if there is nothing against them, let them serve as deacons.
—1 Timothy 3:8-10

"Besides, they get into the habit of being idle and going about from house to house. And not only do they become idlers, but also gossips and busybodies, saying things they ought not to. So I counsel younger widows to marry, to have children, to manage their homes and to give the enemy no opportunity for slander. Some have in fact already turned away to follow Satan."

—*1 Timothy 5:13-15*

"As it is written: 'God's name is blasphemed among the Gentiles because of you.'"

—*Romans 2:24*

"All who are under the yoke of slavery should consider their masters worthy of full respect, so that God's name and our teaching may not be slandered."

—*1 Timothy 6:1*

In the past, have you considered gossip and slander a means of following Satan? ❑ Yes ❑ No

In the future, does this knowledge make you less likely to practice these vices? ❑ Yes ❑ No

The Consequences of a Bad Reputation

The Bible pictures the church as the bride of Christ. Just as on earth a woman traditionally bears the name of her husband, so we now bear the name of Christ. Just as a wife's actions reflect on the name she bears, so our actions reflect on the name of the one whose name we bear. Sinful behavior is a reflection on the honor and integrity of the Lord. It gives Satan a tremendous opportunity to soil the name of Christ before the watching world.

American Christianity has certainly fallen into that same trap. George Barna surveyed Christians and non-Christians regarding their attitudes, opinions, values, and behavior on issues that impact societal life. He discovered that in only 7 out of 66 categories did Christians differ significantly from the values of the world.[7] Those claiming to be Christians basically believed and did the same things in the same proportion as unbelievers. This behavior gives Christians a bad reputation among unbelievers and creates at least two consequences.

First, a bad name destroys the willingness of unbelievers to listen to the message of Christ. When we adopt the same vices as the world, we create a lack of respect, and the world becomes unwilling to listen. How many times have you heard someone refer to the behavior of a Christian and say, "Well, if that's what it means to be a Christian, I'm just as good as _____" or maybe "The reason I don't go to church is because it's so full of hypocrites!" Every time a church member lives in sin, the world shuts out the message along with the messenger.

Paul knew how a Christian's behavior affected unbelievers' receptivity to listen. Read Romans 2:24 and 1 Timothy 6:1.

No wonder Paul said: "Everyone who confesses the name of the Lord must turn away from wickedness" (2 Tim. 2:19b). Those who claim to be Christians but don't live differently should not tell anyone! They are irreparably damaging the name of the one they claim to know.

The decades of the misrepresentation of Christ's name have led to a loss of respect for God. In times past, even though many Americans did not believe, they at least respected the things of God. Now our culture no longer fears God and instead seeks societal laws that intentionally marginalize Christian influence from public life.

Second, God holds the person accountable who takes His name in vain. The Third Commandment contains a warning: "You shall not take the name of the Lord your God in vain, for the Lord will not leave him unpunished who takes his name in vain" (Ex. 20:7, RSV). *Vain* means empty, worthless, devoid of meaning. God is saying, *Do not claim to be one of My people and then live your life in such a way that you render My name worthless. Do not behave in such a way that to be a Christian is devoid of meaning. I will require accountability of whoever does that.*

Just how serious is God about His name? Let's briefly look at the worst accountability He ever required for taking His name in vain. Read Ezekiel 5:5-15.

Where had God set the nation of Israel? (v. 5) _____

What were her sins? (v. 6) _____

_____

In front of whom was God going to execute His judgments? (v. 8)

_____

What was God's purpose in punishing Israel? _____

_____

God wanted the peoples of the earth to revere His name again. By publicly judging Israel in their sight, she would understand that God's name was holy, and that He was not like those claiming to represent Him. That's exactly what happened when He destroyed Jerusalem. Read Jeremiah 22:8-9.

What does that mean for us today? (Check one or more.)
- ❑ The Old Testament was an underdeveloped view of God. In the New Testament, we learn that He is a God of love, not a God of wrath.
- ❑ God is the same, yesterday, today, and tomorrow. We can be confident that He has not changed. If He required accountability then, He will require it today.
- ❑ God recorded their story for our benefit. We can learn a lesson from their mistakes and not be careless about His name.

This example is a worst-case scenario, but God left it as warning of how serious He is about His name. If He required accountability under the law of Moses, then how much more are we accountable (Heb. 10:28-31)? He wants us to know that grace is not a license to sin. Mercy is not a permission slip to take His holy name and smear it in the mud. God's patience is beyond our imagination, but none should deceive himself into thinking sin offers no consequences.

Practical Application
How can you help your church honor the name of Christ? This week's lessons have been about the enemy's strategies to defeat the church. How can you help your church honor the name of Christ and defend against those schemes?

1. Obey the Lord. While none of us is perfect, we can make sure that the direction and practices of our lives are in keeping with God's com-

> " 'People from many nations will pass by this city and will ask one another, "Why has the Lord done such a thing to this great city?" And the answer will be: "Because they have forsaken the covenant of the Lord their God and have worshiped and served other gods." ' "
> —*Jeremiah 22:8-9*

HOW TO HELP YOUR CHURCH HONOR THE NAME OF CHRIST
- Obey the Lord.
- Get involved with Christians who are struggling.
- Exercise church discipline.

mands. If we practice love and good deeds, the world will respect us and be more receptive to our message.

2. Get involved with Christians who are struggling. All of us experience temptation and weakness. None of us is superhuman. We need each other to spur us on. By praying for each other and challenging each other to do good works, we can overcome the enemy.

3. Exercise church discipline. Paul advised in 1 Corinthians 5:11, "But now I am writing you that you must not associate with anyone who calls himself a brother but is sexually immoral or greedy, an idolater or a slanderer, a drunkard or a swindler. With such a man do not even eat." He specifically said that if someone claims to be a Christian but proactively commits evil, the church should discipline that person.

Immoral lifestyles destroy the credibility of the message, not to mention corrupting others in the church. The purpose of church discipline is not getting even, but restoring. It should only be done in love without a critical spirit. At the same time, we must be diligent to protect the honor of the Lord's name.

To which of these three approaches will you commit? (Check one or more.)
- ❏ Obey the Lord.
- ❏ Get involved with Christians who are struggling.
- ❏ Help to restore a brother or sister who has fallen.

---

[1]John Mark Terry, *Church Evangelism* (Nashville: Broadman & Holman, 1997), ix.

[2]George Barna, *Growing True Disciples* (Ventura, CA: Issachar Resources, 2000), 66.

[3]Ibid, 36.

[4]A. Scott Moreau, *Essentials of Spiritual Warfare* (Wheaton: Harold Shaw, 1997), 19.

[5]Joseph A. Komonchak, Mary Collins, and Dermot A. Lane, *New Dictionary of Theology* (Downers Grove, IL: IVP, 1988), 272-273.

[6]Ibid, 42-43.

[7]George Barna, "The American Witness," *The Barna Report,* November/December 1997, 1-8.

VIEWER GUIDE

1. The church that threatens the enemy is the church that's doing the _____

   _____ .

2. "A house divided against itself _____ stand." (Matt. 12:25)

3. Jesus commanded us to _____ each other.

4. One of the great tests of how much we love our brother is when we see him in

   error, do our hearts _____?

5. Satan's schemes are often broken in the attitude of _____.

6. God puts us in the body so that we don't have to face battles _____.

   In our communities we find strength.

7. Satan succeeds under the cover of _____.

8. Satan tries to disrupt the _____ of church leaders.

9. The church on fire for God will be under _____.

   The way you respond is to stay_____.

Putting On the Armor

SPIRITUAL WARFARE

CASE STUDY

Jody knew that the flashing blue lights in her rear-view mirror weren't a good sign. She was in a hurry to get to work, and she apparently had exceeded the speed limit. She pulled her car off to the shoulder of the road and waited for the policeman to walk toward her.

To her surprise, the man wasn't wearing a uniform. He was wearing street clothes. Nothing clearly indicated that he was a policeman.

If you were in Jody's situation, what would you do? If someone without a uniform claimed authority to stop you, would you roll down your window or step out of the car? If there were no uniform and badge, would you question the person's authority?

On a spiritual level, how important is it that we who claim authority over Satan are wearing the right uniform? What authority do we have if we're not wearing the armor of God?

DAY ONE

YOU HAVE TO PUT IT ON

Now that we've studied how Satan attacks individuals and churches, we need to ask the next logical question: *How do we prepare for and defend ourselves against spiritual attacks?* The early Christians in the region of Ephesus were perhaps asking a similar question, for the apostle Paul told them clearly to "put on the full armor of God" as they wrestled against these powers (Eph. 6:11). Like soldiers who wear appropriate military attire, Christians should wear the right armor. This week our goal is to learn how we can put on the armor of God.

Whose Armor Is It?

Think back to the first week of this study. God fights spiritual battles for us. David found this to be true in his battle with Goliath (see

1 Sam. 17:45-47). David told Goliath, "the battle is the Lord's, and he will give all of you into our hands" (v. 47). Even though the battle is still real for us, we have victory only because God is on our side.

Read Ephesians 6:11 in the margin. Whose armor did Paul tell the believers to wear? _____

"Put on the full armor of God so that you can take your stand against the devil's schemes."
—Ephesians 6:11

Paul told believers to wear the armor of God. The armor that we wear in battle is not our own armor. We can do nothing in our own strength to win spiritual battles, nor can we take any steps in our own abilities or training that will lead us to victory apart from God. Instead, we can win in spiritual warfare because we wear God's armor.

Examine several texts that will reveal the relationship between God and the armor (Eph. 6:14-17).

Match the texts in the right column with the appropriate piece of armor in the left column. Consider how each verse shows God's relationship to the armor.

1. __ "belt of truth" (v. 14)
2. __ "breastplate of righteousness" (v. 14)
3. __ "feet fitted with the gospel of peace" (v. 15)
4. __ "shield of faith" (v. 16)
5. __ "helmet of salvation" (v. 17)
6. __ "sword of the Spirit" (v. 17)

a. 2 Corinthians 5:21
b. John 14:6; 17:7
c. Psalm 28:7
d. Ephesians 2:14
e. John 1:1
f. Matthew 1:21

This exercise should help us realize that we can't separate wearing the armor of God from our daily walk with God. Jesus is the Truth (John 14:6), and His Word is truth (John 17:7). God is righteousness (2 Cor. 5:21). He is our peace (Eph. 2:14). As with the psalmist, we proclaim that God is our shield (Ps. 28:7). Indeed, He is our salvation (Matt. 1:21). Finally, He is the Word (John 1:1), and like a sword, His very Word can "strike the earth" and "slay the wicked" (Isa. 11:4).

Just as David found Saul's armor ill-fitting (1 Sam. 17:39), we must not enter spiritual warfare armed with protection of our own making.

God graciously allows us to wear His armor in battle. The focus of spiritual warfare is not to be on the devil. Our eyes are always to be on God rather than on the enemy.

Why Is the Armor Important?

To answer this question, it might be helpful to remember the general outline of the Book of Ephesians (week 1, day 5). The first three chapters of Ephesians give a theological foundation: we can experience spiritual victory because we are in Christ. The final three chapters of Ephesians focus on practical living. Because we have been saved, we have victory; nevertheless, we still must live out our faith in our personal lives (4:1–5:18), in our homes (5:21-33; 6:1-4), in our churches (5:19-21), and in our workplaces (6:5-9).

Living out our faith daily, though, is not easy, because we are struggling against the powers (Eph. 6:12). The enemy schemes each day to weaken our faith and to destroy our testimony. The only way that we fight these battles is to "put on the full armor of God" each day. Fighting and winning these spiritual battles helps us more fully understand the blessings of being in Christ.

When Paul told the believers in the region of Ephesus (Eph. 1:1) to "put on the full armor of God" (Eph. 6:11,13), the believers had to decide to wear the armor—it was not automatically on them. As believers in Christ, we positionally have His grace and truth in our lives; God makes us righteous when we are converted (2 Cor. 5:21). Practically, however, we still decide each day whether we will fight spiritual battles with God's weapons.

In fact, "putting on the armor" (as revealed in the remaining lessons this week) encompasses all of life. The armor involves daily living in truth, righteousness, and faith; standing firm in our faith, ready to quench the enemy's darts with God's shield; and living in hope, standing ready to tell others the good news about Jesus. Putting on the armor involves knowing, believing, and living God's Word every day.

Do you see why Paul challenged the believers to put on the "full armor of God"? Wearing all the armor of God—indeed, spiritual warfare itself—involves daily lifestyle, not finding some quick fix or immediate solution to struggles in life. Putting on the armor means daily living a life pleasing and honoring to God and being a faithful disciple of Jesus in all areas of life.

What happens if believers do not wear the armor? What are the dangers if we do not live in truth, righteousness, faith, and hope? What happens when the enemy shoots at us and we do not stand firm? The result is obvious: the enemy attacks, and we believers are not prepared to respond. Defeat is almost inevitable—and we become discouraged in our Christian walk.

Do you know believers who seemingly never experience victory in daily life? If so, why might this be the case?

Putting on the armor concerns knowing, believing, and living God's Word every day.

It may be that these believers have never learned how to live daily as a disciple of Christ. Perhaps no one has taught them how to wear the armor of God. When the enemy aims at them, they have few defenses, and they are easy targets. Maybe you have experienced continual spiritual defeat, and no one has yet taught you how to wear the armor of God. Your own patterns of defeat may show you the importance of the armor of God.

Check each statement that applies to you.

❑ No one has ever helped me prepare for spiritual battles; I've faced most of them on my own.

❑ Prior to this study, I really hadn't given much attention to the "armor of God."

❑ I know that Christians should wear the armor, but I am not sure how my life would change if I really wore it.

❑ I am excited about learning how to put on the armor.

❑ I would prefer a quick-fix solution to my struggles—I'm not too interested in learning about daily perseverance in the armor.

❑ I have studied the armor before, but I've not focused on the fact that the armor is God's.

❑ No matter what it takes, I want to wear the armor—I've lost too many battles already.

Putting On the Full Armor

Remember Paul's command to wear the full armor. No one piece is insignificant, and no piece can be ignored. If any piece of the armor is missing, a gaping hole remains—and we are vulnerable to the enemy. Satan aims at vulnerable areas, and he systematically tries to weaken us.

Ask God to help you to put on the full armor—and to remember that the armor is His. Write your prayer in the margin.

DAY TWO

THE BELT AND BREASTPLATE

Maybe you've seen pictures of a typical first-century Roman soldier like the one in the margin. Possibly Paul was shackled to a Roman soldier as he wrote the words of Ephesians 6. We do know that Paul was in prison when he wrote this letter (6:19-20), and he was likely thinking about such a soldier as he wrote.

Some writers give so much attention to the specific physical details of each piece of the armor that they miss Paul's emphasis on daily Christian living. Our goal in the next four lessons is to apply the armor to our lives and to defeat the enemy's schemes through that application.

"Stand firm then, with the belt of truth buckled around your waist."
—Ephesians 6:14

The Belt of Truth (Eph. 6:14)

The belt of a Roman soldier was typically a wide leather belt designed to hold the soldier's tunic in place. The soldier tucked his outer garment under the belt so that the tunic wouldn't hinder his running or fighting. When his belt was tightened, he was ready for battle. On the other hand, a slackened belt meant that the soldier was off duty. Likewise, the Christian who is ready for battle must fix in place his commitment to know, believe, and live the truth.

Satan is a liar (John 8:44), and one of his primary attack strategies is to feed us lies or to entice us to lie to ourselves. Since the time he lured Eve through a half-lie in the garden of Eden ("You will not surely die"—Gen. 3:4), the enemy has promoted lies. The best defense against his lies is truth.

Jesus is the Truth (John 14:6). He embodies truth, and we have truth in us when He dwells in us. When He lives within us, nothing—including the "powers"—can separate us from the love of God (Rom. 8:39). Likewise, God's Word is truth that sets us apart and makes us holy (John 17:17). We can't consistently win spiritual battles if we don't know God's Word.

Paul had more in mind than just theological teachings when he called believers to "stand firm then, with the belt of truth buckled around your waist" (Eph. 6:14). Even though we do have the truth in us when we are Christians, we still must live out truthful lives. Wearing the belt of truth means living a life of integrity and honesty.

On the other hand, we succumb to Satan's temptations when we speak or live anything less than the truth. If we don't know Jesus in a personal way, we can't wear the belt of truth. If we don't consistently tell the truth, we aren't wearing the belt. When we live a life of hypocrisy, the belt is not on us.

Maybe you regrettably know the pain of living a life of lies. A "little white lie" may not have seemed so bad at the time. It may have made sense to lie in order to protect yourself or somebody else, but the first lie led to other lies that led to more lies, and eventually you were caught in a web of your own making. Dishonesty in lifestyle and words leads to bondage—and only the truth will set us free (John 8:32).

Wearing the belt of truth means living a life of integrity and honesty.

Are you wearing the belt of truth? Consider the following questions to evaluate this piece of armor in your life.
- Do you consistently speak the truth? ❑ Yes ❑ No
- Do you give in to temptations to tell "little white lies" or to avoid the truth? ❑ Yes ❑ No
- Are your public and private lives consistent with each other? ❑ Yes ❑ No
- Do you strive to be the same person internally (who no one else sees) as you are externally (when others are watching)? ❑ Yes ❑ No
- Are you currently covering up any lies? ❑ Yes ❑ No
- Do you ever rationalize your wrong, even when you know God is displeased? ❑ Yes ❑ No

- Do you ever lie to convince yourself that your particular sins are sometimes acceptable? ❑ Yes ❑ No

To win the battles of spiritual warfare, we must fight by knowing, believing, and living God's truth. The belt of truth must be buckled tightly about our waist. If you are wearing the belt of truth today, ask God to give you the integrity to wear it every day.

If your life lacks truthfulness and integrity, take time now to confess to God your wrong and ask His forgiveness. Decide now that you will always tell the truth and live a life of integrity.

Write one specific action you will take to be more truthful in your lifestyle.

_____

_____

The Breastplate of Righteousness (Eph. 6:14)

The breastplate of the Roman soldier covered the upper torso, including some of the most vital organs. It offered protection from the enemy's darts and spears. In a similar fashion, the breastplate of righteousness helps protect us from the enemy's attacks.

On one hand, we are protected because God has given us His righteousness (2 Cor. 5:21; Rom. 3:20-22; 5:17). This righteousness is God's gift to us based on what Christ did for us on the cross. In another of Paul's letters, he described it this way: "I consider them [all things lost] rubbish, that I may gain Christ and be found in him, not having a righteousness of my own that comes from the law, but that which is through faith in Christ—the righteousness that comes from God and is by faith" (Phil. 3:9). We can stand on God's righteousness when the enemy seeks to accuse us and condemn us before the Lord (see Rom. 8:33-34; Rev. 12:10).

On the other hand, we must live out a life of righteousness; that is, the work of God in our lives must be evidenced by our daily righteous living. We don't earn God's favor by our good works, but our good works do show that God is working in our lives (Jas. 2:14-18). To put it simply, the person who is wearing the breastplate of righteousness will do what is right according to God's standards.

The apostle Paul understood well that believers wearing the breastplate would live righteously.

Read Ephesians 4:22–5:1,3 in your Bible. List several of Paul's commands for righteous living on the following page. Three examples have been provided for you.

- Put off falsehood and speak truthfully (v. 25).
- Those who have been stealing must stop (v. 28).
- Don't let unwholesome speech come out of your mouth (v. 29).

_____

_____

_____

Perhaps you listed commands such as "don't grieve the Holy Spirit" (v. 30), "don't have even a hint of sexual immorality" (5:3), or "don't get drunk on wine" (v. 18). We hope that you also recognize the positive commands such as "be kind and compassionate" (4:32) and "be imitators of God" (5:1). Believers who wear the breastplate of righteousness not only turn away from wrong, but they also turn to good.

Recall the story of Cain and Abel in Genesis 4:1-10. After Cain killed his brother, Abel, the Lord confronted Cain and reminded him that doing good helps guard against wrong: "If you do what is right, will you not be accepted? But if you do not do what is right, sin is crouching at your door; it desires to have you, but you must master it" (v. 7). Making right choices—righteous living that shows we are wearing the breastplate—helps protect us against temptation.

How do we know which choices are right and which are wrong? To answer this question, remember Paul's command to put on the full armor of God (Eph. 6:11). We cannot fully understand God's standards of right and wrong apart from knowing Christ and His Word. In other words, we need the sword of the Spirit (v. 17) and the belt of truth (v. 14) to complement the breastplate of righteousness. All of God's armor is mandatory for the soldier who seeks to win spiritual battles.

To conclude today's lesson, look again at your list of Paul's commands from Eph. 4:22-5:1. Place a star (*) by any that speak directly to you. Choose to follow the guidelines in the margin. Commit yourself to live righteously.

DAILY PUT ON THE BREAST-PLATE OF RIGHTEOUSNESS:

1. *Confess your wrong and accept God's forgiveness (1 John 1:9).*
2. *Turn away from your wrong (Eph. 4:22).*
3. *Turn to good (Jas. 4:17).*
4. *Live a life worthy of the calling you have received from God (Eph. 4:1).*
5. *Thank God every day for the righteousness He has given you.*

DAY THREE

THE RIGHT SHOES

"Stand firm then, with the belt of truth buckled around your waist, with the breastplate of righteousness in place, and with your feet fitted with the readiness that comes from the gospel of peace."
—Ephesians 6:14-15

Have you ever had a pair of shoes that just didn't fit? Maybe they were too big, making it difficult for you to keep them on your feet. Perhaps they were too small, creating blisters and sore toes as you tried to walk. Or maybe they weren't quite wide enough, and you tried in vain to squeeze your feet into the improper size. If your feet hurt because you were wearing the wrong shoes, did your entire body hurt?

When Paul described the armor we wear for spiritual battles, he also recognized the importance of proper shoes (Eph. 6:15). Some scholars debate the meaning of this piece of armor, but the emphasis on standing firm in the peace of God remains clear. When we face spiritual battles, standing firm requires the right footwear.

Your Feet Fitted—Standing Firm

The Roman soldier usually wore strong boots with heavy soles for protection and studded nails for traction. Particularly because the soldier often fought in hand-to-hand combat, his footing had to be sure—a soldier who lost his footing would be vulnerable to the enemy. Indeed, even a belt and a breastplate wouldn't help much if the soldier were already on the ground!

Read Ephesians 6:11-14 (you're probably becoming quite familiar with these words). Fill in the following missing words.

"Put on the full armor of God so that you can take your

_____ against the devil's schemes." — v. 11

"Therefore put on the full armor of God, so that when the day of evil

comes, you may be able to _____ your ground, and

after you have done everything, to _____." — v. 13

"_____ firm, then, with the belt of truth

buckled about your waist." — v. 14

The same word in all of these passages, translated as *stand,* was a military term meaning "to hold on to a position." Paul was essentially saying to the believers, *Get ready for the battle, and then hold your ground. Don't let the enemy take one inch of the territory.* A firm footing is necessary to stand our ground against the enemy.

Paul was not the only biblical writer who stressed the importance of standing firm against the devil. Read James 4:7 and 1 Peter 5:8-9. Circle the words in those passages that tell us how to respond to the enemy.

"Submit yourselves, then, to God. Resist the devil, and he will flee from you."
—James 4:7

Your authors circled *resist* in both passages as well as *standing firm* in 1 Peter 5:9. In these examples, we aren't told to search for the enemy or to rebuke him. Instead, he is seeking us, and we are to stand firm and resist his advances. We resist him best when our footing is secure—when we are standing on God as our rock (Ps. 92:15).

Feet Fitted with Readiness—Experiencing His Peace

In a passage about spiritual warfare, the reference to the "gospel of peace" might seem out of place. After all, this passage is a call to be ready for war. How does the gospel of peace fit into a battle strategy? Several teachings are applicable.

"Be self-controlled and alert. Your enemy the devil prowls around like a roaring lion looking for someone to devour. Resist him, standing firm in the faith, because you know that your brothers throughout the world are undergoing the same kind of sufferings."
—1 Peter 5:8-9

113

The gospel itself tells a story of peace. As unbelievers, we were spiritually dead in our sins (Eph. 2:1-2). We had no hope, but God in grace saved us through faith (2:8-9). Jesus became our peace and reconciled us to God the Father through His death (2:14-18). For nonbelievers whose minds have been blinded by the "god of this age" (2 Cor. 4:3-4), Jesus offers reconciliation. The truth of His reconciliation is incredibly good news.

Peace does not always indicate the absence of external conflict. David the shepherd faced a very real enemy in Goliath, yet he had confidence in his God to overcome the Philistine giant (1 Sam. 17:1-51). The external conflict was real, but so was David's inner peace: "The Lord who delivered me from the paw of the lion and the paw of the bear will deliver me from the hand of this Philistine" (v. 37). Likewise, Paul could speak of a gospel of peace even as he called believers to prepare for war.

God gives us peace even in the midst of the battle. Jesus promised His disciples that He would give them peace, but He also told them that His peace was not like the peace that the world gives (John 14:27). In fact, after He offered them peace, He encouraged them not to be troubled and afraid. He knew they would face battles, but He also knew they could experience inner peace even when spiritual warfare raged. Somehow, God grants us peace that the world can't understand, no matter how fierce the battle (Phil. 4:6-7).

How, then, do we experience daily peace? How do we stand firm when the battle rages? Trust the promises of God revealed in His Word. When we rest on His promises, we can stand firm in the battle.

Read the following texts, and briefly describe how each truth might bring you inner peace even when the external battle is strong.

Proverbs 3:5-6 _____

_____

Romans 8:28 _____

_____

Philippians 4:13 _____

_____

When we are in the middle of a heated spiritual battle, we need the truth of God's Word to strengthen us. He will give us His strength to do whatever He asks (Phil. 4:13). He directs our steps (Prov. 3:5-6) and brings things together for our good (Rom. 8:28)—even if He does so through the spiritual battles we face. When we know that He will use even the battles themselves to accomplish His plan (see p. 15), we can stand firm with peace in our hearts.

Feet Fitted with Readiness—Sharing Our Peace

The image of *readiness* with this piece of armor implies preparedness—ready to do something. In fact, the text may refer to Isaiah 52:7, clearly emphasizing action: "How beautiful on the mountains are the feet of those who bring good news, who proclaim peace, who bring good tidings, who proclaim salvation, who say to Zion, 'Your God reigns!' "

The implication is that we should be ready at any moment to announce the good news of Christ—including those times when we're caught in a spiritual battle. Think about this challenge. What better witness could you find than a person who has learned to trust and to proclaim God's love even when he is facing spiritual turmoil?

Although we may find it easier to follow God and tell about His goodness when life is going well (remember Job?), people who trust God in the midst of spiritual battles often offer powerful testimonies of God's care. A heart at peace with God both stands firm and moves forward, trusting God and proclaiming a God who is trustworthy.

God expects us to be obedient at all times. When we are obedient—whether to the call to do evangelism or to some other mandate from God—that very obedience weakens the devil's influence in our lives. The worst choice we can make when under spiritual attack is to be disobedient to the God who gives us His armor to win the battle.

"Job replied to the Lord: 'I know that you can do all things; no plan of yours can be thwarted.' "
—Job 42:1-2

Recognizing your responsibility to proclaim the gospel of peace to others who are separated from God, list below the names of two nonbelievers for whom you will pray this week. Ask God to prepare you to share your faith with them.

_____

_____

Mark each statement *T* (true) or *F* (false) to indicate the status of your spiritual footwear.

_____ I am standing firm in my faith in spite of spiritual warfare.

_____ I seem to be under spiritual attack, and my faith is wavering.

_____ I have a sense of peace in my heart that I really can't explain.

_____ I know the good news should bring me peace, but I'm experiencing more inner turmoil than peace.

_____ I am always ready to announce the good news, even when I'm facing spiritual battles.

_____ I'm sure I miss opportunities to share my faith because I get more focused on my struggles than on God.

If your perceived peacefulness needs a boost because the enemy has defeated you, ask God to restore your peace.

DAY FOUR

THE SHIELD OF FAITH

In Ephesians 6 we're not reading the advice of some boot-camp private. We're not taking counsel from a green recruit. Instead, we're gleaning wisdom from one of the most decorated saints in history. Paul was a seasoned veteran in spiritual warfare. When he spoke of taking up the armor, perhaps no other person except Christ had more insight into this matter. We would do well to pay special attention to every word from the most extensive passage Paul ever wrote on the subject. Today we consider verse 16, "above all, taking the shield of faith with which you will be able to quench all the fiery darts of the wicked one."

Take Up the Shield of Faith

How important is faith? The first two words of Ephesians 6:16 give us the clue—above all. You can almost see Paul blowing a bullhorn, shouting in a megaphone, blasting a trumpet, doing back hand-springs—whatever it takes to get our attention. *Whatever else you practice regarding warfare, you better not miss this!* Paul shouts. Why was Paul so adamant about the importance of faith?

In order to answer the question properly, we must realize what kind of warfare Paul was talking about. Paul believed faith was necessary at all times, but particularly when the battle took on two characteristics.

When the battle is intense—Notice that the shield is the only piece of armor for which Paul chose to spell out its function. Although we can reasonably surmise what the belt, breastplate, shoes, helmet, and sword do, Paul left no doubt that faith quenches fiery darts. When the battle is "fiery" or intense, we need this weapon.

When the battle requires endurance—Shields defend against an offensive. Paul expected a satanic onslaught for un undetermined time. He expected faith to be useful in weathering the storm.

Four times in three verses Paul told believers to stand (Eph. 6:11,13-14). He had in mind defending, not attacking; resisting, not retaliating. Paul obviously was referring to the kind of warfare that requires endurance.

What would you list as an example of a "fiery dart" in your experience of spiritual warfare?

Standing Requires the Attitude of Faith

Why is faith especially important in intense, long-term battles? Why is faith required to stand? Let's consider the perspectives of God and Satan. Then we will apply to our lives what we have learned.

God

God has all power and can do anything He desires. He can command that Satan never so much as touch you. God can remove him any time

He wants. He can grant you unlimited authority to execute your every whim against the devil. As a result of this study, have you concluded that God doesn't seem to be overly interested in making the limitation of Satan the basis of our victory? Instead, God prefers responding to those who trust His sufficiency in the midst of their weakness. Hebrews 11:6 says, "Without faith it is impossible to please God."

God is pleased by a person who will reject every voice of circumstance, disobey every message of compromise, and swim against the stream of discouragement in order to trust Him. God grants His power to those who will do this. For example, in Matthew 15:21-28 a Syro-Phonecian woman begged Jesus to cast a demon out of her daughter. Initially Jesus ignored her, then He rebuffed her. When she persisted, Jesus exalted her as one of the few who has great faith. He then cast out the demon.

From God's perspective, those who trust Him bring Him delight.

Satan

Satan is not omniscient. He doesn't know the outcome before the testing. He only knows that the kingdom of God will be advanced or hindered based on whether we stand in faith. Therefore, in endurance trials, all his testing and temptations target your ability to persevere. He knows, "If you do not stand firm in your faith, you will not stand at all" (Isa. 7:9).

From Satan's perspective, the only hope of victory for him is for the believer to cave in to discouragement and lose faith.

Us

In order to illustrate how the attitude of faith causes us to stand, I (John) would like to use a personal illustration. Earlier I mentioned that I experienced eight years of intense spiritual warfare regarding whether I was saved. Nothing changed for five years, but then two things happened.

First, I began to immerse myself in the Scripture, including studying every verse in the New Testament in which some form of the word *faith* appeared. Second, I learned that Martin Luther and John Wesley went through the same experience for several years before God delivered them. Their testimonies helped me cope.

The Word of God convinced me that, regardless of circumstances, God would deliver me as well. Seeing the importance of faith, I tried to adopt the attitude of the saints of the Bible. In a nutshell this was what I said to myself:

> *My inability to change my circumstances matters not one little whit. I don't care how long it will be before deliverance comes. It doesn't matter the length of the road I must walk. I don't care how hard the journey. I know my God will come for me! Shall I cave in to discouragement? Will I quit? No! For I am convinced that in all these things we are more than conquerors through Him who loved us. Neither death nor life, nor angels nor principalities nor powers, nor things present nor things to come, nor height nor depth, nor any*

other created thing, shall be able to separate us from the love of God which is in Christ Jesus our Lord. I will not lose heart. My light affliction, which is but for a moment, is working for me a far more exceeding and eternal weight of glory. Yes, the Lord will bring my soul out of prison, that I may praise His name (adapted from Rom. 8:38-39; 2 Cor. 4:16-18).

When I came to the point that I trusted God on no more evidence than His Word, when I believed though nothing changed outwardly—then He came for me. All the begging and pleading prior to that time had done no good. Instead, He waited for faith so that He could have mercy on me. Then God delivered me and blessed me in ways beyond my wildest imagination.

From a human perspective, faith is the attitude that "I trust God no matter what, no matter how long."

Share an experience when you trusted God on no more evidence than His Word.

_____

_____

_____

Standing Requires the Actions of Faith

God will never fail to be who He promises to be in Scripture. It is a spiritual impossibility for anyone who believes Him ultimately to be defeated. However, someone can misunderstand the biblical concept of faith and miss God. Faith is a verb almost as many times as it is a noun. Unfortunately, many Christians wrongly think of faith only as a mental function. In the Bible true faith cannot be separated from action. James 2:17 declares, "faith by itself, if it is not accompanied by action, is dead." Following are the four cardinal rules for biblical faith in warfare that I (John) learned from my experience.

1. I do not turn inward. When the pain level intensified, I made a common mistake. I focused on my problem because I wanted relief. It consumed me. I studied the issue to the exclusion of other necessary things. I spent a lot of time talking to my friends about it. I constantly tried to resolve the conflict. My struggle became the centerpiece of my universe. Most all my prayers to God revolved around the topic. I missed a great deal of life because I focused on my ordeal. Admittedly, there's a time to discuss personal problems with others, but mine was out of balance because it dictated the agenda of my life for those years.

2. I do not sit down. I spent a lot longer in warfare than I needed to. When I first began struggling, I was ashamed since I thought Christians weren't supposed to have that problem. In any event, over the next few years I often adopted the bunker mentality. In retrospect, I should have kept my eyes on God and continued to be about His business.

When I came to the point that I trusted God on no more evidence than His Word, when I believed though nothing changed outwardly—then He came for me.

The apostle Paul is a prime example of someone who handled warfare successfully. After he received the messenger of Satan to buffet him, he continued to serve God diligently. He didn't decide to look after Paul first. He didn't put the churches' needs on hold until it got better. Instead, he armed himself with the attitude of faith and persevered by being "steadfast, immovable, always abounding in the work of the Lord" (1 Cor. 15:58, NASB). Now, I do not passively wait for deliverance. I do not quit doing good.

3. I do everything I know to do and seek God's perspective. For the next three years I began to make adjustments in my life. I established the habit of prayer and Bible study. I changed my priorities in giving. I began to become involved in missions. Meanwhile, I continued to seek God's perspective concerning His purposes for my life. Even though we never know everything God has in mind, He will tell us enough for us to respond. I began to understand His ways and why He allows trials. I realized that this in no way called into question His love for me. I concluded He would bring me out of spiritual warfare in His time, which is exactly what He did.

Victory in warfare comes not by focusing on it but by focusing on God and continuing to do everything He has told you to do. If we will continue to obey Him one step at a time, then one day we will arrive at the place where He wants us.

4. I began to do the things necessary to get ready for God's deliverance. After seeking God's perspective from His Word and concluding that He would deliver me one day, I made one of the best decisions of my life. I decided that since God was going to deliver me, I didn't want these years to be wasted. Even though I didn't know what He wanted to do with my life, I determined to put as much Scripture in my mind as possible so that He would have something to use when He brought me out of warfare. God did deliver and gave me a grounding in Scripture necessary for the ministry to which He one day would call me. Faith is not a matter of merely believing, but rather of getting ready for what God is going to do.

> **Are you in a trial requiring endurance, or do you know someone who is? Based on what I (John) learned, list the actions necessary to get ready for God's deliverance.**
>
> 1. _____
>
> 2. _____
>
> 3. _____
>
> 4. _____

God Delivers with Unusual Blessing

God loves faith! Whenever anyone so believes Him and adjusts his or her life in the midst of a trial, then God delivers that person with special blessing. Moses believed God would deliver the children of Israel, but God had in mind to make him the one through whom the law came. David believed that God would one day make him king, but God had in mind to give the Messiah through his lineage. Paul knew that God would cause him to be a witness before kings, but God had in mind to let him write nearly half the books of the New Testament.

The way God worked with them is the same way He works with any of His children. Although we may not be called to as great a task or have as great a blessing, the principle holds true. In my life, I (John) believed God would bring me out of warfare one day, but God had in mind to surround me with godly people and to use me in His service. We don't know what God has in mind for our future, but we know that He will do something immeasurably more than all we ask or imagine.

Do you have a faith testimony? If so, share it with an individual or with your group at your next meeting.

DAY FIVE

THE HELMET AND SWORD

"Take the helmet of salvation and the sword of the Spirit, which is the word of God."
—Ephesians 6:17

In this lesson we conclude our look at the spiritual armor. Let's review the other pieces of armor we studied this week.

Match the armor pieces with their application for the Christian life.

1. _____ Belt
2. _____ Breastplate
3. _____ Footwear
4. _____ Shield

a. Stand firm, and be prepared to share the gospel.
b. Trust God's Word and live in faith.
c. Make righteous choices.
d. Live with integrity.

Today we will examine the final pieces of the armor: the helmet of salvation and the sword of the Spirit. The answers to the exercise above are 1. d.; 2. c.; 3. a.; and 4. b.

The Helmet of Salvation

"Since we belong to the day, let us be self-controlled, putting on faith and love as a breastplate, and the hope of salvation as a helmet. For God did not appoint us to suffer wrath but to receive salvation through our Lord Jesus Christ."
—1 Thessalonians 5:8-9

Because the head is a particularly vulnerable part of the human body, people often wear helmets. Construction workers, football players, motorcycle riders, and soldiers wear them. The Roman soldier typically wore a leather or metal helmet designed to protect the head from blows of a sword or club. In Paul's analogy of God's armor, our helmet is essential: it is the helmet of salvation.

To better understand this word picture, read the text of 1 Thessalonians 5:8-9 in the margin. Notice that the helmet in this passage refers to the "hope of salvation." When we speak of *hope,* we usually mean something such as a wishful desire, but Paul used the term in a different way. Christian hope is more a confident expectation that God will accomplish His will. In that sense, the helmet of salvation speaks of a trusting, expecting confidence that God will ultimately save His children through the completed work of Jesus on the cross (Heb. 12:2).

As believers in Jesus Christ who have been saved by His grace (Eph. 2:8-9), we have a hope that nonbelievers don't have. We have been made alive in Christ (Eph. 2:4-5), and we have a "living hope through the resurrection of Jesus Christ from the dead, and into an inheritance that can never perish, spoil or fade—kept in heaven" (1 Pet. 1:3-4). To wear the helmet of salvation is to believe that God guides us today and will ultimately take us to heaven. When we understand our identity in Christ and trust Him to complete His eternal plan in our lives, we have a hope that changes the way we live.

You see, we fight spiritual battles with faith when we have the confident assurance that God will ultimately win the war. Satan tempts us with sin, and we confidently trust that God will provide a way out (1 Cor. 10:13). The enemy entices us to worry about our finances, yet we believe wholeheartedly that God will supply all of our needs (Phil. 4:19). The devil strikes at us with the fear of death, but we trust without question in the resurrection and the return of Christ (1 Thess. 4:13-18). Genuine hope keeps us moving forward, never giving up, and running the race with faith (2 Tim. 4:7).

This issue is, of course, a matter of the mind—and we should not be surprised that the helmet of salvation protects the mind. Do you remember the attention we gave in week 4 to Satan's desire to have our minds? He seeks to influence our thinking in negative ways, but we can always respond with Christian hope.

Which of the following statements best reflects the level of Christian hope in your life? (Check as many as apply.)

❏ I want to trust God with confidence, but sometimes I struggle to accept His promises.

❏ I believe in the hope of salvation represented in the resurrection, but I haven't thought much about having hope in this world.

❏ I get so focused on my immediate needs and wants that I forget that God has an eternal plan for me. I live so much for today that I don't think much about the hope of eternity that God offers me.

❏ My confidence in God is stronger, but I am still learning to fight off Satan by trusting confidently in God and His promises.

❏ I fight battles in my mind more often than I should because I don't yet have enough confidence in God to trust Him completely.

If your confidence and hope in God need a boost because the enemy has defeated you, ask God to restore your hope.

Pray the words of Romans 5:1-5 in the margin. Circle the word *hope* as you focus on this text.

"Therefore, since we have been justified through faith, we have peace with God through our Lord Jesus Christ, through whom we have gained access by faith into this grace in which we now stand. And we rejoice in the hope of the glory of God. Not only so, but we also rejoice in our sufferings, because we know that suffering produces perseverance; perseverance, character; and character, hope. And hope does not disappoint us, because God has poured out his love into our hearts by the Holy Spirit, whom he has given us."
—*Romans 5:1-5*

The Sword of the Spirit—the Word of God

Throughout these lessons, we have emphasized the importance of the Word of God in fighting spiritual battles. In fact, you might want to review some of these teachings as you work through this lesson (see, for example, week 3, day 2).

The sword is both a defensive and an offensive weapon. With the Word, we resist the devil (Jas. 4:7), much as Jesus did when He quoted Scripture to counter Satan's temptations in the wilderness (Matt. 4:1-11). We strike deadly blows to the enemy when we know, believe, and claim the truths of God's Word. Remember, Satan's lies are exposed when we stand on the truth.

At the same time, we offensively enter Satan's domain when we proclaim forgiveness and freedom to those held in darkness (Col. 1:13). The Word of God is "living and active" (Heb. 4:12), and we have God's promise that it "will not return to me empty, but will accomplish what I desire and achieve the purpose for which I sent it" (Isa. 55:11). With our feet prepared with the gospel of peace, we invade the devil's kingdom when we evangelize with the Word of God.

Read Psalm 19:7-11. List statements that describe the nature and the power of the Scriptures. The first two answers are given for you.

VERSE	NATURE	POWER
7	perfect trustworthy	revives the soul makes wise the simple
8	_____	_____
9	_____	_____
10	_____	_____
11	_____	_____

God's Word is perfect, trustworthy, right, radiant, pure, righteous, and more precious than gold. The Word revives the soul, makes wise the simple, and gives joy to the heart and light to the eyes. By His Word we are warned about wrong, and keeping His Word brings great reward.

Interestingly, the sword pictured in Paul's description was not the large, long sword that the Roman soldier usually carried. Rather, the weapon was the short, double-bladed sword used in hand-to-hand combat. Sometimes we stand eye-to-eye with the enemy in spiritual battles, but we always have the sword to use against him. We needn't fear because the Word of God will cause the enemy to flee.

We can use the Word in spiritual battles in many ways. First, we can study the Bible so that we can "correctly handle the word of truth" (2 Tim. 2:15). Second, we must know and live the Word. Simply reciting

God's Word when our patterns are still unholy does little to weaken Satan's hold in our lives. Third, we can tell the good news found in the Word, offering hope to persons held in bondage. Fourth, memorizing Scripture will help us guard against sin (Ps. 119:11). Finally, we can teach the Word to others so that they, too, will know how to use the sword of the Spirit.

Read 2 Timothy 3:14-17. In your own words, what advice did Paul give to Timothy?

_____

_____

Put On the Full Armor

As we finish this week's lessons, remember Paul's command to put on the full armor of God (Eph. 6:11). While we have studied the armaments individually, Paul would not have so separated the pieces. Believers need all of the armor to be best prepared for the battle.

Satan is not alarmed by powerless religious activity. Acts 19:11-16 illustrates this point. Read this story in your Bible.

The sons of Sceva, who likely were exorcists by trade, attempted to cast out the demon by the "name of Jesus whom Paul preaches" (v. 13). The demon in turn admitted knowledge of Jesus and Paul, but he had no knowledge of the sons. Apparently, the spirit was alarmed by Jesus and by Paul, but he had no fear of the exorcists. Indeed, the man who was possessed literally beat the sons to the point of bleeding (v. 16). This somewhat humorous story is also a tragic one that teaches us several lessons.

First, religious activity means little if our lives don't reflect God's power. The sons of Sceva attempted to do something religious—as well as good, for that matter. They seemingly wanted to help the possessed man, and they tried to duplicate the process that they had apparently seen others use. Yet, their own lack of genuine relationship with God limited their power; even the name of Jesus had no authority when they tried to use His name in a magical, formulaic way.

Second, the devil isn't threatened if nothing in our lives causes him to take notice of God's work in us. If our lives lack the evidence of God's life-changing grace, the enemy doesn't become too disturbed. In fact, the devil likely wants us to continue our activity—as long as it is our activity and not God's.

Third, it is dangerous to attempt spiritual warfare if our hearts aren't right with God. There is great danger of taking on the enemy when we haven't prepared to do so. Spiritual warriors who aren't wearing the armor of God face inevitable defeat.

Conclude this week by determining steps you will take to put on the full armor of God. List them on the following page.

"Put on the full armor of God so that you can take your stand against the devil's schemes. For our struggle is not against flesh and blood, but against the rulers, against the authorities, against the powers of this dark world and against the spiritual forces of evil in the heavenly realms. Therefore put on the full armor of God, so that when the day of evil comes, you may be able to stand your ground, and after you have done everything, to stand. Stand firm then, with the belt of truth buckled around your waist, with the breastplate of righteousness in place, and with your feet fitted with the readiness that comes from the gospel of peace. In addition to all this, take up the shield of faith, with which you can extinguish all the flaming arrows of the evil one. Take the helmet of salvation and the sword of the Spirit, which is the word of God."

—Ephesians 6:11-17

Belt of truth _____

_____

_____

Breastplate of righteousness _____

_____

_____

Feet fitted _____

_____

_____

Shield of faith _____

_____

_____

Helmet of salvation _____

_____

_____

Sword of the Spirit _____

_____

_____

"Pray in the Spirit on all occasions with all kinds of prayers and requests. With this in mind, be alert and always keep on praying for all the saints."

—Ephesians 6:18

Action plans are only helpful if you carry them out. If you are not committed to these plans, they easily become ways Satan can seek to discourage you.

The key to keeping these action plans is found in next week's study. As you conclude day 5, read Ephesians 6:18 in the margin. As you pray, ask God to bring to mind daily your commitment to putting on the armor.

―――――

[1]Warren W. Wiersbe, *Classic Sermons on Spiritual Warfare* (Grand Rapids: Kregel Publications, 1992), 153.

VIEWER GUIDE

1. The armor is not _____ on us.

2. We need these virtues of godliness to put on every morning to _____ us.

3. We need each piece of the _____.

4. Match each piece of armor with its description:

belt of truth	covering of our mind, hope
breastplate	right choices
feet shod	integrity
helmet of salvation	offensive weapon, Word of God
shield	stand firm
sword	faith

5. How does a newborn believer know how to put on the armor?

   _____.

6. Systematically _____ every believer is putting on the armor.

Praying Victoriously

SPIRITUAL WARFARE

CASE STUDY

Jack was seriously struggling in his walk with God. One day he received a flyer in the mail advertising a spiritual warfare and prayer conference in his city. The flyer promised he would find victory over the spiritual battles he faced.

At the conference, Jack and other attendees began to discuss the role of prayer in spiritual warfare.

"Prayer is critical—but it must be targeted prayer against the specific demons who oppress us," said one. "General prayer isn't effective in spiritual warfare."

"I've learned that verbally rebuking Satan is the most effective way to pray," said another.

One man reminded Jack, "You can buy books that have specific prayers to break Satan's power. Why don't you get one of those?"

Still another person spoke more about the power of praise than prayer: "I still pray, but I've found that praising God in song is a quick and easy way to overcome the enemy."

If you were Jack, how would you respond to these suggestions? What role does prayer play in spiritual warfare? Should you pray for power over Satan? What does the Bible say about warfare praying?

"Pray in the Spirit on all occasions with all kinds of prayers and requests. With this in mind, be alert and always keep on praying for all the saints. Pray also for me, that whenever I open my mouth, words may be given me so that I will fearlessly make known the mystery of the gospel, for which I am an ambassador in chains. Pray that I may declare it fearlessly, as I should."
—*Ephesians 6:18-20*

DAY ONE

...THEN PRAY

After you've put on the whole armor of God, you still need another component in your lifestyle. Interestingly enough, the apostle Paul concluded the passage on putting on the armor of God with a command for the armed believers to take a certain course of action.

Read Ephesians 6:18-20 in the margin and circle what Paul told the believers to do.

Paul issued a strong call for prayer to the believers in Ephesus. Because he was facing spiritual battles, he wanted intercessory prayer warriors who understood the reality of spiritual warfare. He assumed they would be wearing the armor of God.

This week, we'll be studying prayer as it relates to spiritual warfare. Prayer is foundational; all Christians need to be growing in a stronger prayer life. Prayer connects us with God's power.

Underline the statement that best describes your current prayer life.

- I know I should pray, but I don't.
- I have a long way to go, but my prayer life is growing.
- My prayer life is strong and effective.

The important thing is not where you are but where you are going. None of us has arrived, but if we are making progress on the journey, we are headed in the right direction. If we have ceased growing or are not trying to grow our prayer lives, warning bells should sound.

Take time now to pray. If your prayer life is stagnant or non-existent, ask God's forgiveness and make a commitment to grow in prayer. If your prayer life is strong and growing, ask God to protect your prayer time—and ask Him to allow you to influence others to pray effectively.

The Importance of Prayer

Reread Ephesians 6:18-20 on page 126. Underline each reference to the word *all* or *always*.

You probably underlined four uses of these words. Paul told the believers to pray "on all occasions with all kinds of prayers and requests," always praying for all the saints (v. 18). Apparently, he intended the believers to be in prayer prior to, during, and after spiritual battles. In fact, Paul challenged the believers in another city (Thessalonica) to "pray continually" (1 Thess. 5:17).

Why is prayer so important in spiritual battles? Write your answer in the margin.

> "Prayer is communication with the commander-in-chief during the battle. Our awareness of the battle heightens our sense of need to stay in constant touch with our superior officer, who can resupply us and provide us with our orders."[1]
>
> ## CLINTON ARNOLD

> *"Though we live in the world, we do not wage war as the world does. The weapons we fight with are not the weapons of the world. On the contrary, they have divine power to demolish strongholds."*
> —*2 Corinthians 10:3-4*

Let's examine three primary reasons prayer in warfare is important.

First, prayer signifies a relationship with God—and it is our relationship with Him that threatens the enemy. The motivation for prayer always stems from the desire to relate to God, not to get power over the devil. However, we know when we connect with God, the devil is threatened because of what God will do in us and through us. For example, a garden hose disconnected from the faucet poses little threat to a fire. But when that hose has the power of water flowing through it, the fire cannot continue. Likewise, our connection to Christ in prayer threatens the devil because the Holy Spirit flows through us.

Prayer is communication with God; in fact, it is offering ourselves to Him and quietly allowing Him to speak to us in turn. Praying in a proper spirit, we communicate with Him just because we are in relationship with Him and love Him. We draw closer to Him, listen to Him, learn from Him, and gain strength from Him when we pray. Our relationship with Him grows—and whenever our relationship with God increases, God's working through our lives increases.

Second, the battle we face is spiritual, and we fight spiritual battles by spiritual means. Read 2 Corinthians 10:3-4. Paul indicated that that we live in the world, but "we do not wage war as the world does" (v. 3). Look at how other versions of the Bible translate this same phrase:

- "We do not war after the flesh" (KJV).
- "We do not war according to the flesh" (NASB).
- "We don't wage war with human plans and weapons" (*New Living Translation*).

We battle against supernatural powers and principalities (Eph. 6:12), and no natural, human means can defeat this kind of enemy. Only God's working in prayer will weaken the enemy's holds in our lives. Through prayer, God gives us the strength and power to win the battle.

Jesus taught us to pray that God would " 'deliver us from the evil one' " (Matt. 6:13). This model prayer reminds us that we cannot deliver ourselves from the enemy; we are no match for his schemes and temptations in our own strength. Prayer provides the power for deliverance.

Third, the prayer of a righteous person is powerful and effective (Jas. 5:16). Do you remember the story of Elijah who prayed to stop the rain and then prayed to start the rain again? (see 1 Kings 17–18). The writer of the Book of James used this story to explain the power of the prayers of a righteous man. Elijah, who was "a man just like us" (Jas. 5:17), prayed earnestly, and nature itself was affected (vv. 17-18).

Read James 5:16-18, and meditate upon this text in the light of the spiritual armor of Ephesians 6:13-17. A righteous person wears the helmet of salvation and lives a life of truth, righteousness, and faith. When we daily wear the full armor of God, our prayers can be powerful and effective. It's no wonder, then, that Paul first said for the believers to put on the armor (Eph. 6:11), and then he said "pray also for me" (v. 19).

Pause to pray. Ask God to increase your desire for righteousness and to deliver you from the devil's schemes at work in your life right now.

Satan's Strategies Against Prayer

We've recognized throughout this study that Satan schemes against us. If prayer is so important in spiritual warfare, it makes sense that Satan would strategize to weaken our prayer lives. His methods are numerous, and he doesn't give up easily. In fact, your authors have provided a list of several ways the enemy seeks to hinder our praying.

Maybe he entices us with sin, then so accuses us (Rev. 12:10) that we feel guilty praying. At other times he brings to mind messages of doubt: *You don't really believe God hears your prayers, do you? Prayer really doesn't work—think about all of your prayers that have gone unanswered.* When doubt sets in, we typically pray less often.

One of Satan's most successful ways to hinder our praying is working to keep us from praying at all. Perhaps he leads us to direct our attention away from God (including focusing our attention on "good" things), as we have seen in a previous study (week 3, day 5). At other times, he lures us to complacency about prayer. After all, life is OK, even if we have a few struggles. Our family is intact. We're serving in the church, and things seem to be going well there. Our jobs appear to be secure. Apparently, we can get by pretty well without much praying—so we don't pray. When we don't pray, we cause little concern for the devil.

Maybe you've battled with developing a consistent, effective prayer life. Check any obstacles to effective prayer in your life.

- ❏ too busy to pray
- ❏ don't know how to pray
- ❏ unanswered prayers
- ❏ weakened marriage relationship
- ❏ lack of discipline

- ❏ unconfessed sin
- ❏ doubt
- ❏ pride
- ❏ self-sufficiency
- ❏ complacency

Prayerlessness is a sin of omission (1 Thess. 5:17). It displeases God. We live in disobedience and do not wear the breastplate of righteousness. In the meantime, Satan allows us to rest in our complacency and lulls us to sleep before he strikes. Then when the devil attacks, we are exposed to his arrows.

The soldier who chooses to ignore his ammunition when the battle is raging around him is foolish indeed. Be as wise as a warrior. Put on the full armor of God—and pray!

State here one action you will take this week to improve your prayer life.

_____

_____

_____

DAY TWO

PRAYING AS JESUS PRAYED

Many Christians have memorized the words to the Lord's Prayer (Matt. 6:9-13; Luke 11:2-4). We know well the words that begin with " ' "Our Father who art in heaven" ' " (RSV) but have you thought about the events that led to Jesus' teaching these words to His disciples? Luke's gospel tells us that "Jesus was praying in a certain place. When he finished, one of his disciples said to him, 'Lord, teach us to pray, just as John taught his disciples' " (11:1). In response to this request, Jesus gave the disciples the Lord's Prayer, also known as the Model Prayer.

What better teacher than Jesus to show us how to pray? In today's lesson, we want to examine Jesus' prayer life and look for prayer principles to overcome the enemy. Needless to say, the more we follow Jesus' example, the more likely we will win the battles of spiritual warfare.

Prayer Was Jesus' Lifestyle

Read these verses. Explain what each passage tells us about Jesus' prayer life.

Matthew 26:39 _____

_____

Mark 1:35 _____

_____

Luke 6:12-13 _____

_____

Luke 9:18,28 _____

_____

Luke 11:1 _____

_____

John 6:10-11 _____

_____

John 11:38-41 _____

_____

Jesus modeled a lifestyle of prayer. He had particular quiet places to pray (Luke 4:42; 5:16). He prayed in the morning (Mark 1:35), into the evening (Matt. 14:23), and through the night (Luke 6:12). He prayed before making major decisions (Luke 6:12; Matt. 26:36-46). He prayed prayers of thanksgiving (John 6:10-11; 11:38-41). He taught others to pray (Luke 11:1). He prayed in private (Mark 6:46; Luke 9:18) and with others (Luke 9:28). During times of incredible struggle, He prayed (Matt. 26:36-46; 27:45-46). And He prayed intensely for His followers (John 17:1-25—also known as the "priestly prayer").

Jesus' prayer life teaches us a basic principle about prayer and spiritual warfare. Those who overcome the enemy through prayer are those who "pray continually" (1 Thess. 5:17)—not those who suddenly decide to begin praying when the battle erupts. Remember, it's our relationship with God that threatens the enemy, and a strong relationship with God is marked by consistent and heartfelt prayer.

> Those who overcome the enemy through prayer are those who "pray continually"—not those who suddenly decide to begin praying when the battle erupts.

Based on your study of Jesus' prayer life, write one way you plan to make your prayer life more like that of Jesus.

_____

_____

Jesus Taught Us to Pray About Spiritual Battles

In the Model Prayer, Jesus taught His disciples to pray, " ' "Lead us not into temptation, but deliver us from the evil one" ' " (Matt. 6:13). Though some versions of the Bible use only the word *evil,* the reference most likely refers to Satan. If so, Jesus taught His disciples that prayer is necessary for overcoming the enemy even before the battle becomes intense. Satan is so powerful that we can't defend ourselves against him in our own strength—and we need to realize this truth before we learn the hard way that we can't defeat Him alone.

These Scriptures contain some of the strategies of the evil one. Draw a line from the text on the left to its corresponding meaning on the right.

Matthew 13:19	The evil one entices people to sin.
Matthew 13:38	The evil one sends fiery arrows against us.
Ephesians 6:16	The evil one sows his followers among Christians.
1 John 3:12	The evil one snatches away God's Word after people hear it.

Can you see why we need prayer daily in order to stand against Satan? He aims his darts at us (Eph. 6:16), trying to lure us to sin

(1 John 3:12). He is cunning enough that he can plant his own followers in the church (Matt. 13:38), and he can lead people to forget God's Word even after they've heard it (Matt. 13:19). If we wait to start praying until we are under obvious attack from this conniving and evil enemy, we may already be on the edge of defeat.

When Jesus faced His struggle in the garden of Gethsemane, He told three of His disciples to keep watch as He went aside to pray (Mark 14:32-34). He returned from His praying, only to find them sleeping (v. 37). Jesus awakened them and challenged them to " 'watch and pray so that you will not fall into temptation' " (v. 38). Although they were exhausted from sorrow (Luke 22:45), Jesus gave them a stern warning: if you don't watch and pray now, you're not going to have the strength needed to face coming temptations. We are wise to hear these same words from the Lord.

Jesus not only taught His disciples to pray for protection, but He also personally prayed for their protection from the evil one. Read John 17:15. Have you ever thought about the fact that Jesus is praying for us in spiritual battles? He warned Peter that Satan wanted to sift him, but He also told Peter that He had already prayed for him (Luke 22:31-32). Today, Jesus is our high priest, interceding for us (Heb. 4:14-16; 7:23-25). When we realize that Jesus prays for us in times of spiritual warfare, we can trust that "the Lord is faithful, and he will strengthen and protect you from the evil one" (2 Thess. 3:3).

> *" 'My prayer is not that you take them out of the world but that you protect them from the evil one.' "*
> *—John 17:15*

Jesus is praying for us in spiritual battles.

Because Jesus taught us to pray for God's protection from the evil one, we need to do so. Write your prayer here, and begin this practice daily.

_____

_____

Jesus also modeled for us a commitment to pray for others who will face battles with the enemy. List below the names of persons for whom you will begin praying as Jesus did, "Protect them from the evil one." Take the time to pray for them now.

_____

_____

Jesus Focused on the Father in His Praying

In the Model Prayer Jesus showed us to pray by focusing on God. He is our Father, and His name is holy (Matt. 6:9). The kingdom is His (v. 10). He provides our daily needs (v. 11). He alone forgives our sins (v. 12) and guards us from the enemy's temptations (v. 13).

In Jesus' prayer in John 17, He again focused on God. Indeed, He referred to the Father as "Holy" (v. 11) and "Righteous" (v. 25).

Jesus brought the Father glory by His obedience (v. 4). His own authority came from the Father (v. 2), and He sought to make the Father known (v. 26). He knew that the Father was the One to protect His followers (v. 11).

As we've seen, Jesus mentioned the evil one in both the Model Prayer (Matt. 6:13) and the "priestly prayer" (John 17:15). However, He didn't emphasize the devil; He focused only on God in His praying. Sometimes, people who engage in spiritual warfare talk more in their prayers about the devil than about God. In fact, some people talk more to the devil ("Satan, I rebuke you!") in their praying. If we follow Jesus' model—as we should—we need to keep our focus on God. Ask God now to help you keep your eyes on Him in spiritual battles.

DAY THREE

PRAYING IN BROKENNESS

Today we'll consider the primary way we gain spiritual power: by allowing God to break us through His Spirit and through His Word.

Brokenness is the process by which God sifts us and molds us to make us dependent on Him.

> **How do you react to the words "allowing God to break us" as a strategy of spiritual warfare? Circle the words to indicate your feelings.**

scared	unwilling	excited	offended	eager
repulsed	surprised	anxious	perplexed	angry

Regardless of your feelings at this point, ask God to open you to what He wants to teach you through this lesson.

Power: The Trap of Spiritual Warfare

Listen to phrases you may hear from folks who practice varying kinds of spiritual warfare. "I rebuke the devil." "I take authority over the enemy." "I am reclaiming ground that the enemy took." "In the name of Jesus, I command you to come out!"

In particular contexts, these phrases might reflect a subtle danger inherent in spiritual warfare—that is, sometimes we get more focused on the power in warfare than we do on the God who gives the power. "We prayed, and power came down." Sometimes we want to feel mighty, and using warfare strategies and techniques fills that want.

This temptation to use power for power's sake is not new. Think about the bait that the serpent offered Eve in the garden: "God knows that when you eat of it your eyes will be opened, and you will be like God, knowing good and evil" (Gen. 3:5). Compare that temptation to Satan's offer to Jesus in the wilderness. Showing Jesus all the kingdoms

**REASONS THE POWER OF
SPIRITUAL WARFARE
ATTRACTS US**
1. We long to be in control.
2. We want powerful solutions.
3. We want to feel "spiritual."
4. Powerless people want power.
5. Power itself is a temptation.

of the world, the devil said, "All this I will give you, … if you will bow down and worship me" (Matt. 4:9). In both cases, the enemy dangled the bait of power in front of his target. Eve took the bait, but Jesus rejected it. He knew the devil's offers of power came at too high a price.

Why is the power of spiritual warfare so attractive to many people? **First**, our fallen nature longs to be in control, whether it be over others or over demons. **Second**, people are looking for instantaneous, powerful solutions to the struggles they face. **Third**, some believers like to be more "spiritual" than others. One way to show that we're more spiritual is to take on the demons—to dare to tread where others won't go. **Fourth**, persons who already feel powerless sometimes look for power. People who feel economically disenfranchised, for example, might find the power of spiritual warfare inviting. **Finally**, often we don't recognize that the power itself is a temptation. Satan is so scheming that sometimes he traps us even while we think we're spiritually powerful.

How do we know if we've become enamored with the power of spiritual warfare? This exercise won't completely answer this question for you, but it may alert you to a potential problem. Respond to these statements, marking "always" (A), "never" (N), or "sometimes" (S).

___ I brag to others when I experience spiritual victories.
___ I like the feeling of power I get when I take on the enemy.
___ I'm hoping that God will use me in a way that others will see.
___ I want people to know I know how to do spiritual warfare.
___ I think spiritual warfare is fun—I like the battles.

If you answered *always* or *sometimes* to any of these statements, the caution light should come on for you. Don't let the devil entice you with power for power's sake.

The Power Found in Weakness

Read the story of Paul's "thorn in the flesh" (2 Cor. 12:1-10). Paul had experienced powerful revelations from God, and he might have had reason to boast about his experiences (vv. 1,5). To keep him from bragging, however, God gave Satan permission to torment the apostle with some type of affliction (v. 7). Whatever the affliction was, it was strong enough that Paul pleaded with God three times to remove it (v. 8). God refused to do so, choosing instead to teach Paul that " 'My grace is sufficient for you, for my power is made perfect in weakness' " (v. 9).

God's power is made perfect in weakness? That statement doesn't make sense from the world's perspective. However, the Bible contains many stories of God's using weakness to accomplish His plan by showing His power. Think about some of these examples.

- Moses said he was " 'slow of speech and tongue' " (Ex. 4:10), but God told him He would help him speak and teach him what to say (v. 12).
- God systematically reduced Gideon's army so that they would know that He alone had delivered them (Judg. 7:1-25).

- David had only a sling and a rock, but God directed the rock to take down the Philistine giant (1 Sam. 17:1-50).
- Jeremiah said he was only a child, yet God promised to go with him and rescue him (Jer. 1:7-8).

Think as well about the cross. How did Jesus defeat Satan and his followers? He overcame the enemy forces not by overpowering them, but by surrendering to the cross. Through His obedience to death, Jesus triumphed over the powers and authorities (Col. 2:13-15; Phil. 2:5-11).

How do you respond to the truth that God's power is most evident when we are weak? (Check one or more.)
- ❏ I want whatever God wants; if He wants to break me, I'm ready.
- ❏ I was hoping for an easier way to find spiritual victory.
- ❏ I don't want to be weak, even if God wants it.
- ❏ I think God may be allowing Satan to weaken me, but I'm struggling to see God's purpose in it.

For Paul, the weakness created by the thorn in his flesh ultimately caused him to depend more on God for strength. Paul learned so much in that experience that he concluded, "Therefore I will boast all the more gladly about my weaknesses, so that Christ's power may rest on me" (2 Cor. 12:9). In his anguish, Paul found strength in Christ's power. In his weakness, he experienced power.

If we want to experience spiritual power, the route to that power is not to pray, *Lord, give me strength.* We're too susceptible to ego and self-sufficiency when we think we have enough strength to fight our battles—even when we know that God gave us the strength. The better prayer to pray if we want to be spiritually powerful is, *Lord, make me weak, so that I must always depend on You.*

Do you see what happens when we pray that way? God breaks us in whatever way He wishes. Sometimes He allows Satan access to us to keep us humble, but God always keeps Satan within God's limits. At other times, God permits the difficult circumstances of life to keep us weak (see 2 Cor. 12:10). When God breaks us, we no longer are interested in power for power's sake. We seek only God's grace that is sufficient for every struggle.

How, then, do we win spiritual battles if we're weak? We keep our focus on God who alone is our strength and shield. We stop depending on self, for the self isn't strong enough to win any battles. We pray more because we know we desperately need an intimate relationship with our Creator. We put on the full armor of God, realizing we can't win the battles without it.

In the end, the weakest believer who relies on God's strength is much more a threat to Satan than the "strong" believer who relies on his own strength. How did Paul fight the fight? He fought not in his strength, but in his weaknesses—and thus, in God's strength. He trusted God's hand, wore God's armor, and lived God's way. That's the way to win spiritual warfare.

How do we win spiritual battles if we're weak?

"I am already being poured out like a drink offering, and the time has come for my departure. I have fought the good fight, I have finished the race, I have kept the faith."
—2 Timothy 4:6-7

Take a minute and reflect on the words found in 2 Timothy 4:6-7. These words are Paul's farewell words to his young protégé, Timothy. Paul was ready to die, and he could say with integrity that he had "fought the good fight."

If you're willing to do so, conclude this study by writing a prayer to God that expresses your desire to experience spiritual victories through His strength and your weakness.

_____

_____

DAY FOUR

PRAYING WHEN FATIGUED

Military battles are rarely won carelessly. Most victorious armies know how to handle the two extremes of warfare. **First,** they know how to respond when physical fatigue sets in, supplies are limited, and the emotional stress of a life-and-death situation is overwhelming. **Second,** they know how to keep their focus when victory is easy and they are riding a sense of euphoria on top of the mountain.

Have you ever been between these two extremes in your spiritual life? How do you handle the mountaintop experiences with God? Have you had an experience with God where you wanted to stay forever? How do you respond to the euphoria? Have you been in a spiritual battle in which you felt you just couldn't go on? Today's lesson will shed light on how to pray when you encounter either extreme. Let's see how Jesus handled them.

Jesus Got Away from the Crowds for Prayer

You probably remember from our study two days ago that Jesus often took time to get away to pray. Review some of the texts in Luke's gospel, and fill in the blanks below.

"At daybreak Jesus went out to a _____ place" (Luke 4:42).

"Jesus often withdrew to _____ places and prayed" (5:16).

"One of those days Jesus went out to a _____ to pray" (6:12).

"Once when Jesus was praying in _____" (9:18).

Your version of the Bible may differ somewhat, but the answers from the *New International Version* are "solitary," "lonely," "mountainside," and "private." Jesus customarily got away from the crowds to find a quiet place and pray. We can't be certain, but He may have had specific places to which He retreated when He needed prayerful rest.

Notice the last two words of that previous sentence: "prayerful rest." Jesus didn't retreat just to retreat. He was the Son of God, so we know He wasn't retreating out of fear. He wasn't running from responsibility. He surely wasn't ignoring His call. In His unique status of being fully God and fully human, He simply longed for quiet time with the Father. Apart from the crowds, He found rest and replenishment in prayer. He got away, but He got away to pray.

We, too, need to get away to pray. The spiritual battle does get intense. The enemy doesn't readily back away. Recall from Luke 4:1-13 that Satan tempted Jesus three times before he backed off—and then only until another "opportune time" to attack Him. Satan's arrows are sharp, and even the battle to deflect them with the shield of faith (Eph. 6:16) can be exhausting. "Prayerful rest" is often in order.

Describe a time when you were spiritually exhausted and a prayerful retreat gave you strength to continue. If you have not had such an experience, what plans will you make for a spiritual retreat?

_____

_____

We Need Balance Between the Mountaintop and the Valley

Take the time to read the stories of Mark 9:2-29. Through the lives of Jesus' disciples, these stories show us two extremes of our Christian experience: the mountaintop where miracles happen and the valley where defeat occurs.

In verses 2-12, Peter, James, and John were privileged to see Jesus transformed before them on the top of a mountain. Jesus was "dazzling white" (v. 3) in His changed attire. Out of nowhere, Moses and Elijah also appeared, talking with Jesus. Then God spoke from a cloud! Needless to say, this mountaintop experience was an awesome one for these disciples. So unbelievable was this event that Peter wanted to make the event permanent by building "tabernacles" (v. 5, NASB) for Jesus, Moses, and Elijah. After all, who wouldn't have wanted to stay there? Jesus, though, led the three disciples back down the mountain.

At the foot of the mountain was another story (29:14-18). The remaining disciples had tried to cast a demon from a possessed boy but had been unsuccessful. They had lost a spiritual battle in which the boy's physical well-being was at stake. Only after Jesus came and rebuked the demon did the boy experience healing (vv. 20-29). Jesus came from the mountaintop and did what the disciples could not do.

When the disciples asked Jesus why they had been unsuccessful in casting out the boy's demon, His response to them was simple: " 'This kind can come out only by prayer' " (v. 29).

Why do you think the disciples had failed?

_____

This question raises several possible responses. Mark 9:33-34 tells us that the disciples had been arguing over who was the greatest; in fact, they argued among themselves even as they tried to stop another exorcist who was not one of them (9:38-39). Maybe their proud and argumentative spirits hindered their prayers when they encountered this demon (see Jas. 4:1-3).

Matthew's account of this story indicates that the disciples lacked faith (Matt. 17:14-20). Their faith at that point was not yet the size of a tiny mustard seed. At the same time, Jesus' response in Mark's gospel seems to indicate an additional problem: the disciples had not been praying as they should have been. Maybe they lacked faith, and therefore they didn't pray. Or, maybe they assumed they could conquer the demons on their own—after all, Jesus had given them authority over demons (Matt. 10:1)—and they thought they didn't need to pray. Whatever the reason, the disciples lacked power.

Now let's bring the two stories together. On the mountaintop were three disciples who wanted to stay where God was doing something miraculous. In the valley were other disciples who were failing miserably. The disciples on the mountain wanted to stay where the power was evident, but a hurting boy at the foot of the mountain needed them. Those on the mountain needed to do ministry with power, and those in the valley needed power to do ministry. That is, the mountaintop disciples needed to go to the valley, and those in the valley needed to go to the mountain for a while.

These two experiences teach us several lessons about prayer in warfare.

- Staying where the power seems most real (on the mountaintop) is not acceptable if a hurting world is crying out for God's power in their own lives.
- However, ministry in a hurting world is ineffective if we lack the power to make a difference.
- At times we need a mountaintop experience to be rejuvenated to do ministry, but the mountaintop must always lead us back to the valley, where hurting people need a touch of God's power. When we get weary and ineffective in the valley, it's time to retreat to the mountain.

Do you see the need for balance in our spiritual lives? Spiritual battles are tough, and we need God's strength from the mountain. When God gives us His strength, we're called to "press on" (Phil. 3:14). How do you respond to this call for balance?

Check each statement that applies to you.

- ❏ I need to spend more time on the mountain to find a balance.
- ❏ I need to spend more time in the valley to find a balance.
- ❏ I'm not sure where I need to be at this point, but I know I need to evaluate the balance in my life.

Should You Go Up or Come Down the Mountain?

The focus of this lesson is balancing a prayer life. So where are you? Do you need to go to the mountain, or do you need to come down the mountain? Are you so worn out that you have nothing to give? Or have you stayed too long where there is no one to whom to give?

If You're in a Valley ...

- Set aside time in advance to go to the mountain. Clear your calendar. Try to complete any projects or assignments prior to the retreat so you have little else consuming your attention.
- Enlist prayer partners who will pray for you before and during the retreat. Encourage them to pray for God to recharge your spiritual batteries.
- Choose a quiet place. Avoid as many distractions as possible.
- Start small. You may want to begin with a brief commitment of time (a couple of hours) if you are unaccustomed to this process. Setting your time goals too high will likely lead to failure and frustration.
- Read and pray. Let the Word of God speak to you, and then respond to His leading. Consider recording your thoughts and insights in a journal.
- Be prepared for the battle. When God speaks, the enemy counters. If God reveals sin in your life, assume that the devil will provide you with rationalizations for your sin. When God challenges you to step out in faith, be prepared for the enemy to try to convince you otherwise.
- Be sure to pray for others. Satan's strategies are often designed to put our focus on self. Don't let the retreat become self-centered.
- Give yourself permission to get away with God as Jesus did, but then return to the valley—just as Jesus did.

If You've Been on the Mountain ...

Get back down to the valley where hurting people are waiting for the good news! We can become so spiritually full that we are gluttonous—wanting more of God to selfishly fill ourselves.

If you are not presently involved in a ministry in your church or community, ask God to show you a need that you can fill. Tell your pastor and church leaders of your desire to serve God in a sacrificial way. List one or more possibilities about which you would be willing to pray.

We can become so spiritually full that we are gluttonous—wanting more of God to selfishly fill ourselves.

DAY FIVE

PRAYING EVANGELISTICALLY

I (Chuck) became a Christian when I was 13 years old. A seventh-grade classmate, Randy, told me about Christ's love, His death on my behalf, and His coming return. He challenged me to turn from my wrong and trust God in faith. For almost a year, though, I rejected Randy's words. I wanted to live my own life, and I felt I was too young to make such a drastic commitment. Every day, Randy told me about God, and every day I gave some excuse not to follow Him.

Something happened, though, that changed my heart. I still can't explain it, but I knew I needed to consider Randy's words. I decided to visit a church (primarily so I could tell Randy that I was going to church, to be candid), and God just grabbed my heart. The pastor's words seemed aimed at me. I knew that Randy spoke truth, and I really did need to follow Christ.

As I think back to those days, I remember how many times Randy said, "I'm praying for you." He prayed often, and he prayed with heart-felt concern for me. God heard my friend's prayers. In grace, the Father rescued me "from the dominion of darkness" and brought me "into the kingdom of the Son" (Col. 1:13).

Our goal in this lesson is to look at the spiritual warfare elements in praying for nonbelievers. Ask God to give you a burden for evangelistic prayer—like Randy's—as you complete this study.

The Condition of Unbelievers: Blinded by the Enemy

"Even if our gospel is veiled, it is veiled to those who are perishing. The god of this age has blinded the minds of unbelievers, so that they cannot see the light of the gospel of the glory of Christ, who is the image of God."
—2 Corinthians 4:3-4

Read 2 Corinthians 4:3-4 in the margin and answer the following questions:

What is the state of unbelievers? _____

_____

Who has created this "blindness"? _____

The apostle Paul was committed to telling others about the good news of Christ. In fact, he knew that God had called him to do just that— God would use him to " 'open their eyes and turn them from darkness to light, and from the power of Satan to God, so that they may receive forgiveness of sins' " (Acts 26:18).

Paul also understood that he couldn't change people in his own ability. "The god of this age has blinded the minds of unbelievers" (2 Cor. 4:4), and no human power could change these blinded minds.

"The god of this age" is a reference to Satan, who is also called the " 'prince of this world' " (John 16:11) and the "ruler of the kingdom of the air" (Eph. 2:2). How does the enemy blind the minds of unbelievers? Though there may be several methods, two are most obvious.

He Blinds People by the Lure of Sin

Let's face it—we sin because we are sinful by nature (Eph. 2:3; Rom. 5:12), but we also sin because sin is often fun. The fruit on the tree looks good, and we think it will bring us pleasure. Afraid that we're missing something by not eating the fruit, we bite into it.

That's the way Satan works. As we've seen earlier in this study (week 3, day 3), the enemy lures us to see what we're missing. Then, at least for a little while, we enjoy the pleasures of sin. Disobedience costs us our peace with God, but we seldom consider the long-term consequences when the fruit looks good *right now*.

By nature, unbelievers are without understanding and do not seek God on their own (Rom. 3:11)—they are blinded to the truth of the gospel (2 Cor. 4:4). The pleasure of sin only deepens that blindness. Why should they give up what they enjoy? Maybe, in fact, God just wants them to miss out on something (remember the serpent's words to Eve?). Unbelievers who are still in darkness (Col. 1:13) see the temporary pleasure of sin while failing to understand the eternal consequences.

Satan Gives Unbelievers Lies to Believe

Satan is the father of lies (John 8:44). Observe how several versions of the Bible state this truth:

"When he lies, he speaks his native language" (NIV).

"Whenever he speaks a lie, he speaks from his own nature" (NASB).

"When he speaks a lie, he speaks from his own resources" (NKJV).

Though the specific wording differs, the truth remains the same: the nature of Satan is falsehood. It shouldn't surprise us, then, that Satan blinds unbelievers by giving them lies to believe. Consider these lies that some unbelievers are trusting:

- "I'm good enough. God will accept me."
- "I'll always have tomorrow to follow God."
- "There are many routes to God."
- "God is so loving that He wouldn't judge me."
- "Hell isn't real anyway."

Do you know other lies that unbelievers accept? List one or two below.

_____

_____

THESE PASSAGES MAY HELP YOU TO COUNTER SATAN'S LIES WITH THE TRUTH:
- *"I'm good enough. God will accept me" (Isa. 64:6; Mark 10:18).*
- *"I'll always have tomorrow to follow God" (Prov. 27:1; Luke 12:16-21).*
- *"There are many routes to God" (John 14:6; Acts 4:12).*
- *"God is so loving that He wouldn't judge me" (2 Cor. 5:10).*
- *"Hell isn't real anyway" (Luke 16:19-31; Rev. 20:11-15).*

Let's be clear here. Unbelievers are held accountable for their disobedience to God, both by their nature and by their actions. Unbelief is sin, and all people will give an account before God (2 Cor. 5:10); unbelievers will answer for their wrong. Nevertheless, the devil isn't just sitting idle as unbelievers reject God. He continually works to keep their minds blinded to the truth—and we don't have the power in ourselves to counter his schemes. We must pray for unbelievers!

Praying for the Believer: a Prayer for Boldness

"Pray also for me, that whenever I open my mouth, words may be given me so that I will fearlessly make known the mystery of the gospel, for which I am an ambassador in chains. Pray that I may declare it fearlessly, as I should."
—**Ephesians 6:19-20**

Read Ephesians 6:19-20 in the margin. When Paul concluded the list of the armor, he asked the believers to pray for him. What was his specific prayer? Underline it.

Paul asked the Ephesian believers to pray that he would "fearlessly" tell the good news of the gospel. If we understand the reality of the situation when we share the gospel, we will better understand Paul's request. Unbelievers are in the "dominion of darkness" (Col. 1:13), held under the power of Satan (Acts 26:18). They are already condemned (John 3:18). Though Satan is no match for God's grace, he doesn't easily give up his captives. Evangelism is spiritual warfare—taking the gospel of light into the kingdom of darkness. If we're going to tell unbelievers the good news of Jesus, we'd better be ready for the enemy to fight us.

Paul certainly knew that truth, for he was imprisoned for preaching the gospel (Eph. 6:20). He didn't give up, though. Rather, he asked believers to pray for him so that he wouldn't miss a single opportunity to tell about Jesus. Notice the similarities between Ephesians 6:19-20 and Colossians 4:3-4, another passage Paul wrote from a prison: "Pray for us, too, that God may open a door for our message, so the we may proclaim the mystery of Christ, for which I am in chains. Pray that I may proclaim it clearly, as I should."

Fearlessly and clearly—that's the way Paul wanted to proclaim Christ. He knew, though, that he couldn't do that in his own power. He needed the prayer support of other believers to speak boldly and clearly as the enemy opposed him. Interestingly, Paul asked the Ephesians to pray for him after he told them to put on the full armor of God (Eph. 6:11). In the context of chapter 6, Paul assumed that those persons praying for him would themselves have on the full armor of God. Paul was in a spiritual battle as he evangelized, and those who prayed for him were in the battle, too. Everybody involved needed the armor.

H – *Pray that unbelievers will have receptive hearts.*
E – *Pray that their spiritual eyes and ears will be opened.*
A – *Pray that they will be convicted of God's attitude toward sin.*
R – *Pray that they will be released to believe.*
T – *Pray that their lives will be transformed.[2]*

If Paul needed the prayer support of armed prayer warriors, surely we do, too. Few of us have the boldness of the apostle. Ask God to give you the names of armed believers who will pray for you to be a bold and clear witness. List their names in the margin, and ask them this week to support you in prayer. Using the acrostic in the margin, join with these prayer warriors to pray for others who are held in darkness.

For specific guidelines to implement this type of ministry, see "Praying with Boldness," in *A House of Prayer*, compiled by John Franklin (Nashville: Lifeway, 1999), 90.

---

[1]Clinton Arnold, *Three Crucial Questions about Spiritual Warfare* (Grand Rapids: Baker, 1997), 46.

[2]Adapted from *Praying Your Friends to Christ* (Alpharetta, GA: North American Mission Board, 1998), 16-17.

VIEWER GUIDE

1. Why is developing a consistent prayer life so difficult?

   1) We don't see the _____ to pray.

   2) We don't view prayer as a _____.

2. A slot machine approach to prayer: We pray to _____.

3. There is no way we can win spiritual battles if we are not people of _____.

4. How to get started on growing your prayer life:

   1) get a _____.

   2) create a _____.

5. Fasting is wanting to eat more at _____ table than at _____ table.

   I so long for God that my _____ needs pale in comparison.

6. When the Scripture speaks of breaking, it is talking about severing our

   _____ toward anything else that is ahead of Jesus.

7. Prayer is first _____.

   Prayer is also _____.

   Prayer is _____ to God, as well.

8. God has chosen to _____ through prayer.

Current Issues

CASE STUDY

"That's it!" Jason thought to himself. "Finally, I understand why I've faced so many problems in my spiritual life."

Jason had been a Christian for about five years when his life suddenly took a turn for the worse. His temptations to sin increased. His relationship with his wife soured. His church was in conflict. Because he had never faced so many struggles at once, Jason wasn't sure how to understand this unexpected turmoil.

When his pastor spoke one Sunday about spiritual warfare, Jason began to consider the possibility that some of his battles were spiritual ones. On Monday he went to the local Christian bookstore to buy some books about spiritual warfare.

To his surprise, the number of books available was overwhelming. Some spoke about casting out demons and breaking demonic curses. Others suggested that Christians could be possessed by demons. Still others included prayers for binding and rebuking the devil. Jason wanted direction, but he wasn't sure which books would be most helpful.

How would you have advised Jason? With the increased popularity of spiritual warfare in our society, how do you know which ideas to accept or reject?

DAY ONE

CHRISTIANS ON THE OFFENSIVE

This week we will turn our attention to controversial teachings on spiritual warfare. Depending on which author you read, you will encounter varying opinions. We recognize that much difference of opinion exists on these subjects, even among prominent leaders whom God has used. Therefore, we (John and Chuck) take our positions with much humility and respect for others' opinions.

That stated, however, we feel it would be an injustice to our readers not to forthrightly test popular teaching with biblical verses and patterns

that call certain viewpoints into question. We want to be bold in presenting to you the biblical evidence as we see it.

Much controversy in spiritual warfare revolves around such concepts as "warfare praying," "territorial spirits," and "spiritual mapping." "Warfare praying" essentially uses prayer as a weapon against Satan, particularly against spirits whom Satan is assumed to have assigned to particular regions (hence, "territorial spirits"). "Spiritual mapping" is an extensive research process by which believers seek to determine Satan's influences in a particular area, with the goal of breaking Satan's hold.

A common denominator of these concepts is an approach to spiritual warfare that seeks to gain an upper hand on the enemy in order to defeat him. In this lesson, we want to evaluate whether Christians should go on the offensive when engaging in spiritual warfare.

Did Jesus Go on the Offensive?
The answer to this question depends on how you define the term *offensive*. If offensive spiritual warfare means looking for demons in order to uproot them in preparation for the gospel, the answer is "no." As we'll see, however, this answer isn't the final one.

No biblical evidence suggests that Jesus went hunting for demons. Instead, He simply went about doing good (Acts 10:38). When His ministry brought Him into contact with demons, He dealt with them. Consider the stories in Matthew 9:18-33. In the first story (vv. 18-25), Jesus healed a little girl and a woman with a blood disease. As He left the place where He healed the little girl, He healed two blind men who had been following Him (vv. 27-31). Then, He had little rest before someone brought to Him a man who was possessed and mute (vv. 32-33). Jesus drove the demon out of the man, and the healed man spoke. This pattern is duplicated in the gospels more than once (see Mark 1:21-26; 7:24-30; 9:14-27; Luke 4:31-35). In most cases, demon-possessed persons were brought to Jesus—He didn't go looking for them.

Not only did Jesus not hunt demons but He also didn't have an elaborate exorcism ritual when He confronted demons. Only once did He ask the name of a demon (Mark 5:8-9), and the point of that question was not to gain some sort of magical power over the demon by knowing its name (as some superstitiously believed in Jesus' day). A close look at this story in Luke's account reveals that the demons knew they were defeated before Jesus ever asked their name (Luke 8:28-29).

No biblical evidence suggests that Jesus went hunting for demons.

Jesus' questioning the name was intended only to show that the man possessed was severely possessed—a "legion" of demons inhabited him.

When Jesus did confront demons, His approach was straightforward and concise.

Read the following accounts, and briefly describe Jesus' approach to exorcism.

Mark 1:21-26 _____

Mark 7:24-30 _____

_____

Mark 9:14-27 _____

_____

Jesus didn't have a specific formula He always followed when He encountered demons. Nor did He typically enter into a conversation with them. In fact, they often spoke first. He didn't offensively go looking for them, nor did He ritualistically counter them when they appeared. Jesus simply ordered them to leave, and they did.

On the Other Hand...

> The very fact that Jesus came to the earth indicates that He took the offensive against the "prince of this world."

Just the very fact that Jesus came to the earth indicates that He took the offensive against the "prince of this world" (John 16:11). He came to teach the good news of the kingdom, and that good news included salvation from sin (Mark 2:1-12; Luke 19:10), healing from physical illnesses, and deliverance from demonic powers (Matt. 4:23-24). Just as Satan enticed the first Adam to sin and to lose his life (Gen. 3:1-7), the Second Adam (Christ) came to die and give us life again (Rom. 5:12-17; 1 Cor. 15:45).

Christ's very presence and His preaching took on the enemy and defeated him. Think about it. Jesus came, and demons fled. Illnesses disappeared. Outcasts discovered love (John 4:1-26). Tumultuous seas became calm (Luke 8:22-25). Funerals halted (Luke 7:11-17; 8:51-56). And the enemy met his match (Matt. 4:1-11; Col. 2:15). When the Word became flesh (John 1:14), God was taking the offensive.

His primary method of warfare, though, was not to take on the demons. Instead, it was to proclaim "the good news of the kingdom" (Matt. 4:23) through His actions and His words. He is the Word (John 1:1), and His words carried power that dislodged Satan and changed lives.

In a similar way, we engage offensively in spiritual warfare when we take up "the sword of the Spirit" (Eph. 6:17) and proclaim the good news. Is it surprising, then, that Jesus gave five versions of the Great Commission (Matt. 28:18-20; Mark 16:15; Luke 24:45-47; John 20:21; Acts 1:8)—all that called His followers to imitate His ministry and preach the good news? He expected His followers to overcome the enemy through the power and the preaching of His Word.

So, should we go on the offensive? Our answer is both a "no" and a "yes." There is no biblical mandate for us to search for demons and root them out. On the other hand, there is a clear mandate to go to the world and to preach the good news—and that very act takes on the enemy. As we proclaim and teach, we should always be prepared to deal appropriately with demonic forces if they manifest themselves in the course of our ministry.

Be Alert, Stand, and Resist

If we engage the devil offensively when we do evangelism, we need to be prepared for the battle. In that sense, the best defense prepares us for the offensive battle. Take a look at how a defensive posture in spiritual warfare prepares us and encourages us to go on the offensive. Our primary defensive measures are listed here:

"Be on your guard" (1 Cor. 16:13)—The enemy is "a roaring lion" who wants to devour us (1 Pet. 5:8). We don't want to focus on him; however, we do want to be aware of his schemes.

"Submit to God" (Jas. 4:7)—Only God can grant us the power to win spiritual battles. When we live in submission to Him, our very lives become a threat to the enemy.

"Stand firm" (Eph. 6:11,13; 1 Pet. 5:9)—The word translated *stand* in Ephesians 6 is a military term meaning "take your position and hold it." We can't defend ourselves if we can't stand firm, nor can we launch an offensive attack if our footing is unsure.

"Resist the devil" (Jas. 4:7)—More than simply "rebuking Satan," resistance means submitting to God and actively saying "no" to the devil's temptations. He flees when we resist him—at least for awhile (Luke 4:13; Jas. 4:7).

When we learn in God's grace to submit to Him and to firmly resist Satan, then we're best prepared to enter into offensive warfare through evangelism. Our witness is more pure, our confidence in sharing our faith is stronger, and our trust in God is more complete when we submit to Him and resist the enemy.

What is your offensive warfare readiness? Check all that apply.
___ I am focused on God yet aware of Satan's schemes. (25%)
___ I live in submission to the will of God. (25%)
___ When temptations come, I stand firm. (25%)
___ I flee from tempting situations. (25%)

My offensive warfare readiness is _____ %.

What About Territorial Spirits?

The biblical support most commonly given for the existence of territorial spirits is Daniel 10:1-21. In this text, the Prince of Persia and the Prince of Greece are demonic forces that hindered an answer to Daniel's

A defensive posture in spiritual warfare prepares us and encourages us to go on the offensive.

prayer. A battle in the heavens ensued, and God's angels intervened so that Daniel received his answer.

While this text does suggest that demonic forces may have influence over particular areas, no strategy for countering the demons is given. Daniel didn't attempt to name the demons, break their power, or cast them out. In fact, he didn't even know the battle was going on until it was over. The Bible simply doesn't give us a mandate or a strategy to take on territorial spirits.

DAY TWO

DEMON POSSESSION

One of the most controversial questions regarding spiritual warfare is whether or not a Christian can be possessed by a demon. This question is important because our answer to this question determines how we will respond to a believer who is caught up in intensive spiritual warfare. If we believe that a Christian can be demon possessed, we might attempt an exorcism. If we don't believe that a believer can be demon possessed, exorcism isn't an option. The goal of this lesson is to provide a biblical answer to this important question.

What Is Demon Possession?

Read the following passages and list characteristics of the person who is demon possessed in each account.

Mark 1:22-26 _____

_____

Mark 5:1-5 _____

_____

Mark 9:17-26 _____

_____

From these several characteristics, do you see any common denominator in these stories? Describe what these accounts have in common.

_____

_____

_____

In each of these accounts, the level of demonic influence over the person suggests ownership or control. For example, the evil spirit took control of a man's voice and then shook him violently before leaving (Mark 1:22-26). The demoniac at Gerasenes was so violent and so strong that no one could bind him. In fact, he couldn't even control himself; he cut himself with stones and cried out continually (Mark 5:1-5). The demon in the epileptic boy so strongly controlled him from his childhood that it continually threw him into fire or water to kill him (Mark 9:17-26).

Look again at the story of the demoniac in Mark 5:1-20. Seemingly everything about him was affected by the demon that possessed him. The man was strong enough to break iron chains. He had not worn clothes for a long time (Luke 8:27). His shrill cries echoed day and night. Those who saw him believed he was out of his mind. The enemy owned him—and that's the nature of demon possession. Only Jesus had the answer for such a tragic man.

The Holy Spirit Protects Us Against Possession

The question for this day is essentially, "Can Satan totally control believers?" To answer the question, we must first recognize who does own believers. The Bible isn't ambiguous on this point:

> "Don't you know that you yourselves are God's temple and that God's Spirit lives in you?"—1 Corinthians 3:16-17

> "Do you not know that your body is a temple of the Holy Spirit, who is in you, whom you have received from God? You are not your own; you were bought at a price. Therefore honor God with your body."—1 Corinthians 6:19-20

The significance of these statements becomes most obvious when we know that the Spirit of God is God. His assignment is to seal God's children, "guaranteeing our inheritance until the redemption of those who are God's possession" (Eph. 1:13-14). If God's Spirit is God and He lives within us and seals us, then how likely is it that another spiritual power can possess us? God owns believers (remember, He bought us at a price), and the demon who desires to possess and control a believer must overcome God first. As we've seen throughout this study, Satan isn't strong enough to defeat God. God is too mighty to be overcome (1 John 4:4). As believers, we can rest assured that Satan can't possess us.

The demon who desires to possess and control a believer must overcome God first. Satan isn't strong enough to defeat God.

How do you feel about the truth of God's ownership of believers? (Check one.)
❑ relieved
❑ uncertain
❑ other?_____

What is the implication of this truth for us? We can face spiritual battles knowing that Satan will never gain control of us. We have been transferred from the dominion of darkness into the kingdom of God's Son (Col. 1:13), and Satan can't take us back from God. He will not ultimately win in the believer's life because he can't defeat God. Therefore, Christians cannot be demon possessed. However, those who claim to be Christians but who are not can be demon possessed. Paul warns Titus about imposters of the faith in Titus 1:15-16.

Can Demons Have Any Influence on Believers?

Take a minute to review two texts you have read throughout this study.

"Put on the full armor of God."—Ephesians 6:11

"Be self-controlled and alert. Your enemy the devil prowls around like a roaring lion looking for someone to devour."—1 Peter 5:8

Both of these passages were written to believers. If Satan and his forces could have no influence on believers, why would Paul and Peter have written these words? We don't need to put on armor if the enemy doesn't have ammunition, and we needn't be on the alert if the roaring lion has no teeth.

Our enemy, though, wants to devour us. The darts he shoots at us are "fiery" (Eph. 6:16, KJV). He was brazen enough to attack Jesus, and he surely schemes against us. He can't possess us, but that doesn't mean he doesn't try to harm us any way he can.

What are Satan's limits in the lives of believers? He can go no further than God allows. We are still fully accountable for our choices—but his influence can be incredibly strong. In fact, sometimes he so persistently and powerfully attacks us that our souls seem to be tormented under that attack. Some writers call this state "oppression." Let's look at **four primary ways** the enemy tries to oppress believers.

First, he accuses us and gives us false messages about ourselves: "You're no good." "God doesn't love you, and nobody else does, either." "You're never going to experience victory." "You're wasting your time trying to be a Christian." Messages like these bombard us to the point that no day is free from them. In the end, **we lose hope** and struggle with believing even God's promises.

Second, he leads us to **doubt our salvation,** and the doubts consume us. Satan knows that a doubting person is "like a wave of the sea, blown and tossed by the wind" (Jas. 1:6). The believer who wrestles with doubt often becomes works-driven; that is, he begins to do as many good works as possible to convince himself of his salvation. At the same time, though, he can never work enough to convince himself. Doubts remain, and the accompanying fear can be overwhelming.

Third, he discourages us, and the **persistent discouragement** becomes debilitating. Maybe you've served God but have seen few results from your ministry. Perhaps you haven't seen as many changes in your own life as you want. You might have been emotionally wounded in a bitter church conflict. Maybe you've never found freedom from a particular sin. Discouragement sets in, and the hope of victory decreases. Our joy disappears, and it seems like we will never regain it.

FOUR PRIMARY WAYS THE ENEMY TRIES TO OPPRESS BELIEVERS:
He causes believers to
- *lose hope*
- *doubt their salvation*
- *stay discouraged*
- *face continual temptation*

Fourth, Satan reintroduces sin strongholds in our lives by **continual temptation,** and we lose our will to fight. How great it would be if we could just erase our desire for sin and never again face temptations that have hounded us in the past! Sometimes God allows that kind of change to take place, but more often we still face the temptations. Knowing our vulnerability, Satan attacks, entices, lures, and seduces us in those areas. He doesn't give up; in fact, his onslaught is continual. Often, daily, hour after hour, and seemingly minute by minute, we struggle. If the enemy can convince us that the powerful temptations will never decrease, we are more inclined finally to give in—and the foothold quickly becomes a stronghold.

What Actions Should Believers Take?

If you sense that you are under the persistent, long-term effects of spiritual oppression, these steps may help you move toward freedom:

- Ask your pastor or group leader to help you to evaluate whether you are, in fact, a Christian. Oppressive doubts about one's salvation may be the drawing conviction of the Holy Spirit. We must settle this issue before taking any other steps.
- Enlist a team of prayer partners who will pray for you to experience freedom. Be sure to enlist partners who themselves are walking in the full armor of God.
- Follow the pattern already established for overcoming the enemy: submit to God, resist the enemy, and stand in your faith. Learn to wear the armor of God.
- Confess to God any sin in your life (1 John 1:9).
- Confess your struggles to a trusted believer who will pray for you (Jas. 5:16).
- If the oppression continues, seek the help of a pastor or Christian counselor who might provide longer-term guidance.

> **If you feel you are being oppressed, place a star beside each action you feel God leading you to take this week. If you are not sensing oppression, thank God for His protection and care.**

DAY THREE

BINDING AND LOOSING

Today we will explore binding and rebuking the devil. In order to evaluate this practice, we will give a brief summary of popular teachings on the subject, then examine the teaching in light of Scripture.

Binding in Jesus' Name: The Popular Teaching

Many Christians teach that Satan must be bound in order for them to do God's work—or at least make it easier. Three times Jesus referenced the idea of binding in Matthew—12:29; 16:19; and 18:18. The need for

" 'How can anyone enter a strong man's house and carry off his possessions unless he first ties up the strong man? Then he can rob his house.' "

—Matthew 12:29

"They brought him a demon-possessed man who was blind and mute, and Jesus healed him, so that he could both talk and see. All the people were astonished and said, 'Could this be the Son of David?' "

"But when the Pharisees heard this, they said, 'It is only by Beelzebub, the prince of demons, that this fellow drives out demons,'

"Jesus knew their thoughts and said to them, ' "Every kingdom divided against itself will be ruined, and every city or household divided against itself will not stand. If Satan drives out Satan, he is divided against himself. How then can his kingdom stand? And if I drive out demons by Beelzebub, by whom do your people drive them out? So then, they will be your judges. But if I drive out demons by the Spirit of God, then the kingdom of God has come upon you." ' "

" 'Or again, how can anyone enter a strong man's house and carry off his possessions unless he first ties up the strong man? Then he can rob his house.' "

" 'He who is not with me is against me, and he who does not gather with me scatters. And so I tell you, every sin and blasphemy will be forgiven men, but the blasphemy against the Spirit will not be forgiven. Anyone who speaks a word against the Son of Man will be forgiven, but anyone who speaks against the Holy Spirit will not be forgiven, either in this age or in the age to come.' "

—Matthew 12:22-32

binding Satan can most clearly be seen from 12:29. Read Matthew 12:22-32 to understand the full context in which verse 29 occurs. Notice that:

- Jesus cast out a demon (v. 22).
- When challenged about it, Jesus taught that in order for a strong man's house to be robbed, he must first be bound (v. 29).
- Since Jesus just cast out a demon, and since the discussion revolved around Satan's kingdom, then we can assume that Jesus bound Satan in order to rob his house. That's why he could cast out the demon.

Those who practice binding Satan believe these verses encourage us to do what Jesus did and bind Satan in order to "plunder his house" (v. 29, NASB). This passage leads us to bind Satan when we are praying, especially when we take action to invade his territory.

Those who hold this view say the authority to bind is helpful in preventing potential demonic activity, or in limiting his attacks on us or others. Matthew 16:19 and 18:18 obviously make a connection between what happens in the physical realm to what happens in the spiritual realm. What we bind on earth will be bound in heaven; therefore, it is also wise to exercise this authority in prayer.

A Balanced Perspective

We believe binding Satan misses the mark for several reasons.

First, we disagree with the interpretation of Matthew 12:22-32. The passage is not about an approach to spiritual warfare but rather "Is Jesus the Messiah?" Consider the evidence:

- In verse 23 the people asked if Jesus was the Son of David, the Messiah.
- The Pharisees did not believe He was the Messiah; therefore they explained away His power. They sought to discredit Him by saying His power came from being the devil (v. 24).
- Jesus pointed out that they were wrong for two reasons. First, a kingdom divided cannot stand; therefore Satan wouldn't be fighting himself (vv. 25-26). Second, He asked by whose power everyone else cast out demons (v. 27). In other words, the Pharisees had a double standard.
- Jesus then appealed to the fact that He was the Messiah by pointing out that if He could drive out demons in the power of God, then God's kingdom was coming through Him (v. 28).
- In verse 29 the phrase "again" implies He was going to restate the same idea in different words. Luke 11:22 makes this point even more clear by saying, "when someone stronger attacks and overpowers him." In verses 28-29 Jesus wants them to understand that His superior strength validated who He was.
- In verse 32 He warned them against attributing the activity of God to the activity of Satan. Mark 3:30 says that the reason Jesus commented was because they were saying, "He has an evil spirit."
- Therefore, we can see that Jesus was not trying to prescribe a way to accomplish spiritual warfare but rather appealing to the fact that He was the Messiah who could bind Satan.

Second, nowhere in the Gospels did Jesus bind demons before He cast them out, nor did He bind Satan to limit his presence or activity. He let Satan have access to His life (Matt. 4:1-11; John 14:30), the disciples (Luke 22:31), and Judas (John 13:27). Evidently, Jesus was more concerned with victory through obedience and faithfulness to God rather than through limiting Satan.

Third, if we really could bind Satan in order to limit his influence, then why isn't his influence diminished? So many Christians have "bound' him that by now he should be nothing more than a giant ball of twine. However, he seems to be alive and well.

Fourth, if we bind Satan in the authority of Christ, how is it that he keeps becoming strong enough to get free? Or is binding for a limited time only? Does it wear off? The picture of Revelation 20:1-3 reveals that once God binds Satan, God determines when he will go free.

Fifth, the necessity of binding Satan in order for God's work to be done implies that Satan's power can influence and resist God's power. If this were true, then God would be less than God.

Sixth, the Bible teaches that Jesus has already disarmed Satan at the cross (Col. 2:15). His destruction is assured (Heb. 2:14). Why is there a need to bind, to temporarily limit Satan's power when the Bible pictures a much more severe treatment of him by God? Why should we revert to a lesser tactic when God has already employed a greater one? Why take out a restraining order against Satan when he has already been locked in prison?

Since the scriptural evidence to bind Satan is weak at best and very suspect, we should not develop a theology based on it. While we will not be so dogmatic as to prohibit someone from trying this approach, we encourage a healthy focus on God in order to seek His purposes and guidance in the midst of warfare. The energy spent on trying to limit Satan would be better spent on understanding God in order to fully obey Him.

Put an X on the scale to indicate your attitude toward the statement: energy should not be spent on limiting Satan but rather on understanding God in order to obey Him.

disagree   agree   wholeheartedly agree

Rebuking Satan: The Popular Teaching

Proponents of rebuking Satan say that when Satan is tempting, hindering, oppressing, or attempting to deceive, he should be rebuked and stopped. This view is held for at least two reasons.

First, in the Bible a general principle is that God often rebuked those who were doing evil. Second, more specifically, Satan was rebuked by the Lord on at least two occasions (Matt. 4:10, 16:23). Jesus also rebuked demons (Matt. 17:18; Mark 1:25).

Therefore, those who teach rebuking believe that since we have Christ's authority, we can and should rebuke Satan as well. Therefore, it's our responsibility to use our authority against him in prayer or when we see his manifestations in everyday life.

A Balanced Perspective

The above perspective is troubling for several reasons. First, the words *rebuke, rebuked, rebukes, rebuking* occur in 110 verses in the NKJV translation. In only 8 verses were the words used in connection with Satan. The vast majority of times the word is used God rebuked people, or people rebuked people. Satan receives very little focus.

Second, in every instance where Satan was rebuked, God or Jesus did the rebuking (Zech. 3:2; Matt. 17:18; Mark 1:25; 9:25; Luke 4:35; 4:41; 9:42; Jude 9). Third, of all the biblical prescriptions to deal with Satan, *rebuke* is not mentioned. The main strategies in the Bible are *resist* rather than retaliate (James 4:7; 1 Peter 5:9) and *stand* rather than attack (Eph. 6:11,13-14).

Rebuking Satan does not have much biblical support. The examples are scarce (8 out of 110), and when it was done, God did it. Therefore, we conclude that this lifestyle by believers should not be encouraged. Again, the goal is not to be dogmatic but rather to discourage an unhealthy focus on the devil. When rebuking does become a standard part of someone's prayer life, that person is out of balance.

> **The goal is to discourage an unhealthy focus on the devil.**

Personally, your authors don't practice rebuking the devil nor do we encourage it; however, if we were to allow for the possibility, there are at least two truths about rebuking that are often violated.

a. Many people rebuke Satan generally for anything he might do to create mischief. Their wording is often broad, like "Satan, I rebuke you and all that you're doing in this place." In the Bible, not only is it God who does the rebuking, but He also addresses specific situations (Zech. 3:1; Matt. 17:18; Mark 9:25; Luke 9:42).

b. Many people rebuke Satan with a spirit of arrogance. Tee shirts are printed saying, "Satan is ugly, cause Jesus beat him with a stick"; a popular children's song says, "And if the devil doesn't like it, he can sit on a tack." However, Jude 8-10 mentions a mark of the evil men is their harsh language against celestial beings. Arrogance toward Satan is not biblical. In fact, we see in Luke 10:17-20 that Jesus quickly moved to guard His disciples' attitude when they realized their authority over the demonic. He affirmed that He indeed gave the authority, but quickly tempered their exuberance by reminding them, "However, do not rejoice that the spirits submit to you, but rejoice that your names are written in heaven" (v. 20). Too many Christians have become arrogant, puffed up because of the superiority Christ gives. That is extremely dangerous.

A common mentality among proponents of binding and rebuking is to aggressively engage Satan and limit his power so that the kingdom of God can advance. In Scripture people did not practice binding and rebuking. Instead, Satan's power was broken by the brokenness of saints as they obeyed God. They did not seek power over the devil. They sought faithfulness to God. The by-product of obedience was that God broke the canceled power of Satan through them as they followed Him in their circumstances.

Defensive Methods Do Not Equal Passivity

Hopefully our advice about practicing binding or rebuking has not encouraged you toward passivity. Christians are not to do nothing; rather, we are to spend our energy seeking God and obeying Him rather than focusing on the devil.

In Scripture Satan's power was broken by the brokenness of saints as they obeyed God.

DAY FOUR

GENERATIONAL CURSES

Do you ever find yourself doing something exactly the way your mother or father did, even though you know it's offensive to God and others? Why do you repeat the behavior of your parents, even if you would rather not? Today we will look at a popular explanation for this phenomenon. Many say a "generational curse" may be at work.

Before examining the popular teaching we must first clarify the term. Some people use "generational curse" to mean nothing more than that the behavioral patterns of your parents have influenced yours. They observe that growing up in the same household has tremendous power to mold and shape a young life. This influence is so strong that we tend to imitate naturally, often subconsciously, what was modeled for us in our formative years.

Often a sinful behavior can be imitated in a family line for several generations.

Others use the term *generational* in a different sense. It is this second definition that we want to evaluate today.

Popular Teaching

Varying nuances of this teaching exist, but the core beliefs teach that the sins of the father or mother cause a curse in the form of satanic activity to be passed on to their children. This curse results from the violation of God's moral law that grants Satan legal access to the parents' life. Because of this legal access through the parents, a demon has rights to their offspring. The demon can replicate the same evil in the life of the child that he had in the parent.

Even though someone becomes a Christian, these curses inherited from the parents remain in effect until they are broken. This explains the struggle some Christians have with persistent, overpowering sins. For example, if the father was addicted to pornography, then the demon can make the son become a pornographer, too. The scriptural evidence cited for this position is as follows:

- Curses can be inherited through family lineages. Exodus 20:5; 34:7; Numbers 14:18; and Deuteronomy 5:9 reveal the sins of the fathers were passed to their children. Curses ride on family bloodline.

"You shall not bow down to them or worship them; for I, the Lord your God, am a jealous God, punishing the children for the sin of the fathers to the third and fourth generation of those who hate me."
—*Exodus 20:5*

"Maintaining love to thousands, and forgiving wickedness, rebellion and sin. Yet he does not leave the guilty unpunished; he punishes the children and their children for the sin of the fathers to the third and fourth generation."
—*Exodus 34:7*

"The Lord is slow to anger, abounding in love and forgiving sin and rebellion. Yet he does not leave the guilty unpunished; he punishes the children for the sin of the fathers to the third and fourth generation."
—*Numbers 14:18*

"You shall not bow down to them or worship them; for I, the Lord your God, am a jealous God, punishing the children for the sin of the fathers to the third and fourth generation of those who hate me."
—*Deuteronomy 5:9*

- Curses put on families continue in effect through the offspring for at least three or four generations unless they are broken (Ex. 20:5; 34:7; Num. 14:18; Deut. 5:9).
- Christ's work on the cross creates legal rights to break these curses.
- Christ's work does not become effective in a believer's life until he claims his legal rights to break the power of these curses. This process resembles breaking the power of our sinful natures. Sin has been dealt with positionally, but the flesh must be put to death by appropriating the power of the Holy Spirit. Similarly, Satan's power was broken at the cross, but it is our responsibility to take our authority in Christ and renounce curses inherited from our ancestors.

Those who teach breaking generational curses think a believer must take his authority in Christ and break these curses by declaring to Satan that he no longer has any authority or legal right over him. By so doing the believer will experience tremendous new freedom in Christ.

Scriptural Teaching

Your authors do not believe this teaching is true for several reasons. **First**, the verses used to prove the concept that satanic curses can be passed through family lineage are invalid. Read Exodus 20:5; 34:7; Numbers 14:18; and Deuteronomy 5:9 in the margin. These verses cannot prove the popular teaching because:

- The person visiting the sins of the fathers on the children to the third and fourth generation is God, not Satan. In three of the verses God Himself states He is the one visiting the sins on the children. In the other verse Moses simply quotes God. Why should someone sense the need to address Satan when God Himself has said from His very own mouth that He is the One initiating the action?
- If God is the initiator, then who can claim any power, reverse any action, or cancel anything He has decreed? How likely would it be for someone to be under the curse of God, and then announce to Him that they are breaking what He Himself has set in place? Only God has the prerogative to reverse His decision.

Second, the basic meaning of curse does not conform to the reality of what happened at the cross. As a verb *curse* either causes or invokes evil, misfortune, destruction, ruin or possibly death to the subject of the curse. As a noun, a curse is the wish, evil, destruction, ruin, or misfortune that comes upon someone. As an adjective, *cursed* is someone under the condition of evil, misfortune, punishment, or separation from God. The basic meaning of curse does not reflect what happened at the cross which provided victory and a restored relationship with God.

Third, the cross broke all curses and secured God's blessing (see Gal. 3:13; Col. 2:10-15; Eph. 2:14-16). In Colossians 2:9-15 Paul pointed out the completeness of Christ's work on our behalf.

Read the verses in the margin on the following page and list what Christ has done for you on your behalf.

_____

_____

_____

_____

_____

_____

_____

_____

Christ has dealt with the sinful nature, made us alive with Him, forgiven our sins, removed keeping the law as the basis of righteousness, and disarmed the powers and authorities. Basically, Paul said, *Whatever was against you, God has dealt with—including Satan.*

This disarming of the powers and authorities means that Satan no longer has rights or rule over Christians; therefore, he cannot curse us. Paul wrote in Ephesians 1:3, "Praise be to the God and Father of our Lord Jesus Christ, who has *blessed* us in the heavenly realms with every *spiritual blessing* in Christ (authors' italics)."

The law of the Spirit of life in Christ Jesus has set us free from the law of sin and death. Satan cannot make us sin, nor can he curse us. Revelation 12:10 strengthens this truth by declaring, " 'Now have come the salvation and the power and the kingdom of our God, and the authority of his Christ. For the accuser of our brothers, who accuses them before our God day and night, has been hurled down.' "

Fourth, if God has redeemed you, who can curse you? Ultimately God has the power to curse or bless. Those whom He has blessed cannot be cursed by another. Balaam tried to curse the children of Israel three times, but in all instances he could only bless (Num. 24:10-13). How likely would it be that Satan could curse any child of God? No wonder Paul said in Romans 8:31-39 that no one can condemn those God has justified; nothing can usurp His power over us.

Finally, the unlikelihood of Satan cursing may also be noted from the fact that in all 175 verses where cursing occurred, no record exists that Satan ever cursed anyone. The only time he even was mentioned in a verse with the word *curse* is when God cursed him in Genesis 3:14.

"In Christ all the fullness of the Deity lives in bodily form."
—**Colossians 2:9**

"You have been given fullness in Christ, who is the head over every power and authority."
—**Colossians 2:10**

"In him you were also circumcised, in the putting off of the sinful nature, not with a circumcision done by the hands of men but with the circumcision done by Christ."
—**Colossians 2:11**

"Having been buried with him in baptism and raised with him through your faith in the power of God, who raised him from the dead."
—**Colossians 2:12**

"When you were dead in your sins and in the uncircumcision of your sinful nature, God made you alive with Christ. He forgave us all our sins."
—**Colossians 2:13**

"Having canceled the written code, with its regulations, that was against us and that stood opposed to us; he took it away, nailing it to the cross."
—**Colossians 2:14**

"And having disarmed the powers and authorities, he made a public spectacle of them, triumphing over them by the cross."
—**Colossians 2:15**

Potential Dangers

The teaching of generational curses opens the door to two potential dangers. **First**, someone may focus too much on yesterday's sins and too little on today's issues. A tremendous amount of energy can be consumed on navel gazing, introspection, and dwelling on the past. Any time oppression occurs—or perhaps a person just has a bad day—he may wonder if some demon from his parents is pursuing him.

Second, a person can shift responsibility and blame to others. The sins he commits are not his fault but rather that of dad or mom. An unhealthy attitude of blame, disrespect, or despising can occur. When a person blames someone else, he does not assume responsibility for his own sins. Ironically, when that is the case, he never finds freedom in Christ, even though he may earnestly seek it.

Third, this teaching minimizes the total cancellation of all curses through the cross of Christ. Christ is the focus, not us or our parents.

DAY FIVE

DANGERS TODAY

The goal of the final lesson this week is to examine several areas of concern about contemporary approaches to spiritual warfare. We have previously looked at one concern—the danger of seeking power for the sake of power (week 7, day 3). In day 5 your authors will point out other potential problems with the contemporary warfare movement. As you study this lesson, pray that God will guard you from these dangers.

The Danger of Dualism

Dualism is the belief that God and Satan are equal beings. Since they are equal, no one can be certain which of the two will ultimately win the battle between them. Although we know of no leaders in the spiritual warfare movement who teach dualism, many of their teachings imply it. Some writers so focus on Satan's power that the enemy appears to be almost equal to God.

Others so emphasize our role in the spiritual battle that it seems the ultimate outcome is dependent on us—rather than on God, who is sovereign over all. If we pray the right prayer or discover the right name of the evil spirit, then God will be victorious. Good and evil are equal forces and with just a little help, the scales can be tipped in favor of one or the other. God is attempting to overcome evil, but He simply hasn't been able to do so yet.

As we've seen throughout this study, God and the devil are not equal, nor can Satan weaken God's sovereignty. God is eternal, but Satan was created (Ezek. 28:13). Indeed, God uses the devil to accomplish His will (2 Cor. 12:1-10). Satan now attacks us only with God's permission (Job 1:1-12; Luke 22:31-32).

The enemy's ultimate defeat is already guaranteed (Rev. 20:10). Satan was defeated by the cross (Col. 2:15). Regardless of how intense the battle becomes, we need to remember that Satan never has been, is not now, and never will be equal to God. In fact, he is a defeated foe.

> **Review the chart on page 13 contrasting a sovereign versus an unsovereign God. Underline what you consider to be the strongest arguments for your position.**

The Danger of Denying Personal Responsibility

Maybe you remember the television comedian named Flip Wilson, famous for the line, "The devil made me do it! The devil made me do it!" The character that Flip played continually deflected blame for wrong to the devil, and the joke typically evoked the audience's laughter. We take the same approach when we have a tendency to blame demons for most of our problems.

Think about these indications of this potential problem:

- Finding particular demons for particular sins (for example, a demon of lust causes a person to lust) risks denying personal responsibility.
- Seeking to name demons in order to overpower them tends to neglect needed attention to human responsibility. For example, we might be less likely to call people to repentance, or to turn from sin, when we focus only on the demons.
- Searching for territorial spirits in the air risks missing the problem on the ground—that is, sinful people are the issue more than controlling spirits.
- Some spiritual warfare counseling gives so much attention to root causes of oppression that accountability for actions today is neglected.

Personal responsibility for our actions, regardless of demonic influence, is a clear biblical teaching. The story of David's wrongly taking a census of the people of Israel is a good example of this truth (2 Sam. 24:1-17; 1 Chron. 21:1-17). Both God and the devil had a hand in testing David to take the census. The devil led David to commit the sin, but God allowed the tempting in order to carry out His judgment on the people. At no point, though, was David absolved of his responsibility in the sin.

To see this point, read 1 Chronicles 21:3. Satan enticed David, but Satan's voice wasn't the only one that David heard. His general Joab challenged him not to take the census, setting up a choice for which David would be responsible. Furthermore, David took full responsibility for his sin: "Then David said to God, 'I have sinned greatly by doing this. Now, I beg you, take away the guilt of your servant. I have done a very foolish thing' " (1 Chron. 21:8). In no way did David place the blame on the enemy who enticed him to do wrong. We are wise not to ignore the influence of the demonic, but we're also wise to understand that we are individually accountable for our own actions.

The Danger of Human-Centered Rather Than God-Centered Approaches to Warfare

Think back to week 1 day 1 of this study. In our analysis of the origins of Satan, we discovered that Satan likely was originally an angel whose

"But Joab replied, "May the LORD multiply his troops a hundred times over. My lord the king, are they not all my lord's subjects? Why does my lord want to do this? Why should he bring guilt on Israel?"
—1 Chronicles 21:3

159

"How you have fallen from heaven,
    O morning star, son of the dawn!
You have been cast down to the earth,
    You who once laid low the nations!
You said in your heart,
    'I will ascend to heaven;
I will raise my throne
    above the stars of God;
I will sit enthroned on the mount
    of assembly,
        on the utmost heights of the
        sacred mountain.
I will ascend above the tops of the
    clouds;
    I will make myself like the
Most High.'
But you are brought down to the
    grave,
        to the depths of the pit."
                        —Isaiah 14:12-15

desire for control led him to rebellion against God (Ezek. 28:11-19; Isa. 14:12-15). The personal pronoun *I* referring to Satan echoes throughout the accounts of Satan's fall.

Read Isaiah 14:12-15 and circle the pronoun *I* each time it occurs.

You should have circled five uses of the personal pronoun. Clearly, Satan desired to be the center of the attention. That issue—who is the center of attention?—is the concern here. Few believers who recognize the reality of spiritual warfare intentionally seek to be the center of attention. Nevertheless, sometimes we unintentionally direct the attention to ourselves by our wording: *Satan, I rebuke you. I cast you out. I bind you, Satan. I break any powers that control this area.* Do you hear the focus on self?

At other points, we want others to know just how spiritually powerful we are. Have you ever been tempted to proudly tell others what God seems to be doing through you? Even during this study, have you ever felt that you were on a higher spiritual plane because you are studying spiritual warfare?

The point is not that we should never use the personal pronoun *I* or tell others what God is doing. Rather, the point is that we should conduct spiritual warfare in God's way so that He alone gets the glory. The attention to Him must increase, and any attention to us must decrease.

Often we are unaware of a focus on self unless God brings self-focus to our attention. Take the "I" challenge. When you are in conversation with another person today (or pick a day), challenge yourself to deflect the conversation back to the other person as much as possible. Ask questions that will lead to a response other than "yes" or "no." By so doing, you will train yourself to seek to get to know others rather than seeking to promote yourself.

The Danger of an Overemphasis on Satan

For too long, many believers ignored the reality of Satan. Satan was thought to be only a mythical character or an impersonal force who really didn't affect individual lives. The good news is that the current interest in spiritual warfare has countered that error by reminding us of the reality and the power of the enemy. The bad news is that the same interest has in some ways led to an unhealthy focus on Satan.

Maybe you've read C. S. Lewis's classic work, *The Screwtape Letters.* This fictional book details a series of letters between a senior demon and a junior demon, whom the elder demon is mentoring. In the preface to this book, Lewis warned his readers that human beings usually commit one of two errors in relation to the demons: we ignore them, or we become fascinated with them.[1] Regrettably, the latter problem has now become more common, and we often give the devil more attention than he deserves.

As a result, books and videos that put more emphasis on Satan's power against believers than God's power through the cross are more popular than ever. Paul warned against these factors in Titus 1:10-11. As Christians, though, we must always exalt Christ.

Remember, spiritual warfare is about so focusing on God that we recognize the enemy when he comes in a counterfeit way. Perhaps these general questions will help you to evaluate resources and conferences on spiritual warfare:

Evaluating Resources on Spiritual Warfare
- Has this resource directed my attention more to God or to the devil?
- Do I want to serve God more after having read this book, listened to this tape, or attended this conference?
- Does this resource clearly emphasize God's guaranteed victory, or does it leave me wondering who will win in the end?
- Does this resource stress the cross of Jesus as the site of spiritual victory?
- Do I fear the devil more after having used this resource, or do I love and trust God more?
- Do I have a stronger desire for God, or am I only motivated to fight the devil?

The Danger of Overreacting to the Dangers

We've recognized throughout these weeks of study the potential dangers of the contemporary approach to spiritual warfare. In fact, this particular lesson only reinforces those concerns. On the other hand, our goal is not to react so strongly against the dangers that we miss the needed emphases in today's warfare approaches.

There are several reasons for studying spiritual warfare and promoting that study to other believers. First, emphasizing the reality of Satan is needed in our society, especially since only 43 percent of Christians strongly disagree with the statement "Satan is not a living being but is a symbol of evil."[2] Many spiritual warfare writers focus on using warfare strategies to reach unbelievers, and that commitment to evangelism is an important one.

In addition, helping believers to understand Satan's schemes in order to counter them is essential if we want believers to live victorious Christian lives. Hence, some writers are teaching ideas and concepts that we need to know—we don't want to throw out the truths with the problems.

Do you know of any other contemporary issues or writers on spiritual warfare today that you wish to discuss with your group? Ask your group leader to compile these questions and seek the input of your pastor, church staff member, deacon, Sunday School teacher, or other knowledgeable student of the Bible. Apply the questions in the shaded box on page 161.

Our goal throughout this study has been to approach spiritual warfare from a biblical perspective. We must maintain that goal, even if the biblical truths about demons and warfare stretch us beyond our comfort zone. Biblical truth remains our guide. May God keep you anchored in the Bible, and may He give you His perspective from it. And may God increase your confidence in His eternal victory for you in your salvation in Christ.

---

[1]C. S. Lewis, *The Screwtape Letters* (New York: MacMillan, 1961), 3.
[2]George Barna, *Growing True Disciples* (Ventura: Issachar, 2000), 56.

VIEWER GUIDE

1. We no longer _____ the enemy.

   He really does want to _____ us.

2. Can Christians be influenced by demons?

   Possession implies _____; therefore, Satan cannot possess them.

   However, Christians can be _____ by Satan.

3. The devil is always subservient to the one who created all things.

   He is not _____ to God.

4. God's coming to this world was to take the offense.

   Our call is to go out into this same world to live lives of _____,

   speak the truth, share the gospel, and raise up churches that _____ God.

5. Chuck's fear: We have brought churches together and cocooned ourselves.

   We have put the _____ over our light

   and the _____ goes out.

6. Prayer walking is praying on site with _____.

7. Spiritual warfare is about so knowing _____ that we know the

   difference when the _____ comes.

8. The Christian life is not about responding to the devil.

   It's about _____ with Him.

Discerning God's Voice

CASE STUDY

Susan had a habit of overeating. She had often lost the extra weight, only to gain it back. Lately she was in one of those gain-it-back cycles. Getting dressed one morning she sighed because fudging on her diet (no pun intended) had begun expressing itself in unflattering ways. Susan felt defeated. She knew she was not honoring God by the way she fed her body. She had confessed to the Lord a hundred times and promised to do better, but here she was again in the same old pattern.

Her mind flooded with feelings of worthlessness, guilt, and discouragement. *Why don't I have more self-control? I'm a pathetic failure! The only reason God loves a charity case like me is because it's His job.* Susan wondered if these thoughts were coming from God. She began praying, waiting for God to lower the boom.

One of the most commonly asked questions in spiritual warfare is, *How do I know the difference between the voice of God and the voice of Satan? How do I know if I'm hearing from the right source?* The next five days we will contrast five differing messages that we receive. We will explore how God speaks versus how Satan speaks.

DAY ONE

CONDEMNATION VS. CONVICTION

Has Susan's scenario ever played itself out in your mind? Perhaps food is not your particular weakness. Think about your area of vulnerability. Have you had similar thoughts of guilt and condemnation about your actions? What do you sense God saying to you when you feel you have sinned? How does He convict you?

Does God Speak to Condemn His Own?
God will only speak to you in agreement with His Word. He has some very specific things to say in the Bible about condemnation.

Read Romans 8:1-2 in the margin. How much condemnation does a believer in Christ Jesus face?

❑ 0%   ❑ 33%   ❑ 66%   ❑ 100%

Therefore, when you feel or think thoughts of condemnation, is God speaking to you? ❑ Yes ❑ No

"There is now no condemnation for those who are in Christ Jesus, because through Christ Jesus the law of the Spirit of life set me free from the law of sin and death."
—*Romans 8:1-2*

According to the Scripture, those who are in Christ Jesus are not condemned. If you feel condemned—that is, worthless, hopeless, or without any possibility for change—God is not the voice you are hearing. You may say, *Wait a minute! I always feel condemnation when I sin. In fact, a lot of times I just feel condemned in general even when I haven't sinned. You mean that's not God's voice?*

Let's explain what Paul meant about no condemnation. While it is true we have sinned and deserve to be condemned, God has provided a way of forgiveness. The cross satisfied the requirements of justice and established a new standard of justification. We are justified by faith in Christ. Knowing the truth about our status in Christ grants us permission to reject the voices that condemn us and embrace forgiveness.

The devil often accuses us with the facts. He points to sins we have committed. Fortunately, Satan's accusations are inadmissible in God's court because of the cross. God ultimately determines the evidence against us. Not only have we been forgiven, but now, we are His children. Paul said in Romans 8:33-34, "Who will bring any charge against those whom God has chosen? It is God who justifies. Who is he that condemns? Christ Jesus, who died—more than that, who was raised to life—is at the right hand of God and is also interceding for us." Paul was saying, "If God declared you innocent, who can condemn you?"

The fact that God does not condemn you does not imply that God is unconcerned about your sin. It means that you no longer live under the spiritual sentence of death that your guilt deserves. Your identity is not that of a sinner, nor are you eternally separated from God.

What Is Self-Condemnation?

Feelings of condemnation do not just happen in a vacuum. They stem from an internal belief system that says you are worthy of condemnation. The devil is called the accuser because he constantly points out the evidence of our sin, failures, and shortcomings to convince us of our worthlessness. If we believe him, we have condemned ourselves.

If God does not condemn you for sin, what is the likelihood that self-condemnation is from Him?

If you battle feelings of self-condemnation, what is likely the problem? (Check all that apply.)
❑ I am looking at the evidence of my failures.
❑ I am listening to how the devil interprets the evidence.
❑ I am believing my feelings.
❑ I enjoy feeling guilty. It excuses my behavior.
❑ I am paying attention to what others say.
❑ I am looking at the cross and God's perspective.

Self-condemnation produces feelings of worthlessness and despair. In Susan's case, she felt tremendously guilty for overeating. She knew it was harmful, but she did it anyway. Afterward, she felt terrible. That sickening, inescapable gnawing sensation chewed away at her insides. What person hasn't experienced that feeling—often so strong, it's almost overpowering?

Gaining weight made a statement to Susan about her personhood. She viewed herself as a failure. Other areas of her life also caused her to feel that way. She thought about her cluttered house and her unruly children. A vague sense of inadequacy pervaded her life. She wondered why she couldn't shake those feelings and rise above them.

Have you had similar feelings? ❑ Yes ❑ No

What do you think could help you overcome them?

_____

_____

Susan's self-condemnation produced three negative consequences: **First,** she withdrew from God in shame rather than seeking to restore her relationship with Him. **Second,** her guilty feelings undercut her confidence in God's power to forgive and restore. **Third,** she developed a warped view of God. She saw Him as harsh and continually displeased with her.

Self-condemnation does not lead to repentance and change. Satan knows that and tries to use our disobedience against us. He tries to convince us that we cannot change or that God's power is insufficient to overcome our besetting sin. In addition, Satan leads us to obsess about our guilt. We heap such self-condemnation on ourselves that we have great difficulty climbing out of the abyss.

In a radically different approach to Satan's, God convicts of sin without leaving us with feelings of condemnation. Instead, God's presence is a tender place of compassion and mercy.

How God Speaks to Convict of Sin

Because He is holy, God cannot fellowship with unholiness. If we choose to sin, God will hold us accountable. When we experience God's conviction for sin, remember that His purpose is always repentance and restoration of our relationship with Him. We can recognize His voice of conviction by these outcomes:

1. **We will be convinced of the truth.** Recall from week 4, day 1, that God is concerned about our minds. When He convicts us of sin, He seeks to touch our understanding so that we will be convinced of the truth of what He says. We will recognize our sin for what it is and confess why we were wrong. God's goal is for us to see our sin from His perspective. When that happens, we agree with God about our sin.

2. **We will experience grief.** Instead of feeling condemned for our sin, we will feel grief when we view the sin against the backdrop of a love relationship with God; we are sorry for how it affects the One we love. That's why sorrow is a natural reaction. Condemnation focuses on self instead of God. We are preoccupied with how *we* performed, what *we* did. Fixating on self results in a vicious cycle of replaying failures. That's why grief—not wallowing in guilt—is a work of God's conviction.

3. **Our relationship with Him will grow stronger.** God is love (1 John 4:8). Love by nature seeks the well-being of others. The fact that God convicts us of sin proves His love. If He let us continue in sin, that path would lead to self-destruction. If He dealt with us according to His power, His anger would destroy us. Instead, God works in such a way that His children are built up rather than torn down. By leading us to repentance, He reestablishes fellowship with Him and thereby grants us all the resources of heaven.

> **Based on the three outcomes listed above, which would likely be the voice of God? (Check all that apply.)**
> ❏ You experience feelings of condemnation leading you constantly to replay your failures.
> ❏ You understand how much of a sinner you are. You conclude you'll never be of much use to God. You are a hopeless case.
> ❏ You recognize your sin and know why you were wrong.
> ❏ You feel grief for how your sin has affected your relationship with the Father.

If your lifestyle is characterized by guilt and condemnation, yet you have repented of every known sin, fight this spiritual battle in the same way you would fight any other type of spiritual warfare. Jesus said that man lives on " 'every word that comes from the mouth of God' " (Matt. 4:4). Saturate your mind with the truth that God has forgiven you completely and remembers your sins no more (Isa. 43:25).

Memorizing verses and quoting them in moments of battle will help you reject lies and walk in truth. Learn to discern what is of God and what is not of God. Recognize God's voice when He speaks by daily feeding on His Word.

DAY TWO

DISCOURAGEMENT VS. ENCOURAGEMENT

Two years ago Maria left her church because of a split. Now her present church was experiencing turmoil over changes made by the new pastor. At an unexpected lunch encounter with a church friend, Maria heard more bad news. A group was being formed to confront the pastor at the next business meeting.

Maria felt discouraged. Weren't Christians supposed to love each other? She thought about leaving this church too. Maybe running into her friend was God's way of warning her. Maybe God was calling her to go somewhere else. Was that thought from Him? How would she know?

Discouragement and Encouragement in the Bible

Bible writers typically related both concepts to a person's relationship with God. Discouragement was anything that hindered confidence in God, which led to decreased faith, perseverance, motivation to action, or obedience.

Encouragement was anything that strengthened the heart to stay faithful to God. Bible translators used the words *encouragement, exhortation, comfort,* and *consolation* to translate the one word in Greek that comes closest to our word for *encouragement.*

Discouragement Is not from God

Your authors are not defining discouragement as a temporary dip in your emotions but rather as a state of mind in which God is considered to be limited, powerless, or ineffective. Discouragement is not from God because of the following reasons:

Jesus did not give in to discouragement—Read Isaiah's startling prophecy about the ministry of Jesus. The Hebrew word *discouraged* means *broken.* Jesus certainly had reason to be discouraged. He spent three and a half years pouring His life into others. However, the leaders crucified Him, the people turned on Him, His disciples abandoned Him, and even God turned from Him. He died naked, alone, despised, and rejected, a man of sorrows and acquainted with grief. Yet Jesus did not view God as limited, powerless, or ineffective. He maintained His confidence in God.

God never affirmed discouragement as His will—God never found a discouraged person and said, *It's OK. I know it's been tough lately. You just stay the way you are.* Quite the opposite happened. When He spoke to discouraged people such as Elijah (1 Kings 19:9-18), the nation of Israel (Isa. 50:1-4), or Jeremiah (Jer. 15:18-19), God specifically addressed their state of mind. Sometimes He even became angry when His people caved in to discouragement (Num. 21:4-6; 32:9-13).

If God spoke to discourage, it would violate His nature—God's words do not lead to defeatism, weakness, or demotivation. Instead, they renew our confidence and strength in Him. When God speaks, His words will be truth and will give us life. Sometimes God disciplines us,

The word translated encouragement, exhortation, consolation, *or* comfort *is often* Paraclesis. *In the Gospel of John, Jesus called the Holy Spirit the PARACLETE. These two concepts are taken from the same Greek root.*[1]

" 'He will not falter or be discouraged till he establishes justice on earth. In his law the islands will put their hope.' "
—*Isaiah 42:4*

and those times can seem discouraging. Hebrews 12:5-6 gives us the filter through which we understand God's actions. He only acts in our best interests. Therefore, God does not speak to discourage us.

List a specific way God has encouraged you recently.

_____

Discouragement Is a Form of Spiritual Warfare

Recall the story of Job (see page 11). God asked Satan if he had noticed Job's integrity. Satan responded by saying Job would curse God if He touched Job's body. After receiving permission, Satan returned to earth and afflicted Job with a disease. In his suffering, Job's wife asked him a most interesting question, "Are you still holding on to your integrity? Curse God and die!" (Job 2:9). Satan sought to discourage Job through his wife's words. He urged Job to give up, to throw in the towel, to call it quits. Why should he continue to be faithful to God?

The Bible often uses the word *faint* when describing those who give up (Ps. 143:4). Just as our physical bodies can grow weary, our hearts can lose strength. Those overcome by discouragement collapse in their hearts; they faint. By contrast, encouragement is the refreshing of the heart resulting in steadfastness. When God spoke at the end of the Book of Job, Job's heart turned again toward God (Job 40:1-5; 42:1-6).

Have you encountered this type of spiritual warfare? Upon seminary graduation, I (John) pastored in a transitional community. I lived below the poverty line, and I had no close friends. Over time, my mind began dwelling on the pain, and I put limits on how much access God could have to my life. Knowing my situation, my brother paid for me to go to a conference as a getaway. The leader spoke about the difficulties in which the biblical character Joseph found himself. Because Joseph's heart remained open to God, he received a tremendous blessing.

During the sermon I realized that discouragement and bitterness had crept into my heart. I renewed my commitment for God to have access to every part of my life. God's victory in my spirit led to a renewed fellowship with Him. In this situation God spoke through my brother, a preacher, and Scripture to encourage my heart in perseverance.

In the margin, describe a time when discouragement raged in your soul.

Think of someone who might be in a similar situation. Does God want you to be available to make a phone call, send a card, write a letter or email, or take some other action to strengthen him or her? Write the name of the person and the action you will take.

_____

"My son, do not make light of the Lord's discipline, and do not lose heart when he rebukes you, because the Lord disciplines those he loves, and he punishes everyone he accepts as a son."
—Hebrews 12:5-6

"Consider him who endured such oppositions from sinful men, so that you will not grow weary and lose heart."
—Hebrews 12:3

We need to clarify two points about encouragement. **First,** do not think that someone who discourages you from a particular plan of action is necessarily the voice of Satan. Often God sends others to warn us when we are about to make unwise decisions. The issue is whether someone is discouraging you in your relationship with God. One of the ways you can discern the voice of Satan is by the resulting fruit. If the fruit produces a lower resolve to follow God, you are not hearing God's voice.

Second, changing plans is not necessarily a sign of a discouraged quitter. There is no glory in sticking with a plan that God is not blessing. The key is discerning God's leading.

Why Are We Susceptible to Discouragement?

At certain times we are more susceptible to discouragement than at other times. Below are five factors that contribute to discouragement.

Unmet expectations—Genesis 4 records that God accepted Abel's offering but not Cain's. As a result Cain became "very angry, and his face was downcast" (4:5). His unmet expectation led to disappointment with God. Because Cain refused to repent, his bitterness led him to murder his brother. First John 3:12 records the spiritual warfare involved by saying "Cain ... belonged to the evil one." When we have certain expectations of God that are unrealistic or unfounded, we can feel discouraged when God does not "come through" for us.

Pain—Satan struck Job with painful sores from head to toe (Job 2:7). When his friends came to see him, they sat with him for seven days without saying a word because they saw his great suffering (2:13). The pain level added to Job's sense of God's injustice (13:24), thereby making him more susceptible to discouragement. Spiritual pain can be even more dangerous than physical pain. Both Jeremiah and Baruch encountered discouragement because of internal hurt (Jer. 15:18; 45:2-3). When our souls carry pain, we can lose heart and become discouraged in our relationship with God.

Hardships—In 1 Thessalonians 3:1-5 Paul sent Timothy to check on the Thessalonian church. He knew they were encountering difficulties, and his greatest fear was that "the tempter might have tempted you" (v. 5) and their labor would have been useless. Of course, the church stood the test, but we should not miss the principle. Paul knew that hardships create a great danger for someone to become discouraged in their relationship with God. Paul knew that Satan could have an opportunity to attack.

Fatigue—Elijah battled the evil kingdom of Ahab. At the moment when the nation was poised to return to God, Queen Jezebel tried to squelch the movement and kill Elijah, who fled for his life. He became so discouraged that he prayed he might die. God did not grant his request. Instead, He let him sleep and angels fed him (1 Kings 18-19). Elijah's greatest immediate need was rest. Fatigue contributed to his susceptibility to discouragement.

Focusing on circumstances—The children of Israel refused to go into the promised land because 10 spies reported that they could not conquer it. The people responded in Deuteronomy 1:28 by saying,

"Where can we go? Our brothers have made us lose heart. They say, 'The people are stronger and taller than we are; the cities are large, with walls up to the sky. We even saw the Anakites there.' " The people became discouraged when they focused on the size of the inhabitants and the height of the walls. Because they looked at circumstances and not God, they wandered in the wilderness for 40 years.

Which of these most often causes you to be susceptible to discouragement? (Check one.)

❏ unmet expectations ❏ pain
❏ focusing on circumstances ❏ hardships
❏ fatigue

How does discouragement affect your relationship with God? Write your response in the margin.

The Nature of God Is to Encourage

Read Romans 15:4-5 in the margin. Paul made the point that the Bible was written to teach us, so that we might endure and be encouraged. In fact, the intent to encourage so characterizes God that Paul called Him "the God who gives endurance and encouragement." When we are encouraged in spiritual things, we should immediately sense that God is speaking to us, whether through reading Scripture, talking with a friend, or reading His Word.

"Everything that was written (in Scripture) in the past was written to teach us, so that through endurance and the encouragement of the Scriptures we might have hope. May the God who gives endurance and encouragement give you a spirit of unity among yourselves as you follow Christ Jesus."
—Romans 15:4-5

Mark the following statements with the letter *E* for encouragement or *D* for discouragement.

1. _____ I watch the news and see there's no hope for our country.
2. _____ I read the Bible and conclude I can never be as good as the saints of old.
3. _____ Scripture tells me that God is a very present help in time of trouble.
4. _____ A lost family member rebuffs my attempts to witness. I conclude that God is probably finished with them.
5. _____ I can't control my tongue. I guess that's just my personality.
6. _____ A friend gave me some advice that solved my problem!
7. _____ The sermon motivated me to be more diligent in prayer.

Answers 1, 2, 4, and 5 are *D*. Answers 3, 6, and 7 are *E*.

DAY THREE

CONFUSION VS. CLARITY

Brad resigned a good job six months ago to start a ranch for disadvantaged children. He had enjoyed his job, but Brad was restless and wanted to impact the next generation. When the opportunity for the ranch arose, Brad and his wife Paige prayed about it. Every indication led them to believe God had opened a door.

However, sponsors withdrew support, and the ranch began operating in the red. Brad dipped into their personal savings. He was determined to trust God but wondered why God would let finances become an issue if He had called them to this work. Had they heard God correctly? To complicate matters, his former employer contacted him about possibly returning.

Paige shared Brad's desire for the ranch, but she knew it would be financially wiser for Brad to take his former job. Was God testing them? She certainly didn't want to fail a test, but neither did she want to lose their savings. Her thoughts went back and forth like a ping-pong ball. Both Brad and Paige were in a state of confusion.

God's Voice Does Not Produce Confusion

What is the source of confusion? Read 1 Corinthians 14:33.

According to the verse, does God's voice create confusion?
❑ Yes ❑ No

> *"God is not the author of confusion but of peace, as in all the churches of the saints."*
> —*1 Corinthians 14:33 (NKJV)*

God is not the author of confusion. His voice does not fill your life with indecision, blurry thinking, or chaos. Satan, on the other hand, does seek to confuse and distort.

What Is Confusion?

The dictionary tells us that *confusion* is a compound of the prefix *con* meaning "with" and the noun *fusion* meaning "mixing together." Hence *confusion* suggests any mixing, blending, or adding together that blurs identities and distinctions. The synonyms of *confusion* are *disarray, clutter, jumble, snarl, muddle,* and *chaos.* Confusion suggests a mixture that creates disorder.

What Causes Confusion?

Humans are mental, emotional, physical, and spiritual beings. These four realities produce a rich mixture of ideas, opinions, values, feelings, desires, goals, motives, and preferences in every individual and relationship. Confusion is created from these elements in two ways.

When we cannot order them—We couldn't function if all these elements were allowed free reign in our lives. We must be able to sort them by their priorities. Our brains must put together each one in an interlocking way like someone putting together the pieces of a puzzle. Until the brain can organize differing components in such a way that the puzzle makes sense, we will remain confused and uncertain.

For example, Paige was trying to make sense of several different elements: impacting the lives of young boys, being faithful to her husband, and worrying about finances. These multiple thoughts were not yet sorted in her mind according to priorities, so she felt confused.

Not everyone who is confused about God's will is under the influence of Satan's voice. Confusion at certain times and in certain ways is a normal part of our growth in the Christian life. However, God doesn't want us to stay confused. His process is to bring us to peace regarding the issues and decisions of life.

When they compete with each other—Confusion is not a mental process alone. Many times we end up in internal conflict because we want to have our cake and eat it too. When one or more conflicting desires, emotions, or fears exist, they compete with one another, throwing us into turmoil. Paige wanted to do God's will, but she wanted God's will to be financially secure. She was having trouble reconciling the two, but she wanted both. The competition created chaos.

Confusion is not just an individual problem but a corporate one as well. Acts 19:29-32 (NKJV) records a riot in Ephesus, "The whole city was filled with confusion" and "Some therefore cried one thing and some another, for the assembly was confused, and most of them did not know why they had come together." In this case confusion was a disruption in the harmony of the citizens of Ephesus. People were at odds with each other because they didn't know what was happening. The relationships in the city could be restored again when they could make sense of the turmoil.

In the same way, a church can be thrown into confusion by disagreement, varying opinions, or gossip. The ensuing turmoil is a state of chaos. Peace is restored when members seek clarity and unity.

Place an X on the scale to describe your typical inner life.

confusion   clarity

Establish Guiding Principles

When you are experiencing confusion, establish guiding principles from which to make choices or to discipline desires. The opposite of disorder is order. The opposite of confusion is harmony. Guiding principles can prioritize our thoughts and desires. For example, athletes know which foods to eat based on the principle of what best conditions their bodies.

Because He had settled the principles that would guide His life, Jesus was never confused. When Satan tempted Him, He was so familiar with the principles that He instantly recognized how they would be violated. Therefore, He never lost His compass.

Determining your guiding principles simplifies life. You don't spend enormous amounts of time or energy trying to make decisions. You are not overly dependent on others for advice. You need only a few guiding principles for most decisions in life. Four key guiding principles follow:

Love for God—Will my relationship with God be stronger before or after this decision?

Love for others—Will others be helped or hindered? Am I seeking personal gain or the best interests of others even if I have to pay a price?

Kingdom advancement—How will this decision impact my desire to advance the kingdom? Will it advance or deter the cause of Christ?

DETERMINING GUIDING PRINCIPLES
Love for God
Love for others
Kingdom advancement
Character

Character—Will I compromise the standard of holiness in any way? Is this in agreement with the nature and character of God?

A person without guiding life principles stands defenseless against a satanic onslaught. Those who are casual about studying the Bible should not be surprised if they are confused about knowing God's will.

If you are not grounded in God's Word, you may be deceived about the truth. If you can't refute doubts or lose sight of the truth through the bombardment of differing views, you may succumb. Settling your key principles enables you to discern truth when the world presents you with new propositions.

Identify a decision you recently faced that caused confusion at the time. Apply the four principles listed above to your decision.

Decision: _____

Did it help or hinder love for God? ❑ Yes ❑ No

Did it contribute to love for others? ❑ Yes ❑ No

Did it advance the kingdom? ❑ Yes ❑ No

Did it promote character development? ❑ Yes ❑ No

What other guiding principles informed your thinking? Thank God for principles that guide you to the truth when you are making difficult choices.

Seeking Clarity

Christians can expect Satan to seek to subvert them through confusion in at least one of three ways. We will examine these tactics and suggest ways to seek clarity.

Bombarding your mind—Often Satan will bombard your mind with multiple thoughts. When you need to make a decision, suddenly your mind will be flooded with thoughts such as, *How will I know if this will turn out right? What will so-and-so think? How will this affect me a year from now? Why do these things happen to me?* You will find it more difficult to focus on the right course of action. You are also likely to become overwhelmed and unable to function at all. When your mind is being bombarded, God is not the source of confusion. Return to your guiding principles. Let them determine your questions. Sometimes writing them on a sheet of paper will help organize your thinking.

Forgetting the truth—The writer of Psalm 78 recited the disobedience of the Israelites in the desert and gave a key reason for it.

"The men of Ephraim, though armed with bows, turned back on the day of battle; they did not keep God's covenant and refused to live by his law. They forgot what he had done, the wonders he had shown them."

—Psalm 78:9-11

Read verses 9-11 in the margin and circle the words that indicate why Israel sinned.

Obviously the Israelites forgot; they did not remember what God had done for them. Spiritual amnesia of the past created an inability to have clarity in the present. Probably the Israelites never set out to forget God. but the crisis of the moment created confusion, chaos, disorder, and distraction. In the same way, Satan knows that if he can create enough confusion, you will likely forget who God is and what He has done.

Once you forget God's past actions on your behalf, you will have difficulty resisting satanic schemes. To counter this tendency, find practical ways to recall God's past faithfulness, such as a family faith scrapbook, oral and written family histories, and remembrances at special family gatherings such as holidays, weddings, and funerals.

Questioning the truth—If Satan cannot succeed in the first two tactics, he often will try to create doubt as to the truth or challenge it. In Genesis 3 he asked Eve, "Did God really say...?" He wanted Eve to second-guess the validity of God's command.

Satan will seek to create doubt in your mind as to the truth of God's Word. Recall the subtle ways Satan tempts us to sin (see page 53). As you stay grounded in God's Word and seek His will in daily decisions, your confusion will give way to clarity as God enlightens your mind.

DAY FOUR

FEAR/WORRY VS. PEACE

Bill's son, Aaron, attended a local college. In high school, involvement in drugs had landed Aaron in juvenile court. For the last year, however, Aaron had been active in the youth group in his church, and he was dating a Christian. In addition, many of his Christian friends attended his college.

God had done much good in Aaron's life, but Bill knew Aaron needed time to let the changes solidify into character. At the end of the first semester, Bill heard through the grapevine that Aaron was pulling back from Christians on campus and hanging out with a crowd of questionable character. Fear filled Bill's heart. Was the rumor true? If so, was God warning him to take immediate action?

God's Voice Does Not Lead to Fear

We develop fears because of life experiences. Fear is a common human inclination. We have all had enough bad things happen to us that we expect painful experiences to regularly invade our lives.

In the middle of our logic—supported by life experiences—God constantly commands us not to fear. For example, in the Book of Matthew God told Joseph not to be afraid to take Mary as his wife (1:20). Jesus rebuked the disciples' fear when He calmed the Sea of Galilee (8:26). Jesus told His disciples not to fear those who could kill the body (10:28). When He walked on the water, He told the disciples not to be afraid (14:27). At the mount of transfiguration Jesus addressed their fear (17:7). When prophecing about the end times, He told them not to be troubled (24:6).

Scripture encourages boldness in response to fear. Second Timothy 1:7 confirms, "For God has not given us a spirit of fear, but of power and of love and of a sound mind" (NKJV). Many of the verses that address prayer have the words *confidence, boldness, faith,* or *expectation* in them. We are told to come to the throne of grace boldly; the confidence we have in Him is that He hears; we have boldness to enter the Holy of Holies; we ask in faith. All these words indicate the opposite of fear. If fact, one of the manifestations of having been with Jesus is boldness (Acts 4:13).

When you have thoughts that lead to fear, what is the likelihood that they are from God?

Strong likelihood   Unlikely

God did expect people to fear Him with holy reverence. Many texts say essentially "fear God" (Lev. 19:14; 25:17). Fear and reverence for God is quite different from fear of man or what man can do to us. In fact, the more we fear God, the less we will fear other things. God's Word assures us that we shouldn't be afraid when God is leading us.

Jesus Lived Free from Fear

No record exists that Jesus was ever afraid, even when He should have been by any reasonable human standard. For example, Jesus wasn't frightened by storms that threatened others. Peter, James, and John were professional fishermen. They had spent their entire lives fishing the Sea of Galilee. They knew a life-threatening storm when they saw it. When they gave their professional advice to Jesus that they were perishing, no one in all Israel was more qualified to render that opinion. But the first words out of Jesus' mouth were, " 'You of little faith, why are you so afraid?' " (Matt. 8:26).

When Jesus was about to be thrown off the cliff at His hometown, He simply looked at the people and passed right through them (Luke 4:28-30). When He was on trial, the only one who became afraid was Pilate (John 19:8). Jesus is our example. We can have the same confidence in God that Jesus displayed on every occasion.

In the margin read an excerpt from Jesus' most famous sermon (Matt. 5–7). Circle the words *worry* or *worrying* every time they appear.

How many words did you circle? _____
What value did Jesus give to worry? ❏ None ❏ A lot

These verses contain five examples. Two times Jesus prohibited worry. Three times He framed it as a leading question. The God who commands us not to fear also commands us not to worry.

" *'Therefore I tell you, do not worry about your life, what you will eat or drink; or about your body, what you will wear. Is not life more important than food, and the body more important than clothes? Look at the birds of the air; they do not sow or reap or store away in barns, and yet your heavenly Father feeds them. Are you not much more valuable than they? Who of you by worrying can add a single hour to his life? And why do you worry about clothes? See how the lilies of the field grow. They do not labor or spin. Yet I tell you that not even Solomon in all his splendor was dressed like one of these. If that is how God clothes the grass of the field, which is here today and tomorrow is thrown into the fire, will he not much more clothe you, O you of little faith? So do not worry, saying, "What shall we eat?" or "What shall we drink?" or "What shall we wear?" For the pagans run after all these things, and your heavenly Father knows that you need them. But seek first his kingdom and his righteousness, and all these things will be given to you as well. Therefore do not worry about tomorrow, for tomorrow will worry about itself. Each day has enough trouble of its own.' "*
—*Matthew 6:25-34*

Worry Is a Form of Fear

Worry is actually a form of fear. The motive for worry stems from fear of the negative consequences. Notice the examples Jesus used in His sermon. He addressed peoples' fears that they would not have enough to eat, drink, or wear.

Why does God want us to avoid worry? Think of it from God's perspective. If we walk with God, and if He never leaves us or forsakes us (Heb. 13:5), then how can anything good or bad come into our lives that is not filtered through the heart of God? He has all power to do anything for us or to keep us from evil. He knows everything that will ever happen from all eternity. His heart is completely toward us. What then do we have to worry about? When we worry, we call into question the love, power, and foreknowledge of God.

Since God promised to provide for our needs, think how insulting it must be to God when His children worry. How would you react to a son or daughter who said every day to friends at school, *I wonder if my parents are going to feed me tonight. I know they've done it every day since I've been born, but what if they changed their minds today?* You would be upset because your child would actually be questioning your heart toward him or her. God views our doubt of Him the same way. That's why the apostle Paul said, "Do not be anxious about anything" (Phil. 4:6). We can trust God.

Although worry might not be as emotionally intense as fear, it is still a form of it. Worry cannot be based on fact. It can only be based on possibility.

Satan's Tactics Lead Us to Worry

Worry begins with our thought patterns. Often Satan uses key phrases or words to trip us up. Three examples include *what if, maybe,* and *perhaps.*

Satan often plays the "what-if" game in my (John's) life. If I start entertaining questions that begin with those two words, I am usually opening myself to spiritual attack. *What if I fail? What if I don't have enough money?* These questions lead to mental energy about a future I cannot control, regarding a possibility which may or may not happen. None of these questions promote confidence in God. They could come from Satan, my own fears, or be encouraged by others' fears, but they do not come from God.

The "what ifs" are only asked by those who don't know the future. God cannot express uncertainty because He already knows what will happen. God does not have to guess. Nothing has ever just occurred to Him. Therefore, He would not ask a question based on the unknown. When God uses the word *if* in the Bible, it's often in a conditional sense, "If My people who are called by My name will ... then I will" (2 Chron. 7:14, NKJV). When Satan uses the word *if,* he tries to create doubt and uncertainty leading to fear.

God's Voice Creates Peace

Worry cannot coexist with truth. The best way to dispel it is to remember what God has said. For example, if you are worried about finances, you can quote Philippians 4:19, "And my God will meet all your needs according to his glorious riches in Christ Jesus." If you are tempted to worry about your children turning from God, you can take comfort in Proverbs 22:6, "Train a child in the way he should go, and when he is old he will not turn from it." If you are intimidated by your supervisor or meeting an important person, you may want to quote Isaiah 51:12, "I, even I, am he who comforts you. Who are you that you fear mortal men, the sons of men, who are but grass?" Meditating, memorizing, and reminding ourselves of the truth breaks the grip of worry. It frees us from the tyranny of its unproductive demands.

Perhaps you might want to take the freedom challenge today. As you go throughout the day, any time you notice fear or worry creeping into your life, write down the thought that triggered it. Often you can see a pattern in your thinking that leads you in that direction.

Write a verse that addresses the worry and carry it with you today. Here are some verses to consider:

"The Lord is my light and my salvation—whom shall I fear? The Lord is the stronghold of my life—of whom shall I be afraid?" —Psalm 27:1

"God is our refuge and strength, an ever-present help in trouble. Therefore we will not fear, though the earth give way and the mountains fall into the heart of the sea, though its waters roar and foam and the mountains quake with their surging." —Psalm 46:1-3

"We know that in all things God works for the good of those who love him, who have been called according to his purpose." —Romans 8:28

"No, in all these things we are more than conquerors through him who loved us."—Romans 8:37

"Finally, brothers, whatever is true, whatever is noble, whatever is right, whatever is pure, whatever is lovely, whatever is admirable— if anything is excellent or praiseworthy—think about such things." —Philippians 4:8

Experiencing God's Peace

Jesus said, " 'Peace I leave with you; my peace I give you. I do not give to you as the world gives. Do not let your hearts be troubled and do not be afraid' " (John 14:27).

The world's peace is based on circumstance. God's peace is based on relationship. The only way we can have peace in the storms of life is to know intimately the One who calms the seas.

Conclude today's study by thanking God for the confidence you have in Christ. Write your prayer in the margin.

DAY FIVE

COERCION VS. COOPERATION

Rick squirmed in the pew. Another sermon about the love of God. He recognized the vast chasm between what a love relationship with God ought to be and what he experienced. Frankly, he could count on his hands the number of times he really sensed God's love.

The pastor asked, "What mental image do you have of God?" Rick knew that for the most part he saw God as a taskmaster he had to please. He felt there was more he could and should do. He knew his shortcomings and failures displeased God, and he felt compelled to do better. If Jesus paid the ultimate price for him, then he ought to do more for Jesus. He wondered why he wasn't a better Christian and why he didn't have any joy. Instead, he seemed to be driven by duty. In fact, that word *driven* best described how he felt about his Christian experience. Why did he feel so joyless?

God Doesn't Drive, He Leads

Rick could be set free by learning that God does not drive or coerce us. Instead, God relates to us on the basis of our cooperation. Of course, He could rule by compulsion. His authority and power are such that He could force us to do anything He wanted. However, God's methods in the Bible are drawing, guiding, and leading.

> **Read the verses and circle the verb in each sentence that best describes the manner in which God directs our lives.**

"The Lord appeared to us in the past, saying: 'I have loved you with an everlasting love; I have drawn you with loving-kindness.' " —Jeremiah 31:3

"No one can come to me unless the Father who sent me draws him, and I will raise him up at the last day." —John 6:44

"When he, the Spirit of truth, comes, he will guide you into all truth. He will not speak on his own; he will speak only what he hears, and he will tell you what is yet to come." —John 16:13

"Because those who are led by the Spirit of God are sons of God." —Romans 8:14

Did you notice God draws, guides, and leads? God wants a love relationship. Love by nature must be free to love. It must choose the object of its affections. Therefore, God does not desire to drive, hammer, or coerce us. He seeks our response based on the motive of love. Although God may speak urgently or insistently, He does not compel us contrary to our willingness.

Satan, on the other hand, routinely uses coercion. In Revelation 13:16-17 a beast arose and tried to force everyone to receive his mark. If anyone did not receive the mark, they could not buy or sell. In demon possession, Satan dominates the victim's faculties and takes them as his own. Nowhere in the Gospels do we find a demon-possessed person wanting to remain possessed. Satan seeks to control others for his own selfish purposes. God does not.

The Source of Drivenness

Satan can create an atmosphere of drivenness in your life by capitalizing on at least five areas.

1. Sense of duty—In its best sense duty calls us to fulfill our responsibilities. In its perverted sense duty leads to a sense of coerced obligation. If you feel driven to obey Christ, most likely these words pepper your mind: *should, must, supposed to, ought to, have to,* or *need to.* For example, *I should read the Bible more. I need to witness to my neighbors. I'm supposed to be nice to everyone. I must pray more than I am. I ought to have more will power.*

The issue is not whether these represent good intentions. The issue is legalism: *I should or must do these things to gain God's favor.* If Satan can cause you to pursue perfection in the hope of experiencing God's grace, then you will likely see God as a taskmaster and have trouble experiencing freedom in Christ.

2. Sense of inadequacy—Many people are driven by a desire to measure up. Children who are told all their lives that they are "less than" others often become compulsive achievers. By accomplishment they seek to prove to themselves and others that they are adequate. Unfortunately, no matter how much they do, an insidious voice always whispers in their ears, *It's not enough.*

3. Need to please others—Many people feel compelled to take certain courses of action that will make people like them. They skirt offending or causing waves, often going to great lengths not to rock the boat. Unfortunately, those adept in manipulation can use tactics like guilt, condemnation, or withholding approval against them to control reactions and behavior.

4. Busyness—When our lives become overfilled, the demands and pressures of juggling multiple responsibilities scream for our attention. We feel hurried, pushed, and pulled. Our criteria for accepting responsibilities should be identifying what God has assigned us. By learning to listen only to God, our work falls into perspective, and He supplies the energy to meet the challenges. If we don't depend on God, we are left to our own resources, driven from one event to the next.

5. Impulsiveness—Have you ever made a rash decision? Impulsively rushed headlong into action? Emotion, greed, desire, or fear takes over. In a sense, impulsiveness is a cousin to drivenness. Some other factor overrides our better judgment.

In the Bible, God was deliberate (although not slow) and intentional. That means a voice leading to impulsiveness is not God. The Bible warns against hastiness in actions and words.

The Cure to Drivenness

Feeling driven stems from the thought patterns of the mind. The solution for transformation is the renewing of the mind (Rom. 12:1-2). The process for renewing the mind follows a four-step process.

Identify the patterns in your life that lead to drivenness—What does your mind dwell on? All of us pick up bad mental habits. By recognizing negative thought patterns, we can stop them before they start. Evil cannot coexist with light; it operates best under the cover of darkness. By exposing it, the first step to defeating evil has begun.

Refuse to be manipulated—Don't let thoughts or circumstances obligate you before you have asked God's opinion.

Affirm the truth—Applying the truth of God's Word to our lives proves the most effective way to stand in spiritual battles.

Live it—Practice develops character. Over time, you will learn not to respond to compulsive thoughts. Repetition of God's truth is the key.

Cooperating with God

God wants to work with and through you to do His will. He will speak to you about many things over the course of your life, but the way He speaks will not cause you to feel driven. He wants your cooperation, not coercion.

Paul understood that God desires for us to have willing spirits. In collecting an offering from the Corinthians, he mentioned twice that God desires a willing heart (2 Cor. 8:12; 9:7). He wants us to cooperate with Him of our own volition.

God's voice may be persuasive, admonishing, encouraging, or rebuking, but His purpose is to increase our willingness. What a different picture of God than that of a taskmaster pushing and pulling us against our wills. Thank God for the privilege of serving Him. When you feel rushed or tired, ask yourself whether you are serving in His strength or yours (see week 1, day 5).

Closing Thoughts

This week we have focused on recognizing the voice of God. Jesus said, " 'My sheep listen to my voice; I know them, and they follow me' " (John 10:27). Listening to His voice is a factor of being in a daily personal relationship with Him.

Our prayer has been that this study has strengthened your relationship with God. We intentionally tried to write it in such a way that it focuses on Him. We acknowledge that Satan is real. Christians need to be aware of his schemes and respond appropriately, but we believe victory ultimately results by being grounded in God rather than fixating on Satan. Victory comes from focusing on God.

"The plans of the diligent lead to profit as surely as haste leads to poverty."
—Proverbs 21:5

"Do you see a man who speaks in haste? There is more hope for a fool than for him."
—Proverbs 29:20

"The weapons we fight with are not the weapons of the world. On the contrary, they have divine power to demolish strongholds. We demolish arguments and every pretension that sets itself up against the knowledge of God, and we take captive every thought to make it obedient to Christ."
—2 Corinthians 10:4-5

---

[1]Spiros Zodhiates, Th.D., *The Complete Word Study Dictionary, New Testament* (Chattanooga, TN: AMG Publishers, 1992), 1105-1107.

HOW TO BECOME A CHRISTIAN

The essence of spiritual warfare is whether you choose to serve God or self.

The essence of spiritual warfare is whether you choose to serve God or self. Serving self is Satan's nature. When Satan tricked Adam and Eve into disobeying God, sin entered the world. In essence, sin is the propensity to serve self. Because of our sinful nature, all of us willfully choose to sin and are separated from God.

The justice of God demands we be punished by spending eternity in hell without Him, but God is rich in mercy and is not willing for "anyone to perish, but everyone to come to repentance" (2 Pet. 3:9). God provided a solution so that justice was served but He could still save us. He sent His Son, Jesus, to bear our punishment by being executed on a Roman cross. The Bible says it this way: "God demonstrates his own love for us in this: While we were still sinners, Christ died for us" (Rom. 5:8). Now you can be saved by simply trusting God's promise and embracing Christ as your Lord. That's what Romans 10:9-10 means: "That if you confess with your mouth, 'Jesus is Lord,' and believe in your heart that God raised him from the dead, you will be saved. For it is with your heart that you believe and are justified, and it is with your mouth that you confess and are saved."

Believing indicates you trust that God does not lie. He has promised to save you, and He will. Confessing with your mouth that Jesus is Lord signifies two things. First, you submit your life in obedience to Him, no longer seeking a lifestyle of serving self. Second, you publicly take your stand to identify with Him. When you enter a relationship with Jesus, He promises to never leave you or forsake you in this life and to take you to be with Him in heaven forever when you die. The way you begin this relationship is by simply asking Him in prayer.

Call upon the Lord now as you pray this prayer:

Dear God, I know I have sinned against You by breaking Your laws, and I ask for Your forgiveness. I believe that Jesus died for my sins. I want to receive new life in Him. I will follow Jesus as my Lord and seek to obey Him in all that I do. In the name of Jesus I pray. Amen.

To grow in your new life in Christ, continue to cultivate this new relationship through reading the Bible, God's blueprint for a godly life; through maintaining a regular time of talking to God through prayer; and through fellowshipping with other Bible-believing Christians in a church near your home.

God will teach you how to follow Him in times of spiritual warfare.

As a child of God you will want to learn all you can about your Father. One of the things He will teach you is how to follow Him in times of spiritual warfare. He will also give you a desire to share your new faith with others. We pray this study will help you grow in each area of your new life in Him.

LEADER GUIDE

This leader guide will help you facilitate an introductory session and eight group sessions for the study of *Spiritual Warfare: Biblical Truths for Victory*. Group sessions are designed for 50 minutes to 1 hour in length. If you have more than 1 hour, extend the time allotted for discussion.

Supplies and Room Arrangement

Have on hand an attendance sheet, extra Bibles, pens or pencils, and member books. For the first couple of sessions, supply name tags.

Arrange the room with chairs in a semicircle facing the TV-VCR. Sit as a participant in the circle to the right or left of the television screen. Place a markerboard in a visible location or plan to use tear sheets that can be mounted on a focal wall. Have on hand markers, an eraser, and/or masking tape.

Video

Before each session, arrange for a TV-VCR in your meeting room. Preview each video and complete the viewer guide in each week's study. Time the videos to better prepare your lesson plan for each session.

This study will interest church leaders, laypeople, and persons outside your church. Play the enlistment video on Tape One in Sunday School departments, for the church in a worship service, and at other churchwide gatherings. A promotional video for cable/broadcast TV use is also included.

In addition, authors John Franklin and Chuck Lawless are featured in a short Message to Pastors. This segment is located after the promotional and enlistment video and before the Introductory Session on Tape One. In this segment they explain their reasons for writing this study and their commitment to biblical support for each topic.

The Introductory Session video consists of two segments and is approximately 25 minutes in length. The eight session videos are also divided into two segments. The first is a review of content from the week's study. The second is a dramatic vignette that shows the spiritual warfare struggles of a typical American family. Together the session segments will take approximately 15 minutes.

The optional unit, week 9, does not have video support.

Promotion and Enlistment

Begin your publicity at least six weeks in advance of the introductory session. Since this subject will appeal to persons who do not attend your church, place fliers or posters in businesses and offices near your church. Also make use of free advertising in newspapers and on television and radio stations. To order a broadcast-quality tape of the promo video, call 615-251-5926. Promote the study in worship bulletins, church newsletters, and on hallway bulletin boards. Send invitations to church and Sunday School leaders, deacons, and ministry leaders.

Order member books three weeks in advance. See page 2 of this book for ordering information.

Prayer Support

Bathe the study in prayer! Because of the nature of spiritual warfare, enlist prayer partners who will pray from the time the study is announced until it concludes. As persons sign up for the study, encourage them to begin praying for themselves, other group members, and the group leader. Consider gathering in the room where you will be meeting for a time of prayer prior to the introductory session.

INTRODUCTORY SESSION

1. Provide a sign-in sheet and a pen. As participants enter, have them sign in and attach a name tag to their clothing. Give them a copy of *Spiritual Warfare: Biblical Truths for Victory*. Collect money if they are paying for their books.
2. Open with prayer. Introduce yourself, giving a brief Christian testimony. Explain your interest in this subject and your excitement about what this study can mean in the life of your church.
3. Allow time for participants to introduce themselves. Ask them to include in their introduction a question they are seeking to have answered as a result of this study. List these questions on a tear sheet or markerboard in a visible location.
4. Ask participants to open the book to page 3. Review the eight session titles. Then invite the participants to follow along with you as you review the information in Meet the Authors and About the Study on pages 4 and 5.
5. Show the first segment of the introductory session video.

6. Following the video, ask members for questions or comments about what they've seen. Use the following as discussion prompters as needed:
    1) What prompted the authors' interest in the subject of spiritual warfare?
    2) How did they define the terms *spiritual warfare* and *victory*?
    3) Why did the authors approach this topic in the way that they did?
    4) What did the authors say was the main thing that they hoped participants would get from this study? (growth in their personal relationship with God through Jesus Christ)
7. Ask participants to turn to page 6 and quickly skim week 1. Assign week 1 to be completed by the next group session. Encourage participants to complete the learning activities as an important part of personalizing the study.
8. Show the second video segment for the introductory session, a dramatic vignette from the life of a typical American family.
9. Discuss these issues from the dramatization. Allow varying interpretations. You are building interest in the story at this point.

    1) How did Peter get distracted from his church commitment?
    2) What obstacles did Peter encounter once he began to cultivate his relationship with God?
    3) Would you say Peter is experiencing spiritual warfare? If so, in what ways?
    4) Do you identify with Peter's story thus far? If so, in what ways?

10. Close the session by praying for God's presence, power, and protection as you begin this study.

WEEK 1

1. As participants enter, have them sign the attendance sheet and attach a name tag to their clothing. Have on hand extra copies of *Spiritual Warfare: Biblical Truths for Victory*. If members are paying for their books, collect money from those who did not pay at the introductory session.
2. Open with prayer. Praise God for being a sovereign God who rules with both justice and mercy.
3. Ask members to complete the viewer guide on page 25 as you play the first video segment for week 1.

4. Ask members to share answers to the viewer guide. If a difference of opinion arises, use group consensus to determine the best answer.
5. Discuss the following key ideas from week 1:

Day 1
1) Review the definition of *spiritual warfare*. (p. 7)
2) Summarize the differences that separate the opposing wills of God and Satan. (p. 7)
3) What do we learn about Satan from the biblical names given to him? (p. 7)
4) What are the two reasons given for why Satan fell? (p. 8) Do humans face similar temptations?
5) Since Satan has been defeated, why does the war continue ? (p. 9)
6) What is the fundamental question raised in day 1? (p. 10)

Day 2
1) According to the authors, what is the foundational question of spiritual warfare? (p. 10)
2) Call for responses to the learning activities on pages 12 and 13.

Day 3
1) How does God use warfare to accomplish His will? Give a biblical example and a personal example. (pp. 14-16)
2) How does God use warfare to reveal His glory? (pp. 16-17)
3) Review the information in the sidebar on page 17.

Day 4
1) Review the four-step process that advances the kingdom through warfare. (pp. 19-21)
2) Call for responses to the learning activity at the bottom of page 21.

Day 5
1) Ask volunteers to share their responses to the learning activity at the bottom of page 23.
2) What difference does it make to be "in Christ"? (p. 24)

6. Play the second video segment for week 1, a dramatic vignette from the life of a typical American family.
7. Discuss these issues from the dramatization:
    1) What led to Peter's decision to have family devotions? What family crises followed?

2) Why is Peter upset by Susan's decision to seek employment?

3) What influences Peter to think that his family might be experiencing spiritual warfare?

8. Assign week 2 to be completed during the coming week.

9. Use the remaining time for prayer requests and prayer for individuals and for this study.

WEEK 2

1. Place the attendance sheet and name tags (optional) by the door. Greet members as they arrive. Have extra copies of the member book and pens available.

2. Open with prayer. Thank God that He has chosen to work through us as He seeks to extend His kingdom. Pray for wisdom and insight during the session.

3. Ask members to turn to page 45. Have them complete the viewer guide as you play the first video segment for week 2.

4. Share responses to the viewer guide. If a difference of opinion arises, use group consensus to determine the best answer.

5. Use the following questions/statements as discussion starters for a review of week 2.

Day 1

1) Respond to the question, *If God loves you, why does He leave you here?*

2) What does "authority" imply when it comes to spiritual warfare? (The authority to cooperate with God in achieving His purposes)

3) Review the mistaken assumptions listed at the top of page 30. What biblical responses can we give to these assumptions?

Day 2

1) What do we learn about exercise of authority from the story of the demon-possessed boy in Mark 9:14-27? (See pages 31-32.)

2) What is the common denominator for the use of authority by Jesus, the disciples, and the early church leaders? (being on mission with God)

3) Under what circumstances, then, can we claim Christ's authority in spiritual warfare?

Day 3

1) How did you respond to the learning activity at the top of page 34?

2) Why do Christians often react against God's using negative or painful experiences to develop character?

3) What lessons for life did you glean from John Franklin's testimony about his period of spiritual warfare? (See pages 35-36.)

4) Review the blessings of character development in the margin of page 37.

Day 4

1) How do the lives of Joseph and Job reflect the principle that character development requires endurance? (p. 38)

2) Review the four stages in character development from the visual on page 41.

3) React to this statement (p. 39): "The end of the process is that God takes believers to new levels of maturity."

Day 5

1) What was your initial reaction to the statement (p. 41) that God sometimes chooses Satan as a means of disciplining wayward believers?

2) What is the purpose for God's discipline? (p. 43) Note that the purpose is not punishment but restoration to God's fellowship and kingdom purposes.

3) Share responses to the learning activity on page 44.

4) Do you think Christians would take sin more seriously if they knew God might use Satan to discipline them?

6. Play the dramatic vignette video for week 2.

7. Discuss these issues from the dramatization:

1) What was your reaction to Peter's "Spiritual Warfare Kit"?

2) Describe Sally and Sunshine. Characterize their relationship with each other.

3) What decision was Sally facing? How does her dilemma relate to character and spiritual warfare?

8. Assign week 3 to be completed before the next group session.

9. Use the remaining time for prayer requests and prayer for individuals and for the group.

WEEK 3

1. Place the attendance sheet by the door. Greet members as they arrive.
2. Open with prayer. Thank God that He has chosen to develop His character in us. Pray for wisdom and insight during the session.
3. Ask members to turn to page 65. Have them complete the viewer guide as you play the first video segment for week 3.
4. Share responses to the viewer guide. If a difference of opinion arises, use group consensus to determine the best answer.
5. Use the following questions/statements as discussion starters for a review of week 3.

Day 1

1) Why is Satan not our greatest adversary?
2) Read Romans 7:15-23 (p. 47). Ask a volunteer to summarize Paul's dilemma.
3) Share responses to the learning activity on page 47.
4) What is the basic root of all sin? (p. 48)
5) Why does God allow Satan to test us at the very points where we are most vulnerable? (p. 50)

Day 2

1) Why does Satan attempt to distort God's Word?
2) What was Satan's scheme with Eve and with Jesus in His temptation experience?
3) Discuss your response to the learning activity at the bottom of page 54.

Day 3

1) What problems might occur when we engage Satan in conversation?
2) Illustrate ways Satan seeks to focus us on what we are missing by following God.
3) Review "How Do I Respond to Temptation?" in the margin of page 57.

Day 4

1) How is forgiveness an issue of spiritual warfare?
2) Share a forgiveness testimony or call on someone you enlisted before the session.
3) How can prayer/accountability partners help us be more forgiving persons?
4) Can a person who refuses to forgive expect to win spiritual battles and be on mission with God?

Day 5

1) What key to victory in spiritual warfare is mentioned on page 61?
2) Share your responses to the learning activity at the top of page 63.
3) What brings victory in spiritual warfare?
4) Review the ways to focus on God on page 63.

6. Play the dramatic vignette video for week 3.
7. Discuss these issues from the dramatization:

1) How does Satan attempt to use Peter's conversation with Joe to discourage him?
2) What did the family learn about spiritual warfare from watching football and baking cookies?

8. Assign week 4 to be completed before the next group session.
9. Use the remaining time for prayer requests and prayer for individuals and for the group.

WEEK 4

1. Place the attendance sheet by the door. Greet members as they arrive.
2. Open with prayer. Thank God for giving us such intricate and capable minds. Pray for wisdom and insight during the session.
3. Ask members to turn to page 85 and complete the viewer guide as you play the first video segment for week 4.
4. Share responses to the viewer guide. If a difference of opinion arises, use group consensus to determine the best answer.
5. Use the following questions/statements as discussion starters for a review of week 4.

Day 1

1) Ask volunteers to review the six reasons that the mind is Satan's most important battlefield.
2) Explain why Satan wants your mind.

Day 2

1) Define the word *stronghold*. What are the two strongholds of wrong thinking mentioned in week 4? (p. 71)
2) How does low self-esteem become a stronghold? What frees us from low self-esteem?
3) How does pride become a stronghold? What frees us from pride?

Day 3

1) What does *giving Satan a foothold* mean?
2) React to this statement: "the more space we give to the devil, the more likely it is we will lose a spiritual battle." (p. 75)
3) Review the visual "The Development of a Stronghold" on page 76.
4) Review the questions that suggest a stronghold may be developing. (p. 77)

Day 4

1) Explain the difference between a truth encounter and a power encounter. (p. 78)
2) Why is it not enough to simply know the Word of God? (We must live the Word.)
3) Review reasons to memorize the Bible. (p. 79)
4) React: "Strongholds are broken when we choose in His power to be *obedient* to His revealed truth." (p. 80)

Day 5

1) Read 2 Corinthians 10:4-5 (p. 81). How do we take thoughts captive?
2) How does thinking thoughts that are pleasing to God help to break strongholds of sin?
3) Share responses to the learning activities on page 83.
4) Summarize the key points from the article, "Declaring a War Already Won" by Chuck Lawless. (p. 84)

6. Play the dramatic vignette video for week 4.
7. Discuss these issues from the dramatization:

   1) What strategy of Satan did we see illustrated in this vignette?
   2) What feelings of worthlessness did Peter experience?
   3) What thoughts kept Susan from experiencing victory?

8. Assign week 5 to be completed before the next group session.
9. Use the remaining time for prayer requests and prayer for individuals and for the group.

WEEK 5

1. Place the attendance sheet by the door. Greet members as they arrive.
2. Open with prayer. Thank God for giving us churches with brothers and sisters in Christ. Pray for your church. Then pray for wisdom and insight during the session.
3. Ask members to turn to page 105 and complete the viewer guide as you play the first video segment for week 5.
4. Share responses to the viewer guide. If a difference of opinion arises, use group consensus to determine the best answer.
5. Use the following questions/statements as discussion starters for a review of week 5.

Day 1

1) Ask volunteers to review each of the three reasons Satan wants to attack the church.
2) Share responses to the learning activity at the bottom of page 88.
3) Discuss the relationship between warfare for individuals and warfare for churches.

Day 2

1) Discuss the four common reasons churches experience division. (pp. 90-92)
2) What is a deadly consequence of division? (lack of evangelism and zeal for the lost)

Day 3

1) Why does Scripture place a high value on doctrine?
2) Recall that deception is one of Satan's main strategies. How does Satan use doctrinal error as a scheme against the church?
3) Share responses to the learning activity on page 95.
4) Explain two ways Christians are deceived. (p. 97)

Day 4

1) Why does Satan want leaders to fail?
2) How does Satan test leaders? (pp. 99-100)
3) Review three ways leaders and followers can help each other at times of testing.

Day 5

1) What is one of the main reasons our culture does not listen to the Christian perspective? (We have lost our good reputation in the eyes of many non-Christians.)
2) Share responses to the learning activities on pages 101-102.
3) How seriously does God take the abuse of His name? Are we individually and as a church accountable for the reflection we cast on His name? Why or why not?

4) How can you help your church honor the name of Christ? (pp. 103-104)

6. Play the dramatic vignette video for week 5.
7. Discuss these issues from the dramatization:

   1) What did Peter call a "sneak attack" from Satan? (conflict in the church)
   2) How did Greg interpret what was happening at his church?
   3) What constructive action was taken by the people at the party? (They prayed.)

8. Assign week 6 to be completed before the next group session.
9. Use the remaining time for prayer requests and prayer for individuals and for the group.

WEEK 6

1. Place the attendance sheet by the door. Greet members as they arrive.
2. Open with prayer. Thank God for giving us His armor to wear. Pray for wisdom and insight during the session.
3. Ask members to turn to page 125 and complete the viewer guide as you play the first video segment for week 6.
4. Share responses to the viewer guide. If a difference of opinion arises, use group consensus to determine the best answer.
5. Use the following questions/statements as discussion starters for a review of week 6.

Day 1
   1) What is the significance of the fact that the armor is God's armor?
   2) Why do we have to put it on?
   3) What happens if we don't wear the armor?

Day 2
   1) Explain the significance of the belt to a soldier. What is its significance to a Christian?
   2) What are some ways we may fail to live truthful lives?
   3) What are some actions we can take to live more truthful lives?
   4) Explain the significance of the breastplate to a soldier. What is its significance to a Christian?
   5) Review the guidelines in the margin of page 112.

Day 3
   1) Explain the significance of proper shoes to a soldier. What is its significance to a Christian?
   2) How does the gospel of peace fit into a battle strategy? (p. 114)
   3) Why is it essential for Christians to share the gospel of peace?
   4) Take a moment to pray for unsaved friends and loved ones identified in the learning activity on page 115.

Day 4
   1) Explain the significance of a shield to a soldier. What is its significance to a Christian?
   2) Illustrate a "fiery dart" from page 116.
   3) Share responses to the learning activity on page 118.
   4) What are some 'faith actions" mentioned in day 4 that can help you get ready for God's deliverance from a fiery trial?
   5) Call on volunteers to share a faith testimony with the group. (See page 120.)

Day 5
   1) Explain the significance of the helmet to a soldier. What is its significance to a Christian?
   2) Explain the significance of a sword to a soldier. What is its significance to a Christian?
   3) Share responses to the learning activity on page 124.

6. Play the dramatic vignette video for week 6.
7. Discuss these issues from the dramatization:

   1) What are some life lessons about the armor that Peter recalled from his notes?
   2) Having on the wrong uniform would embarrass each of us. How do Christians have on the wrong uniform at times?
   3) Susan was well-intentioned, but she was not open to Matthew's input. How are we often like Susan in our relationship with God? with other Christians who seek to give us counsel?

8. Assign week 7 to be completed before the next group session.
9. Use the remaining time for prayer requests and prayer for individuals and the group.

WEEK 7

1. Place the attendance sheet by the door. Greet members as they arrive.
2. Open with prayer. Thank God for the privilege of talking to Him through prayer. Pray for wisdom and insight during the session.
3. Ask members to turn to page 143 and complete the viewer guide as you play the first video segment for week 7.
4. Share responses to the viewer guide. If a difference of opinion arises, use group consensus to determine the best answer.
5. Use the following questions/statements as discussion starters for a review of week 7.

Day 1
1) Why do all Christians need to be growing in a stronger prayer life?
2) Review the three primary reasons prayer is important in spiritual warfare. (p. 128)
3) How does Satan seek to hinder us from praying? (p. 129)

Day 2
1) Describe Jesus' prayer life.
2) Does it encourage you to know that Jesus is praying for you as you encounter spiritual warfare?
3) React to this statement: "Jesus taught His disciples to pray for protection." (p. 132) Discuss the need to begin or continue this practice daily. Ask, Do we also need to pray for others who are facing or who will face spiritual battles?
4) Where was Jesus' focus when He prayed for Himself: on God or on Satan?
5) Emphasize the need to follow Jesus' model and keep the focus on God.

Day 3
1) Why is the power of spiritual warfare so attractive to many people?
2) What is the problem with seeking power in spiritual warfare?
3) How is power found in weakness?
4) React to this statement: "The weakest believer who relies on God's strength is much more a threat to Satan than is the 'strong' believer who relies on his own strength." (p. 135)

Day 4
1) Explain why we need balance between the mountaintop and the valley.

2) Review the material in the shaded box on page 138.
3) Share personal experiences of mountaintops and valleys.
4) Why is staying on the mountaintop not the goal of victorious Christian living? (p. 139)

Day 5
1) Why should we pray for a burden for evangelism?
2) How does the enemy blind the minds of unbelievers? (p. 141)
3) Review the HEART acrostic on p. 142.

6. Play the dramatic vignette video for week 7.
7. Discuss these issues from the dramatization:

1) Why was Sunshine upset? What does she think would solve her problems?
2) What did Peter discover was the best and only thing he could do for Susan and Sunshine?

8. Assign week 8 to be completed before the next group session.
9. Use the remaining time for prayer requests and prayer for individuals and the group.

WEEK 8

1. If this is your last group session, do not use an attendance sheet. Greet members and let them know how much you appreciate their attendance and participation in the group.
2. Open with prayer. Thank God for the Bible and its importance in keeping us grounded as we deal with controversy. Pray for wisdom and insight during the session.
3. Ask members to turn to page 163 and complete the viewer guide as you play the first video segment for week 8.
4. Share responses to the viewer guide. If a difference of opinion arises, use group consensus to determine the best answer.
5. Use the following questions/statements as discussion starters for a review of week 8.

Day 1
1) Review the case study on page 144. With the increased popularity of spiritual warfare in our society, how do you know which ideas to accept or reject?

2) How did the authors answer the question, *Should Christians go on the offensive when engaging in spiritual warfare?* How do you answer the question?

3) How do we prepare ourselves for offensive warfare? (p. 147)

Day 2

1) How did the authors answer the question, *Can believers be demon possessed?* How do you answer the question?

2) React to this statement (p. 149): "We can face spiritual battles knowing that Satan will never gain control of us."

3) Review the four primary ways the enemy tries to oppress believers. (pp. 150-151)

4) Review the actions believers should take if they sense spiritual oppression. (p. 151)

Day 3

1) Discuss the popular teaching and the authors' conclusions about binding and loosing Satan. (pp. 151-153)

2) Discuss the popular teaching and the authors' conclusions about rebuking Satan. (pp. 153-155)

3) How would you counter the argument that the authors' positions encourage passivity toward Satan and his schemes? (p. 155)

Day 4

1) Discuss the popular teaching and the authors' conclusions about generational curses. (pp. 155-158)

2) React to the concept that generational curses shift the responsibility and blame for individuals' actions to others.

Day 5

1) Discuss each danger the authors identified:
   dualism
   denying personal responsibility
   human-centered approaches to warfare
   overemphasis on Satan
   overreacting to the dangers

2) Although there are dangers, what reasons do the authors give for promoting the study of spiritual warfare? (p. 161)

3) If members have listed other issues they wish to discuss, make plans for how you will pursue addressing these issues. Apply the questions in the shaded box on page 161.

6. Play the dramatic vignette video for week 8.

7. Discuss these issues from the dramatization:

   1) What strongholds did Peter uncover in Sunshine's life? (hopelessness and despair)

   2) What did Peter offer Sunshine as the only hope for her predicament?

   3) Does Peter view finding a job as the solution to his family's spiritual battles?

   4) In future situations the family will face, what does Peter hope will be their response?

8. If you are meeting for the optional study, assign week 9 to be completed before the next group session.

9. Use the remaining time for prayer requests and prayer for individuals and the group.

WEEK 9 *(Optional Unit)*

1. Greet members. Thank them individually for their participation and faithfulness to the study.

2. Open with prayer. Thank God for His voice that we can hear and obey. Pray for wisdom and insight during the session.

3. On a markerboard or tear sheet, draw a line down the middle to form two columns. Label the left column Voice of God and the right column Voice of Satan.

4. As you discuss the key ideas from each day, write the appropriate words under each column.

5. Summarize by saying that recognizing God's voice requires hearing it often! Encourage members to cultivate their prayer lives.

6. Close with prayer. Consider standing in a prayer circle and saying sentence prayers of thankfulness to God and the group.

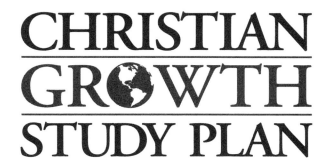

CHRISTIAN GROWTH STUDY PLAN

In the **Christian Growth Study Plan (formerly Church Study Course)**, this book *Spiritual Warfare* is a resource for course credit in the subject area Personal Life of the Christian Growth category of diploma plans. To receive credit, read the book, complete the learning activities, show your work to your pastor, a staff member or church leader, then complete the following information. This page may be duplicated. Send the completed page to:

Christian Growth Study Plan
One LifeWay Plaza; Nashville, TN 37234-0117
FAX: (615)251-5067; E-mail: cgspnet@lifeway.com
For information about the Christian Growth Study Plan, refer to the Christian Growth Study Plan Catalog. It is located online at www.lifeway.com/cgsp. If you do not have access to the Internet, contact the Christian Growth Study Plan office (1.800.968.5519) for the specific plan you need for your ministry.

Spiritual Warfare
COURSE NUMBER: CG-0621

PARTICIPANT INFORMATION

Social Security Number (USA ONLY-optional)	Personal CGSP Number*	Date of Birth (MONTH, DAY, YEAR)
– –	–	– –

Name (First, Middle, Last)	Home Phone
	– –

Address (Street, Route, or P.O. Box)	City, State, or Province	Zip/Postal Code

Please check appropriate box: ☐ Resource purchased by self   ☐ Resource purchased by church   ☐ Other

CHURCH INFORMATION

Church Name

Address (Street, Route, or P.O. Box)	City, State, or Province	Zip/Postal Code

CHANGE REQUEST ONLY

☐ Former Name

☐ Former Address	City, State, or Province	Zip/Postal Code

☐ Former Church	City, State, or Province	Zip/Postal Code

Signature of Pastor, Conference Leader, or Other Church Leader	Date

*New participants are requested but not required to give SS# and date of birth. Existing participants, please give CGSP# when using SS# for the first time.
Thereafter, only one ID# is required. **Mail to:** Christian Growth Study Plan, One LifeWay Plaza, Nashville, TN 37234-0117. Fax: (615)251-5067.

Rev. 3-03